Heather Duckworth

Shy Children,
Phobic Adults

Shy Children, Phobic Adults

Nature and Treatment of Social Phobia

Deborah C. Beidel
Samuel M. Turner

American Psychological Association
Washington, DC

First Printing December 1997
Second Printing February 1999

Published by the
American Psychological Association
750 First Street, NE
Washington, DC 20002

Copies may be ordered from
APA Order Department
P.O. Box 92984
Washington, DC 20090-2984

In the UK and Europe, North Africa, and the Middle East, copies may be ordered from
American Psychological Association
3 Henrietta Street
Covent Garden, London
WC2E 8LU England

Typeset in Minion by EPS Group Inc., Easton, MD

Printer: Data Reproductions Corporation, Auburn Hills, MI
Cover Designer: Minker Design, Bethesda, MD
Technical/Production Editor: Catherine R. Worth

Library of Congress Cataloging-in-Publication Data
Beidel, Deborah C.
    Shy children, Phobic adults : nature and treatment of social phobia / Deborah C. Beidel and Samuel M. Turner.—1st ed.
      p.   cm.
    Includes bibliographical references and index.
    ISBN 1-55798-461-1 (acid-free paper)
    1. Social phobia. I. Turner, Samuel M., 1944– . II. Title.
RC552.S62B45   1998
616.85′225—dc21
                                                 97-33477
                                                 CIP

British Library Cataloguing-in-Publication Data
A CIP record is available from the British Library.

Printed in the United States of America

Contents

Acknowledgments

Many individuals kindly contributed their time and effort to the development of this book. First and foremost, we would like to thank our patients and their families who have contributed their time and taught us so much about this disorder and how to treat it. Second, we would like to thank Carrie Masia, Dan McNeil, Tracy Morris, Scott Spaulding, and Melinda Stanley for their review and comments on the initial draft of this manuscript. Third, we extend our appreciation to John Denning II, Mary Anne Haynes, Kasey Hamlin, and Agnes Siebert for their technical assistance in the completion of the manuscript. Finally, we would like to thank Peggy Schlegel, Beth Beisel, and Catherine Worth of American Psychological Association Books for their consistent support, good humor, encouragement, and suggestions.

Introduction

*"I didn't know anyone else felt like me. You mean that there really
is a name for this? Other people have it?
And somebody knows how to treat it?"*

**An adult patient with social phobia during an initial
interview at our clinic.**

The experience of social anxiety and fear appears to be a universal aspect of the human condition. For most individuals, episodes of anxiety are mild and transitory, but for others, the fear is more severe, pervasive, and enduring. The recognition and discussion of the problem of social fears dates back to at least the time of Hippocrates, but in America social phobia did not become an officially recognized diagnosis until publication of the third edition of the *Diagnostic and Statistical Manual* (*DSM-III*; American Psychiatric Association, 1980). Under-recognition of maladaptive social anxiety is apparent in the above comments from one of our patients. Although the problem of social anxiety is well known, the tendency has been to see this condition as merely a developmental phase in the case of children or as a problem that everyone has at sometime experienced in the case of adults. Thus, prevailing views among professional and lay persons alike have been to minimize the significance of this problem or to attribute it to just a case of shyness. Perhaps that is why many social phobics did not seek treatment and why they tended not to reveal the extent of their distress to others. In 1985, Liebowitz referred to social phobia as the "neglected anxiety disorder," and indeed, this was an apt description. Although there is considerable overlap with the construct of shyness, and the exact relationship between these two conditions has not been determined, when current diagnostic criteria for social phobia are applied, the disorder differs considerably from shyness with respect to epidemiology, course, severity of symptoms, and clinical correlates.

SOCIAL PHOBIA AS A CLINICAL SYNDROME

Even after recognition of social phobia as a diagnosable disorder in *DSM-III*, acceptance as a significant clinical syndrome was slow. Thus, researchers had to overcome skepticism regarding the significance of social phobia as a clinical syndrome by clinicians and by those reviewing grant applications for the National Institute of Mental Health (NIMH). Over the past 15 years, a considerable body of research has emerged demonstrating that social phobia is a highly prevalent and serious disorder in the general population. In fact, on the basis of available epidemiological data, it is the most common anxiety disorder in the population. Research into phenomenology and clinical features revealed that people with social phobia suffer significant emotional distress, social isolation, and occupational maladjustment. Those with social phobia also were found to suffer from depression and increased suicidal ideation. In addition, they frequently suffer from other conditions such as generalized anxiety disorder, avoidant personality disorder, and obsessive–compulsive personality disorder. In short, the data show that the condition is much more severe than had been thought originally. In fact, *DSM-III* criteria initially described social phobia as a "relatively" circumscribed condition. However, when the revised version of the *DSM-III* (*DSM-III-R*, American Psychiatric Association, 1987) was published, the description had changed as a result of research findings. In this version of the *DSM*, two different patterns of social phobia were acknowledged; one characterized by a relatively circumscribed pattern of fear and avoidance and one characterized by a pervasive pattern. This description of social phobia was maintained in *DSM-IV* (American Psychiatric Association, 1994).

From its introduction into the *DSM* nomenclature, social phobia was considered to be an early onset anxiety disorder, appearing most often in mid-adolescence (most other major anxiety disorders had been considered adult onset conditions). However, reports of earlier onset from socially phobic patients and research with younger adolescents and children revealed that social phobia was quite prevalent in childhood. Beidel and Turner (1988) reported the diagnosis of social phobia in children as young as age 8. Social phobia has been estimated to occur in about 1% to 2% of children (McGee et al., 1991), but specific descriptions of childhood social phobia were included in the diagnostic system for the first time in *DSM-IV*. Because descriptors of social anxiety have been removed from the diagnostic criteria of other conditions, and are now attributable to social phobia, the prevalence of the condition in children no doubt is considerably higher. Features of social phobia in childhood are remarkably similar to those seen in adults. Thus, it is clear that some individuals with social phobia manifest the condition in early childhood and remain affected into adulthood.

Although the exact cause of social phobia is not known, its early onset and its familial pattern have raised the question of genetic or biological causation. Similarly, shyness and social anxiety have been studied for their relationship to the early appearing temperamental style known as behavioral inhibition. Examination of the literature, however, reveals numerous other ways in which social phobia might develop, and it is hypothesized in this volume that there are multiple pathways to the development of the disorder.

THE TREATMENT OF SOCIAL PHOBIA

Although the etiology of social phobia is uncertain, the results of treatment studies conducted over the past decade and a half have shown that adult social phobia is a highly treatable condition. In addition, the literature has progressed substantially to the point that recommendations regarding both drug and psychological treatment can be made. Although the amount of research is small, a number of studies indicate that childhood and adolescent social phobia can be effectively treated with psychological strategies similar to those used to treat adults, but the status of drug treatment is less certain. We discuss the current drug and psychological treatments, outlining their implementation and, in the case of drug treatments, explicating guidelines promulgated by pharmacotherapists for the safe use of medication in children.

Empirical research on the syndrome of social phobia and its treatment has grown rapidly since the disorder was included in the official diagnostic system. Because of this, it is a particularly appropriate time for an integrated examination of the nature of social phobia and its treatment across the age span. This book is designed to discuss the syndrome of social phobia across the ages—its various clinical presentations, demographic characteristics, theories of etiology, and empirically supported treatment strategies. In some cases, we have integrated the discussion of child, adolescent, and adult presentations into one chapter; in others, separate chapters for adults or children and adolescents seemed more appropriate. We have endeavored to enrich the discussion by integrating our clinical experience with adults and children with the findings from empirical studies and by presenting case material from our clinical and research practice to illustrate important points regarding the syndrome as well as its assessment and treatment.

THIS VOLUME

The first section of the book focuses on the psychopathology of social phobia. Chapters 1 and 2 address the clinical syndrome and differential diagnosis in adults and children, respectively. These are followed by chapters on epidemiology (chapter 3) and etiological and developmental factors (chapter 4). We then turn to issues of measurement across the various ages (chapter 5), including assessment for the purposes of diagnosis, treatment planning, and determining treatment outcome. Chapter 6 addresses overall clinical management, including patient management and, in the case of child and adolescent patients, child management. Chapter 7 reviews the pharmacological treatment in adults and children, and finally, chapters 8 and 9 review the behavioral and cognitive–behavioral treatments for adults and children and adolescents, including how these strategies are implemented.

This book was written for the clinician, researcher, and student. We have endeavored to present an integrated discussion of the nature of social phobia in children and adults, as well as a discussion of how the nature of the syndrome affects the manner in which treatment is conducted. Each chapter includes a review of the relevant literature. As often occurs in psychology, different speciality areas develop parallel lines of research, but there often is little communication among the various speciality areas. Thus, clinical, developmental, experimental, and social psychologists all have made contributions to the literature on social fears. In only a few cases have the contributions from one field been recognized and used by another. Therefore, in this book we have attempted to integrate these relevant literatures in order to present a more comprehensive presentation of the disorder.

In addition to integrating the diverse psychological literatures on the nature of social anxiety and fear, and discussing etiological variables, a primary aim was to make this book practical. Therefore, the reader will find case vignettes, clinical examples from our own practice, actual assessment instruments, examples of other clinical material, and case examples of how we conduct assessment and treatment of child and adult social phobia. In addition, the chapters on treatment implementation describe the parameters associated with how to make these interventions work and common problems associated with implementation. We believe this practical focus will be useful for clinicians who treat patients with social phobia. Likewise, researchers should find this clinical material useful for enhancing their understanding of the problems faced by patients and the clinicians who treat them. Finally, for students, the clinical presentation should provide a richer understanding of the patients and the challenges faced in understanding and treating this condition. It is our hope that the contents of this volume will serve to educate the clinician about the clinical characteristics of social phobia, provide assistance to the implementation of successful treatment, provide the researcher with helpful insight into the nature of the disorder, stimulate thought about areas of controversy, and point out many of the areas where we are in need of additional inquiry. As for the student, we hope the contents of this book will stimulate interest in this disorder, provide the foundation for understanding the nature of the condition, and give guidance in how its treatment should be approached.

1

Clinical Presentation of Social Phobia in Adults

Elaine is a 40-year-old advertising executive. She is well educated, enjoys a high income, and lives in a fashionable neighborhood. Elaine came to our clinic because of a conversation with the owner of her company. He told her that he had decided to retire and wanted to turn over the business to Elaine. Although tremendously excited by the opportunity to own her own business, she was upset because for many years she had avoided securing accounts and other social aspects of her upper management position, constantly arranging her schedule to work in the background. As a result, she minimized her distress in social situations by avoiding almost all social contacts, while still performing her duties exceptionally well. The prospect of assuming the leadership of the company frightened Elaine so much that she was seriously considering resigning. According to Elaine, the tasks associated with assuming ownership were almost all social in nature, and the thought of assuming the role evoked considerable anxiety. The distress associated with her dilemma increased her general anxiety such that she suffered from constant tension and muscle aches and

pains, and complained of difficulty sleeping, crying episodes, and
anergia.

This scenario is not atypical for those who suffer from social phobia. Although able to maintain employment, people with social phobia
often find their occupational choices and roles dictated or constrained
by social fears. Similarly, the personal lives of those with social phobia
are characterized by extensive social avoidance. Frequently, individuals
seek treatment when they no longer are able to maintain their avoidant
lifestyle; when they become dissatisfied with the inability to reach their
goals; when a significant life event forces a change in their occupational,
personal, familial, or social responsibilities; or when a significant other
decides that he or she is unwilling to continue living the severely restricted lifestyle adopted by someone with this disorder. Often times,
as was the case with Elaine, those with social phobia are considered
reserved or shy, but others rarely understand the extent of their social
inhibition or the personal distress that they endure. Patients with social
phobia frequently suffer dysphoric mood and sometimes frank depression, and, as was the case with Elaine, high levels of general anxiety
and other somatic symptoms are common. This chapter will discuss
the symptoms, detrimental effects, comorbidity, and differential diagnosis of social phobia in adults.

DIAGNOSIS

Recognition of the syndrome of social phobia dates back to at least the
time of Hippocrates (Marks, 1985). Although Marks and Gelder (1966)
and Marks (1970) described the syndrome as it is currently conceptualized, social phobia as a formal diagnosis did not enter the American
psychiatric nomenclature until the publication of the third edition of
the *Diagnostic and Statistical Manual of Mental Disorders* (American
Psychiatric Association, 1980). The criteria for the diagnosis of social
phobia essentially were those outlined by Marks and Gelder (1966) and
Marks (1970). Despite some minor revisions during the last decade, the
clinical description has remained generally unchanged. In fact, the most
significant change has been the wording of criteria to allow for two

subtypes known as the generalized and specific. The essence of social phobia is extreme social inhibition and timidity. The more specific description found in the fourth edition of the *Diagnostic and Statistical Manual of Mental Disorders* (*DSM-IV*; American Psychiatric Association, 1994) is discussed in the following sections.

The *DSM-IV* characterizes social phobia as "a marked and persistent fear of one or more social or performance situations in which the person is exposed to unfamiliar people or possible scrutiny by others" (American Psychiatric Association, 1994, p. 416). Virtually any situation that includes the possibility of observation or scrutiny by others may be feared by those with social phobia. Common socially distressful situations include formal speaking, interacting with others, attending social events, maintaining social dialogue, and eating or writing in front of others. Less common but nonetheless distressful situations reported by those with social phobia include being observed while typing or using photocopying equipment, using public restrooms, or merely saying one's name at a public meeting. Leisure activities also may be distressful. For instance, some adults with the disorder describe anxiety and avoidance when playing golf, dancing, or walking down the aisle at church, again because of the fear of observation and evaluation by others. However, the disorder is not limited to situations where one's performance is under specific scrutiny by others. Rather, it often involves anxiety and dread whenever any type of social interaction is anticipated. Thus, individuals with social phobia frequently do not associate with others at work and do not attend social events such as parties or meetings where social exchange would be expected. In addition, a relatively rare but often particularly debilitating form of social phobia is fear of using public restrooms. In these cases, fear is not generated by concern about cleanliness or contamination by germs but rather is related to concerns about social evaluation and the process of bodily elimination.

A second characteristic of social phobia is that "exposure to the feared social situation almost invariably provokes anxiety, which may take the form of a situationally bound or situationally predisposed panic attack" (American Psychiatric Association, 1994, p. 417). Although most clinicians were aware of it earlier, *DSM-IV* criteria officially recognized that individuals with any type of anxiety disorder could have panic attacks. In fact, those with social phobia often describe experiencing panic attacks when in a social encounter or even when anticipating a social event. The physical symptomatology of these attacks is the same as those of panic disorder and can be quite severe. In addition, the pattern of the physiological response when in a distressful social situation is one of the features that differentiate those with social phobia from individuals who have "normal" speech anxiety (Turner, Beidel, & Larkin, 1986). Specifically, assessment of blood pressure and pulse rates among those who do not meet criteria for an anxiety disorder (i.e., nonphobic controls) indicate that when initially asked to give a speech, their blood pressure and heart rate increase. After approximately 3 to 5 minutes, physiological responses return to normal baseline levels. The physiological response of those with social phobia differs from that of nonphobic controls. The blood pressure and pulse rate of those with social phobia also increase at the start of a public speaking task. However, these responses remain elevated until the task's completion. Thus, those with social phobia never experience the decrement in physiological arousal characteristic of those without the disorder. This difference in physiological response to social settings also has been found in rhesus monkeys and behaviorally inhibited children (Turner & Beidel, 1989).

Finally, in regard to social phobia, the *DSM-IV* states, "The person recognizes that the fear is excessive and unreasonable" (American Psychiatric Association, 1994, p. 417). Those with social phobia often present for treatment by saying "I know it is crazy to feel this way, but I cannot help it." That is, those with the disorder recognize that often there is no reasonable basis for their fears, but this knowledge does little to alleviate their anxiety. This criterion helps to distinguish social phobia from other conditions such as paranoid personality disorder. Patients with paranoid personality disorder, although experiencing considerable social anxiety, often believe that others are thinking critically about them or may actually be planning to embarrass or humiliate them (see section on differential diagnosis). It is important to note, however, that young children often cannot acknowledge the irrational basis of their fears. Thus, lack of recognition of the unreasonableness of the fear is more common in children and adolescents with this disorder than in adults (see chapter 2 in this volume).

Many of those with social phobia live in constant fear that they will embarrass themselves, appear foolish, or appear less intelligent than others. The most common difficult situation for those with social phobia is public speaking (Holt, Heimberg, & Hope, 1992; Schneier, 1992; Stein, Walker, & Forde, 1994; Turner, Beidel, Dancu, & Keys, 1986). As noted, other commonly reported fears include eating or drinking in public, writing in public, informal social settings such as parties, and a variety of other social performance situations (Turner, Beidel, Dancu, & Keys, 1986). The significant distress experienced in these situations frequently leads to avoidance behavior (Turner, Beidel, Dancu, & Keys, 1986). Avoidance may be overt and sometimes quite dramatic (as in Elaine's case) or rather subtle. As an example of the latter, one of our patients related how she avoided drinking in public. Unable to pick up a glass because of her fear of trembling, she would always order a very large glass of iced tea. Because of the size of the glass, she felt that it was appropriate to slide the glass toward her (rather than pick it up) and, using a straw, bend over to sip from it. This example illustrates the extreme strategies that patients may use to manage or hide their distress. It also illustrates how subtle avoidance behaviors may be. Finally, most people with social phobia, particularly the generalized subtype (see discussion of social phobia subtypes below), are unable to form and maintain satisfying interpersonal relationships, and they have a chronic restricted range of social activities (Turner & Beidel, 1989). Table 1 lists common fears and avoidance behaviors seen in social phobia.

Although difficulty making public speeches is a problem for a large majority of those with social phobia, the disorder typically is not restricted to speech phobia. As noted previously, socially distressful situations need not be limited to those where a person performs some action or activity in front of others. Even chance activities such as meeting a new neighbor over the back fence can cause considerable distress. When interviewing an individual with social phobia, it is important to

Table 1

Situations Commonly Feared by Adults With Social Phobia

Situation	Turner, Beidel, Dancu, and Keys (1986) ($n = 21$)	Turner, Beidel, Borden, et al. (1991) ($n = 88$)
Formal Speaking	88%	99%
Informal Speaking/Meetings	76%	88%
Eating in Public	33%	—
Drinking in Public	5%	—
Eating/Drinking in Public	—	39%
Writing in Public	19%	31%
Taking Tests	10%	—
Initiating Conversations	—	60%
Maintaining Conversations	—	64%
Parties	—	76%
Using Public Restrooms	—	8%

From Turner, S. M., Beidel, D. C., & Townsley, R. M. (1992b). In S. M. Turner, K. S. Calhoun, & H. E. Adams (Eds.), Handbook of Clinical Behavior Therapy (pp. 13–37), New York: Wiley.

remember that the situations that provoke distress may be quite extensive and will vary with each person. Similarly, not all patients with social phobia experience the exact same pattern of physical symptoms or negative cognitions. For example, one patient might experience the full set of typical somatic symptoms (blushing, rapid heart rate, shaking, and trembling), whereas another might only experience general tension and stuttering when in performance situations. Additionally, children might only report having a "sick stomach" or just not feeling well (see chapter 2 in this volume).

It is important to note that although the condition is defined by anxiety and fear associated with specific situations, a patient's social fear is not defined strictly by the physical parameters of those situations. Many individuals who have speech phobia, for example, may only experience distress under certain circumstances. One patient treated in our clinic only had difficulty if the audience included individuals he considered to be authorities in his field. His high performance anxiety was fueled by his concerns about his abilities. This is an important point with respect to treatment and will be addressed further in chapter 8 when we discuss the selection of *core fears* for exposure treatment. Components of the fear will be as unique as each individual who seeks treatment. In any discussion of social phobia, it is important from the outset to distinguish this clinical disorder from behavior that is usually labeled as "shyness," as we do in the next section.

SOCIAL PHOBIA AND SHYNESS

The term *shy* is used by professionals and laypersons alike to describe those persons who are socially reticent. Shy persons are not considered to suffer from an emotional disorder but rather are considered to be temperamentally reserved. Although socially reticent, less gregarious, and less socially inclined than others, shy individuals can socially engage when necessary at the interactional as well as specific performance levels. To date, there are no formal studies available examining the relationship of shyness to social phobia. One hypothesis is that shyness might be on a continuum such that those at the upper extreme meet criteria for social phobia and those at the lower extreme do not. Alternatively, the two conditions, though sharing similar features, could be completely independent. Finally, the term *shy* could be merely a generic label describing a host of conditions characterized by social reticence.

Most studies on shyness have been conducted with children, adolescents, and college student populations, and these data will be discussed in chapter 2. There are, however, reports of follow-up data on adult outcomes of children identified as shy at pre-adolescence (Caspi, Elder, & Bem, 1988; Kerr, Lambert, & Bem, 1996) that will be considered here. Caspi et al. (1988) studied American children, whereas Kerr et al. (1996) examined a Swedish sample. Among both groups of boys, those who were shy when they were 8–10 years old married later and became fathers later than boys who were not shy. Swedish boys did not manifest the occupational impairment in adulthood found in the American cohort of boys. Among girls, marriage and motherhood did not differentiate either the American or Swedish shy sample from their non-shy counterparts. However, both groups of shy girls did show lower levels of academic achievement than non-shy girls. This was particularly striking in the Swedish sample where the rate of college attendance for the non-shy girls was 44% in comparison to 0% for the shy girls. Thus, shyness appeared to result in some long-term impairments similar to those found in samples of socially phobic patients, although the overlap between these conditions is not clear. In an overall review of the empirical literature on these two conditions, Turner, Beidel, and Townsley (1990) examined the shyness and social phobia literature across six different dimensions of functioning: somatic features, cognitive characteristics, behavioral responses, daily functioning, clinical course, and onset characteristics. The review indicated that populations described as shy or socially phobic had similar somatic symptoms and cognitions when in distressing settings. They differed, however, on social and occupational functioning, onset of the disorder, course of the disorder, and overt behavioral characteristics. On each of these dimensions, outcome for those with social phobia was more severe than for those who were labeled shy. There were epidemiological differences as well. Whereas up to 40% of college students reported feelings of shyness, only 2% of adults met diagnostic criteria for social phobia in the Epidemiologic Catchment Area survey (ECA; Robins et al., 1984). About 8% met criteria for social phobia in the National Comorbidity Study (NCS; Kessler et al., 1994; see chapter 3 in this volume, on epidemiology). Turner, Beidel, and Townsley (1990) concluded that the two syndromes are not identical but do overlap on some core characteristics. Thus, these terms, or the representative participant samples, cannot be used interchangeably. The question of whether these two conditions share common etiological factors or are otherwise related remains to be examined.

DETRIMENTAL EFFECTS

As noted above, those with social phobia suffer significant emotional distress, and the results of studies over the past decade show that the disorder is much more serious than was thought previously. When engaged in or in anticipation of social encounters, those affected experience increased somatic arousal similar to the pattern noted for agoraphobics (Amies, Gelder, & Shaw, 1983; Turner, Beidel, Dancu, & Keys, 1986). However, social phobia is characterized by a particular constellation of physical symptoms mediated by the beta-adrenergic system, including heart palpitations, trembling, sweating, and blushing (Gorman & Gorman, 1987). In the 1980s, this characteristic physiological response generated substantial interest in the use of beta-blockers as a treatment for this disorder (see chapter 7 in this volume).

Originally dismissed as a minor problem affecting only public speaking situations, available data indicate that those with social phobia report increased suicidal ideation and suicide attempts as well as increased use of alcohol, anxiolytics, and other drugs, often to meet daily demands of living and working (Amies et al., 1983; Liebowitz, Gorman, Fyer, Campeas, et al., 1985; Schneier, Johnson, Hornig, Liebowitz, & Weissman, 1992; Turner, Beidel, Borden, et al., 1991; Turner, Beidel, Dancu, & Keys, 1986). With respect to social functioning, Liebowitz, Gorman, Fyer, Campeas, et al. (1985) and Turner, Beidel, Dancu, and Keys (1986) reported that inability to work, incomplete educational attainment, lack of career advancement, and severe social restriction were common features of the disorder. Turner, Beidel, Borden, et al., (1991) surveyed 99 individuals with social phobia regarding the severity and type of impairment they experienced. Among this sample, 91% reported academic impairment as a result of their social fears. For example, some patients reported that they received low grades in school as a result of lack of class participation (i.e., they could not speak in class and thus demonstrate their knowledge of the material), chose to avoid classes thought to require class participation or presentations, decided not to attend graduate or professional school, or based the decision regarding their college major on their social fears. In an extreme example, one patient described enrolling and dropping out of three different colleges to find one that did not require a speech class for graduation. Another patient who had waited until the last term to take a required speech class dropped the class and had to return for an extra semester to finish. When he again was unable to complete the course, he sought treatment.

Similar to the extensive academic impairment, 96% of the sample reported occupational impediments. In most instances, this consisted of refusing promotions (as Elaine was considering) or deliberately selecting careers that required only minimal social contact. In severe cases, patients have described hiding in office lavatories or behind filing cabinets to avoid speaking to coworkers or joining them for lunch in the cafeteria. In addition, there is evidence suggesting that there is lost productivity among those with this disorder (Van Amerigen, Mancini, & Streiner, 1994). For example, Schneier and his colleagues (Schneier, Johnson, et al., 1992) used the ECA survey data to examine some of the consequences of social phobia. Results from this survey of a community sample suggested that individuals with social phobia were more dependent on others and relied more heavily on public assistance. Those with specific or nongeneralized social phobia had rates of financial dependency (welfare or disability payments) that were significantly higher than controls who had no disorders (22.3% vs. 10.6%; Schneier, Johnson, et al., 1992). However, this level of dependency has not been reported for clinic samples.

Of the Turner, Beidel, Borden, et al. (1991) sample, 80% felt that their disorder had resulted in impairment of their social relationships. Many patients felt stymied in their attempts to join clubs or organizations in which they had an interest because of the need to introduce themselves to others or participate in social activities affiliated with the organization. Some who had managed to do so then faced additional difficulties as they often would be nominated for leadership positions that they could not assume. Among patients who were unmarried (n = 29), 79% felt that their heterosocial interactions had been restricted by their fears, leaving them unable to date or establish meaningful intimate relationships. Even among those who are married, marital conflict regarding socialization and social activities is common. Patients report that spouses often are unhappy with the patients' preference to stay home and watch television rather than socialize with other couples or go to a restaurant. Similarly, some parents report fearing that their social impairment may affect their children's opportunities for socialization as well, thus leading children into the same cycle of social distress and isolation (see chapter 4 in this volume for a discussion of this issue).

Further complicating matters, alcohol use has been linked to social phobia. Alcohol and other substances, such as anxiolytics, sometimes are used by those with this disorder in a deliberate attempt to minimize their distress. Turner, Beidel, Dancu, and Keys (1986) reported that 46% of a socially phobic sample used alcohol to feel more sociable at a party. In addition, 50% intentionally used alcohol prior to social encounters such as parties or meetings in order to "get themselves there." Another 13% used anxiolytics specifically for this purpose.

Other research has addressed the relationship between the disorders of alcoholism and social phobia. For example, five studies (Bowen, Cipywnyk, D'Arcy, & Keegan, 1984; Chambless, Cherney, Captuto, & Rheinstein, 1987; Mullaney & Trippett, 1979; Smail, Stockwell, Canter, & Hodgson, 1984; Stravynski, Lamontagne, & Lavallee, 1986) reported that rates of social phobia among alcoholic inpatient populations ranged from 8% to 56%. As noted by Heckelman and Schneier (1995), these rates are equal to or higher than the rates of social phobia in the general population. Similarly, among opiate abusers in Australia, 18% to 25% had scores on the Fear of Negative Evaluation Scale and the Social Avoidance and Distress Scale that were within the clinically significant range for social phobia (Grenyer, Williams, Swift, & Neill, 1992). Conversely, Schneier, Martin, Liebowitz, Gorman, and Fyer (1989) reported alcohol abuse among 16% of a socially phobic sample. Rates of alcohol abuse have been reported to be higher among those with social phobia than among those with other anxiety disorders (Kushner, Sher, & Beitman, 1990). Furthermore, the presence of comorbid social phobia increases the risk of alcohol abuse in patients with panic disorder (Kushner et al., 1990).

The high rate of comorbidity among those with either a primary diagnosis of social phobia or alcoholism, in addition to the reports that alcohol often is used to diminish social distress, fuel speculation of an etiological link between these disorders. Clinically, we have seen a number of patients who traced their alcohol use back to their adolescent years, after the onset of their social phobia. Similarly, Kushner et al. (1990) found that among individuals on an alcoholic inpatient unit, most reported that the abuse of alcohol began after the onset of social phobia and that alcohol was used as a form of self-medication for their social distress. Despite these observations, the exact nature of the relationship between social phobia and substance abuse remains unclear. What is clear is that social phobia results in significant impairment in many areas of life functioning and can result in outcomes as severe as limited occupational achievement, restricted social interactions, suicidal ideation, and alcohol and drug abuse.

SOCIAL PHOBIA SUBTYPES

Current diagnostic criteria allow for the designation of two social phobia subtypes: generalized and specific (the latter is sometimes also known as nongeneralized or circumscribed). Generalized social phobia is characterized by anxiety in, and frequent avoidance of, many different social situations. This often includes performance situations as well as common social interactions. For example, Walter came to our clinic initially because he had difficulty giving formal presentations that were part of his job as the head of computer operations at his company. However, during the diagnostic interview, Walter revealed that he also was anxious when in a private meeting with a superior or when chatting with coworkers in the cafeteria. He noted that his wife had complained that he always made excuses whenever she suggested that they go out to dinner or to a movie with another couple. Approximately 70% of patients seeking treatment for social phobia meet the generalized criteria (Turner, Beidel, & Cooley, 1994).

Specific social phobia is characterized by a more circumscribed pattern of fear, frequently in just one situation such as public speaking. Another situation also characteristic of specific social phobia is illustrated by Gail, who did not have any difficulty speaking before groups. She was, however, a member of the "Sweet Adelines," the women's version of a barbershop quartet group. She experienced performance anxiety when her group was in a singing competition (that is, when the audience was very knowledgeable about music). In fact, on one occasion her group was heavily favored to win the competition, but Gail "froze" and they did not even place in the top 10. Specific social phobia may be quite circumscribed but still severe.

Although the exact diagnostic distinction for the subtypes is ambiguous, and different investigators have defined the subtypes in slightly different ways, the subtype distinction can be made reliably (Heimberg, Hope, Dodge, & Becker, 1990; Turner, Beidel, & Townsley, 1992a). Various comparative studies examining characteristics of the subtypes reported similar findings (Herbert, Hope, & Bellack, 1992; Holt, Heimberg, & Hope, 1992; Turner, Beidel, & Townsley, 1992a). The generalized subtype, by far the most common type seen in clinics (approximately 70%; Scholing & Emmelkamp, 1993b; Turner, Beidel, & Jacob, 1994), is associated with more severe anxiety, depression, social inhibition, fear of negative evaluation, avoidance, fearfulness, and self-consciousness than the specific subtype (Bruch, 1989; Heimberg et al., 1990; Herbert et al., 1992; Holt, Heimberg, & Hope, 1992; Turner, Beidel, & Townsley, 1992a). Furthermore, in comparison with the specific subtype, those with generalized social phobia were found to be less educated, less likely to be employed, and more likely to have an additional Axis I or II diagnosis (Herbert, Hope, & Bellack, 1992; Turner, Beidel, Borden, et al., 1991). Thus, it is clear that the generalized subtype differs from the specific on a number of demographic variables and is more severe than the specific on various clinical parameters.

Until recently, the primary distinction between the generalized and specific subtypes was pervasiveness of fear and degree of symptom severity. However, there is increasing evidence that the subtypes may differ on other dimensions as well. For example, Holt, Heimberg, and Hope (1992) reported that individuals with generalized social phobia have an earlier age of onset ($M = 10.9$ years) than the specific subtype ($M = 22.6$ years). Also, Davidson (1993) noted that early onset social phobia particularly is associated with a pattern of increased severity and chronicity during adulthood. McNeil, Ries, Taylor, et al. (1995) used the Stroop color-naming task to assess differences in response latency of those with the specific subtype, the generalized subtype, or the generalized subtype with avoidant personality disorder. Patients with the specific subtype (e.g., speech phobia) had longer response latencies to speech words but not to words associated with general social interactions. There were no differences based on word type in the latter two groups. These data further support the distinctiveness of the specific and generalized subtypes.

As we discuss in chapter 2, onset of social phobia prior to age 11 predicts nonrecovery as an adult. In examining developmental background, Bruch and Heimberg (1994) found that those with generalized social phobia reported more severe shyness symptoms and a family social style characterized by social isolation than did individuals with the nongeneralized (specific) subtype. In a study from our clinic, Stemberger, Turner, Beidel, and Calhoun (1995) reported a number of subtype differences, including greater neuroticism, more frequent history of childhood shyness, and more introversion among the generalized subtype when compared with the specific subtype and controls with no disorders. Taken together, these findings suggest that the generalized subtype has characteristics, some of which may be biologically influenced, that lead to an earlier onset and a more severe clinical picture. When these findings are combined with others, they suggest that the subtypes are qualitatively different.

In perhaps one of the few areas where those with the generalized subtype are less severely affected, those with the specific subtype manifested greater autonomic reactivity in social performance tasks (Heimberg, Hope, et al., 1990; Hofmann et al., 1995). Heimberg, Hope, et al., (1990) found that when asked to perform in front of others, those with the specific subtype had higher physiological reactivity than those with the generalized subtype. In addition, Hofmann, Newman, Ehlers, and Roth (1995) reported that those with the specific subtype had higher heart rates during an impromptu speech task than did those with the generalized subtype. These differences in physiological response further suggest that the two subtypes might be qualitatively different. One hypothesis put forth by Stemberger et al. (1995) to account for this difference is that specific social phobia might represent a true conditioned emotional reaction with the typical associated autonomic features. On the other hand, the generalized subtype might be the result of a more insidious onset resulting from a long history of social inadequacy. Another possibility is that generalized social phobia is related to the Axis II dimension of avoidant personality disorder. In other words, the specific subtype is a "true" phobia, whereas the generalized subtype has some phobic features but might be a variant of personality disorder, and in particular avoidant personality disorder. Some researchers (e.g., McNeil, Ries, & Turk, 1995) have conceptualized subtype differences by differentiating the terms *anxiety* and *fear*. In this context, fear responding is described as physiologically robust (highly reactive) and closely tied to a specific situation. Anxiety responding is considered to be more diffuse and less consistent with measures of psychopathology (such as physiological reactivity). If one applies these labels to the physiological responses of the specific and generalized subtypes, then one might speculate that generalized social phobia may be more characteristic of an anxiety response, whereas specific social phobia is more characteristic of a fear response. As we have noted, available data indicate that the generalized subtype is more severe, more common, and may have a different developmental course than the specific subtype. In addition, physiological response to anxiety-producing situations may differentiate the subtypes. However, further research in this area is necessary to confirm initial findings.

Despite differences in symptom presentation, to date no study of behavioral or cognitive–behavioral treatments has deliberately set out to examine the effects of treatment for the two subtypes. Our preliminary studies (to be discussed in detail in chapter 8 in this volume) suggest that current treatments are less efficacious for the generalized subtype, the most commonly occurring pattern seen in clinics. For example, in 1994, we published a major outcome study comparing exposure (flooding), atenolol, and pill placebo groups (Turner, Beidel, & Jacob, 1994). Although not a part of the final published report, we retrospectively conducted an analysis of the specific versus generalized subtype on the treatment outcome. This analysis revealed that the symptoms of the generalized group were significantly more severe at pretreatment across virtually all dimensions of functioning. In addition, although both groups improved significantly over treatment, the post-treatment scores for the generalized subtype were still higher than the specific subtype scores at pretreatment, indicating that the generalized group, despite statistically significant improvement, still was impaired substantially at posttreatment (see Table 2).

SOCIAL PHOBIA AND SOCIAL SKILL

Existing data reveal clearly that the generalized subtype is more severe and complex than the specific, with a higher frequency of comorbidity with other Axis I and II conditions (see above). Another area of differentiation may be the presence of social skill deficits. Although data from extant studies are mixed, it appears that those with the generalized subtype are deficient in social skills (i.e., they lack many of the skills necessary to engage in effective interpersonal discourse). In an early discussion of social phobia, Marks (1985) distinguished between what he termed "pure social phobics" and those he thought to be suffering from avoidant personality disorder (APD). According to Marks, pure social phobics do not evidence skill deficiencies, whereas those with APD do. Recent reports of subtype differences lend some empirical support for Marks' contention. Before presenting those data, a discussion of the diagnostic classification difficulties of social phobia and the related condition of APD should prove helpful. Because the boundary between generalized social phobia and APD is unclear (cf. Heimberg, Holt, Schneier, Spitzer, & Liebowitz, 1993; Turner, Beidel, & Townsley, 1992a), and because there is overlap in diagnostic criteria, many of the patients whom Marks termed APD no doubt also met criteria for generalized social phobia. *DSM-III-R* as well as *DSM-IV* allow APD and social phobia to be diagnosed concurrently. Empirical studies have shown that the generalized subtype is highly comorbid for APD (Herbert et al., 1992; Turner, Beidel, & Townsley, 1992a) and that APD is present in the generalized subtype significantly more often than in the specific. Thus, Marks' pure social phobics likely were the specific subtype, and his APD group probably was mixed and comorbid for gen-

Table 2

Pre- and Posttreatment Scores for Specific and Generalized Social Phobics Treated With Flooding

Instrument	Specific	Generalized
Self-Report		
SPAI Difference score		
Pre	72.9	110.8
Post	48.1	94.3
SAD		
Pre	7.7	20.6
Post	3.3	18.2
FNE		
Pre	13.0	25.1
Post	13.4	22.1
FQ-Social Phobia		
Pre	10.6	21.4
Post	3.0	15.3
Behavioral Assessment		
Speech Length (minutes spoken)		
Pre	6.2	4.7
Post	8.8	7.9
SISST-Positive		
Pre	41.8	26.8
Post	52.8	35.3
SISST-Negative		
Pre	41.6	51.9
Post	25.0	32.1
Independent Evaluator Ratings		
HAM-A		
Pre	18.0	24.0
Post	6.0	17.0

Table 2 (Continued)		
Instrument	Specific	Generalized
Independent Evaluator Ratings		
CGI-Severity		
Pre	3.9	4.6
Post	2.0	3.3

eralized social phobia. If Marks' distinction is correct, this would support the contention that skill deficits and general social deficiency are part of the clinical picture of generalized social phobia.

In addition to the usual skill deficiencies in areas such as maintaining conversations, initiating conversations, and perceiving social cues, our clinical experience is that those with the generalized subtype tend to have a number of very specific deficiencies perhaps unique to social phobia. One such deficit is an inability to listen in social settings because of an overactive cognitive system. That is, when in a social encounter, those with social phobia are so worried about the perception of their behavior by others, they spend their energy trying to formulate a "perfect" response rather than attending to the details of the conversation. Thus, when it is their turn to speak, they often do not know what to say or whether their "perfect" response now is appropriate because they have not followed the conversation. Other social skill deficits that may be particular to the syndrome include difficulty conceiving of places where normal social discourse can occur and the inability to actively plan social activities. Given the data indicating that generalized social phobia has a long insidious onset and course (Holt, Heimberg, & Hope, 1992), and an earlier age of onset, one can speculate that social skill deficits result from the long history of lack of socialization experiences and, in particular, the lack of recurring socialization experiences. Several intervention strategies (Turner, Beidel, & Cooley-Quille, 1995; Wlazlo, Schroeder-Hartwig, Hand, Kaiser, & Munchau, 1990) have been designed to address these general and specific social skill deficiencies (see chapter 8 in this volume).

Patient performance during in vivo social interaction tests support the idea that those with the generalized subtype of social phobia are deficient in social skills. These deficiencies are evident in both molar and molecular behaviors. For example, as part of our standard assessment battery for social phobia, patients participate in two unstructured in vivo social interactions: one with a confederate of the same sex and one with a confederate of the opposite sex. Interactions are rated with standard 5-point Likert rating scales for social skill (facial gaze, speech length, vocal tone, and overall skill; cf. Turner, Beidel, Dancu, & Keys, 1986). Based on an analysis of 53 patients with generalized and 23 patients with specific social phobia, comparisons between the groups indicated that for each variable those with the specific subtype were more skilled, although the difference only reached statistical significance on one variable and approached significance on another (speech length, $p < .01$, and overall skill, $p < .06$). However, this study did not address the specific social skill deficits that have been just recently identified and that are discussed above.

In an earlier report (Turner, Beidel, Dancu, & Keys 1986), patients with APD diagnosed according to *DSM-III* criteria were significantly different from those with *DSM-III* social phobia without APD on a host of social skill measures. The sample was not divided into subtypes because *DSM-III* criteria did not allow for subtyping, but many of the patients in the former group may have also met criteria for generalized social phobia. In contrast, Herbert et al. (1992) did not find differences in social skills between those with generalized subtype and those with APD, but this study did not include a group composed of those with the specific subtype. Because overlap of the generalized subtype and APD is extensive, one might not expect differences between these two groups. Differences in social skill are more likely found when the latter two groups are compared with a group with the specific subtype and a group with no disorder. As previously indicated, there are at least two primary reasons why reports regarding social skill deficits in individuals with social phobia have been mixed: Patients have not been divided along the specific–generalized dimension in all cases, and the measurement strategies that have been used were not developed specifically for deficits commonly found in social phobia.

A final indication of the presence of social skill deficits in patients with social phobia is that social skill training has been used successfully in the treatment of this disorder (see chapters 8 and 9, this volume). These outcome data further bolster the small amount of descriptive psychopathological data and clinical observation that inadequate social skills are part of the clinical presentation of this syndrome. Because social phobia is a relatively early onset anxiety disorder, one can speculate that social anxiety and resulting avoidance of social situations might prevent the development of normal prosocial behavior. In this regard, Rubin, LeMare, and Lollis (1990) reported that, in children, shyness and social isolation lead to a withdrawn behavior style, restricted peer interaction, and impairment in social skills and interpersonal relationships (see chapter 4 in this volume for an extended discussion).

COMORBIDITY AND DIFFERENTIAL DIAGNOSIS

One of the most frustrating interactions for those with social phobia is confiding to someone about how anxious they become when they give a speech or when they have to attend social events. Most lay persons are likely to respond by saying, "That's not unusual. Everyone gets nervous when they give a speech," or, "Everyone gets nervous from time to time." Just as it is difficult for laypersons to differentiate social phobia from normal public speaking fears, it often is difficult for patients and clinicians to differentiate social anxiety from social phobia. That is, individuals with many different Axis I or II disorders may experience social anxiety and social withdrawal. However, in these cases, the reasons for their distress are different from those that are characteristic of social phobia. Differential diagnosis is necessary to establish a proper treatment plan. In other instances, patients with social phobia may have secondary comorbid conditions. Below, we detail other conditions that often are found to coexist with social phobia. In addition, we review other disorders for which social anxiety might be part of the clinical presentation and discuss how to make the diagnostic distinctions.

Comorbidity and Differential Diagnosis With Other Axis I Disorders

Among adults, social phobia has a high rate of comorbidity with other Axis I disorders (Sanderson, Rapee, & Barlow, 1987; Turner, Beidel, Borden, et al., 1991). For example, Sanderson et al. (1987) reported that 58% of their socially phobic sample had at least one additional disorder, primarily simple phobia, dysthymic disorder, or panic disorder with agoraphobia. On the basis of a sample of 71 patients with social phobia, Turner, Beidel, Borden, et al. (1991) reported that 33% met criteria for generalized anxiety disorder (GAD). In addition, 11% also met criteria for simple (specific) phobia, whereas 6% met criteria for dysthymic disorder, 3% for panic disorder, 3% for major depressive disorder, and 1% for obsessive–compulsive disorder. Interestingly, the most common comorbid Axis I disorders found in adults with social phobia (GAD and specific phobia) also are the most common disorders found in children and adolescents with social phobia (overanxious disorder/GAD and specific phobia; see chapter 2, this volume). Although other re-searchers also have reported a substantial number of coexisting con-ditions in those with a primary diagnosis of social phobia, specific rates for the comorbid disorders often differ somewhat by the particular site. These differences likely are due to different referral patterns and screen-ing practices at various clinics. Nevertheless, it is fair to conclude that a substantial number of patients with social phobia have clinical presen-tations complicated by the presence of one or more additional disorders.

Panic Disorder

Because the anxiety disorders have become more commonly recognized by clinicians and the lay public, differential diagnosis among the various anxiety diagnostic categories has become much easier. However, Heck-elman and Schneier (1995) noted that the diagnostic distinction be-tween panic disorder with agoraphobia and social phobia still may be difficult because patients with panic disorder often avoid social settings. For example, a patient comes to a clinic and describes fear and anxiety when in social situations or when in a shopping mall but also reports panic attacks in both of these settings. Does the patient have social phobia, panic disorder, or both? In such instances, we always have found the distinction made by Marks (1970) to be useful in guiding diagnostic decisions: Those with panic disorder fear the crowd, whereas those with social phobia fear the individuals who make up the crowd. Also, *DSM-IV* indicates that for a diagnosis of social phobia to be appropriate, the avoidance of social situations must not be due to fear of panic symptoms. Careful questioning of the patient described above disclosed that the feelings of anxiety occurred even when the mall was virtually deserted and that what the patient feared was meeting an acquaintance and then having to engage in small talk. Panic attacks did not occur unless the patient recognized (or appeared to recognize) a familiar face. This clinical presentation would rule out a diagnosis of panic disorder as the primary condition.

Differential diagnosis of panic disorder and social phobia also can be made on the basis of several empirically established differences between the groups. Panic attacks in those with social phobia are believed to be situationally bound, whereas they often are considered spontaneous or uncued in those with panic disorder (American Psychiatric Association, 1994). Although the idea that these attacks actually are uncued is debatable (Craske, 1991), individuals with panic disorder do experience panic attacks in nonsocial settings. Among the earliest studies to compare physical symptomatology, Amies et al. (1983) reported that blushing and muscle twitching were more common among individuals with social phobia, whereas changes in respiration, dizziness, palpitations, headaches, blurred vision, and ringing in the ears were more common in patients with panic disorder. Gorman and Gorman (1987) noted that blushing, trembling, heart palpitations, and sweating were the physical symptoms most commonly characteristic of social phobia. Less commonly experienced are symptoms associated with respiratory distress (difficulty breathing, shortness of breath, chest pain). Symptoms of respiratory distress are more commonly associated with panic disorder. Finally, Mannuzza, Fyer, Liebowitz, and Klein (1990) noted that those with social phobia had an earlier age of onset (mid-teens as opposed to early or mid-twenties) and that the gender ratio was more likely to be equivalent for social phobia, whereas the gender ratio was more likely to be predominantly female for panic disorder with agoraphobia.

A final issue is that panic disorder patients frequently develop social fears subsequent to the onset of panic. The question is whether a second diagnosis of social phobia is required. Most of the secondary social phobia seen in panic patients appears to be a feeling of embarrassment and concern over negative evaluation resulting from panic. In our view, although functionally the behavior appears to be the same as for other patients with social phobia, a diagnosis of social phobia should not be made according to the criteria in *DSM-IV*. Although there are no data available to address this issue, we suspect that once panic is controlled, there will be no need to address social phobia separately. In other words, the social fears are secondary to panic attacks.

Other Anxiety Disorders

Social phobia can be distinguished from GAD because the latter diagnosis includes unreasonable worries about a broad range of events (personal finances, family members health, minor matters), whereas worries in social phobia are restricted to fears of evaluation in social settings. However, a number of patients with primary GAD have social phobia as a coexisting disorder (Brawman-Mintzer et al., 1993), suggesting that social fears are pervasive in the latter group. Similarly, patients with obsessive–compulsive disorder (OCD) often are apprehensive in social encounters because they fear others will detect their ritualistic behaviors or fear they might be contaminated by others. However, this distinction is fairly easy to make because those with social phobia ordinarily do not have frank obsessions and compulsions. Conversely, those with OCD do not fear that they will do or say something that will be humiliating or embarrassing (unless the "something" is the ritual).

Depression

Sometimes when we have advertised available treatment programs for individuals with social avoidance, some who seek treatment for social isolation actually meet criteria for major depression. Those with depression often exhibit social withdrawal and avoidance (Dilsaver,

Qamar, & Del Medico, 1992), but social withdrawal in most of these cases is due to depressed mood, anhedonia, and lack of interest in social activities. In many cases, these problems are eliminated when depression is treated. In such cases, it does not appear that an additional diagnosis of social phobia is warranted. Furthermore, individuals with depression usually describe premorbid histories that are dissimilar to social phobia (i.e., these individuals typically have "normal" socialization patterns prior to the development of their depressive state). In contrast, some patients with social phobia describe dysphoric mood secondary to the social restrictions brought on by their social avoidance and isolation. Once again, closer examination usually reveals a very different set of motivational circumstances that drive the avoidance behavior for these cases.

There is an additional reason why attention to comorbid Axis I disorders is important. As noted previously, the addition of a comorbid condition in patients with social phobia increases the likelihood of suicidal ideation and suicidal attempts as well as affects treatment-seeking behavior (Schneier, Johnson, et al., 1992). Those with social phobia and a comorbid disorder reported a substantial number of thoughts about death and had higher rates of suicidal ideation and suicide attempts than those without a comorbid disorder. In comparison with controls who had no disorders, even those with uncomplicated social phobia more often thought about death, but they did not have higher rates of suicidal ideation or suicide attempts. Thus, clinicians need to be aware of the presence of these factors and the clinical complications they might present.

Comorbidity and Differential Diagnosis With Axis II Disorders

As with Axis I disorders, social anxiety is common among those with several different Axis II disorders. However, with respect to the differential diagnosis of social phobia and Axis II disorders, there are no clinical studies that have attempted to differentiate any of these conditions except those that have addressed the issue of APD. APD and obsessive–compulsive personality disorder (OCPD) are common comorbid conditions in social phobia. Although the presence of these two personality disorders may make the process of treatment more difficult, their presence usually does not preclude treating patients with social phobia using the standard interventions. However, additional treatment directed specifically at the personality disorder might be needed after social phobia is treated successfully. On the other hand, the presence of other Axis II disorders, such as paranoid personality disorder, does preclude a diagnosis of social phobia. Therefore, interventions commonly used for this disorder are not appropriate. Some guidelines that have proved useful in our clinical setting are offered in the next section.

Avoidant Personality Disorder

As noted, APD and OCPD are the most common comorbid Axis II conditions diagnosed in patients with social phobia (Turner, Beidel, Borden, et al., 1991). In a sample of 68 patients with a primary diagnosis of social phobia, 22% met criteria for APD. Another 53% exhibited features of APD even though they did not meet full diagnostic criteria. Others have found similar rates of comorbidity (Herbert et al., 1992; Holt, Heimberg, & Hope, 1992; Schneier, Spitzer, Gibbon, Fyer, & Liebowitz, 1991). This is not surprising given the extensive overlap in the diagnostic criteria between the two conditions (Turner, Beidel, & Townsley, 1992a). *DSM-IV* diagnostic criteria for APD include avoidance of occupational activities that require interpersonal contact, preoccupation with being criticized or rejected by others, and inhibition in new interpersonal situations because of feelings of inadequacy (American Psychiatric Association, 1994). The overlap between these diagnostic descriptors and those for social phobia are quite obvious. Several researchers have compared the clinical presentation of social phobia with and without comorbid APD (Herbert et al., 1992; Holt, Heimberg, & Hope, 1992; Turner, Beidel, & Townsley, 1992a). Overall, these studies revealed that those with comorbid APD had more severe scores on a host of self-report and clinician rated variables, including specific social phobia symptomatology and general measures of anxiety, depression, and social functioning. As summarized by Turner, Beidel, and Townsley (1992a), the similarity in the *DSM-III-R* (American Psychiatric Association, 1987) diagnostic criteria for social phobia and APD suggests that those with the generalized subtype may differ primarily on the basis of the severity of their social fears and degree of social impairment. The criteria for APD in *DSM-IV* do not alter this conclusion. Below, we discuss how the additional diagnosis of APD may affect the treatment outcome for social phobia.

Over the past few years, it has been our observation that patients with APD do not respond well to intensive imaginal treatment, in vivo exposure treatments, or both. Psychologically, they do not tolerate the intensive arousal well, and there appears to be an increase in general anxiety and depression. Also the dropout rate, or need for nonprotocol treatments for this group, appears to be greater. In analyzing the effectiveness of flooding treatment with this group, outcome probably is less positive. We have found a graduated, rather than an intensive, approach to exposure therapy to be somewhat helpful but not entirely satisfactory, leading us to the use of alternative interventions such as social skill training.

Those patients with social phobia who also have APD tend to have greater deficiencies in interpersonal skill and greater general inhibition, are less prepared vocationally, and frequently are less educated. They often have poor work histories and a lifelong pattern of reclusiveness and failure to develop social networks (see section on social phobia and social skill in this chapter). Although empirical study of social skill deficits in those with social phobia have produced mixed results (there are few studies), the generalized–specific dichotomy has not been explored. As a result, the type of deficits manifested by those with social phobia may not be detected by standard paradigms for assessing social skill. Thus, despite the lack of clarity from research studies, it is our clinical impression that a skills training strategy is essential for patients with social phobia with APD (see chapter 8 in this volume).

Obsessive–Compulsive Personality Disorder

A second common comorbid Axis II disorder is OCPD (Turner, Beidel, & Townsley, 1992a). Approximately 13% of those with primary social phobia meet criteria for OCPD. In addition, another 48.5% had subsyndromal features of this disorder. Although not sharing many diagnostic criteria with social phobia, those with the comorbid OCPD condition are perfectionistic; devoted to work (perhaps to avoid social interactions); overconscientious; scrupulous; inflexible about matters of morality, ethics, or values; and rigid or stubborn. Those with this set of behavioral characteristics are known to have interpersonal difficulties. Similarly, individuals with social phobia frequently are overly concerned about their outward behavior, believing that it must be perfect or others will think negatively of them. Such behavior has similarities with the perfectionistic beliefs of those with OCPD. Although current data do not allow a determination of whether OCPD or features of OCPD are a predispositional or correlational component of social phobia, it is notable that children with social phobia frequently have very rigid behavioral styles as well (Beidel, 1991; see chapter 2 in this volume).

One of the most important findings from our ongoing research program is the presence of significant obsessive features in many patients with social phobia. The features range in degree of severity from relatively moderate to actually meeting diagnostic criteria (Turner, Beidel, Borden, et al., 1991). It is interesting to speculate what role obsessionality might play in the genesis of social phobia. In our view, it is unlikely that these features are pathonogmonic by themselves, but they likely combine with other vulnerability factors (i.e., high general anxiety and traumatic conditioning) to produce the disorder.

It has been our experience that patients with social phobia who have significant obsessional attributes present a considerable challenge for treatment. They may be less able to use imagery, which makes imaginal exposure more difficult to implement (see chapter 8 in this volume). Even more problematic for the exposure strategies is that these patients frequently use projection and rationalization to explain their deficiencies. Thus, if an exposure session consists of being placed in a situation where negative expectations are realized, the patient will blame someone else or rationalize that the situation is unnatural and thus unimportant. Although we have not attempted their use with these patients, our clinical experience suggests that the defensive strategies adopted by patients with OCPD probably would make the implementation of cognitive strategies difficult at best.

We also have made a number of other observations, with respect to psychopathology as well as treatment, about the patient with OCPD who also has social phobia. The problem is whether social distress is a true comorbid condition or whether patients with OCPD have problems with social anxiety because of their personality attributes. We will illustrate why this distinction is important. Although those with OCPD fear negative evaluation, they do not attribute the failure of a social interaction to their own behavior. Rather, they tend to attribute the problem to other individuals or physical aspects of the social setting (e.g., the room was too hot). Those with social phobia always blame themselves, sometimes when it is not even warranted. We think this is a significant issue if using some type of exposure treatment, primarily because in cases where the patient externalizes the source of the distress, exposure to the situation tends not to elicit arousal.

As noted previously, APD and OCPD represent the most common comorbid Axis II disorders in individuals with social phobia (Turner, Beidel, & Townsley, 1992a), and the presence of either Axis I or II comorbid disorders results in a more severe syndrome than social phobia alone (Turner, Beidel, & Townsley, 1992a; Turner, Beidel, Wolff, Spaulding, & Jacob, 1996). Other personality disorders that appeared with less common frequency in a sample of patients with primary social phobia included histrionic (4%), antisocial (3%), dependent (1.5%), paranoid (1.5%), narcissistic (1.5%), and borderline (1.5%), and it is to some of these disorders that we now turn our attention.

Paranoid Personality Disorder

Those with paranoid personality disorder frequently seek treatment because they are having significant interpersonal distress, but the basis of their social distress is different from those with social phobia. The person with paranoid personality disorder has difficulty developing trust because of a distorted perception about the motives of others. It is crucial that these patients be identified because, in our experience, they respond poorly to behavioral interventions for social phobia. For example, in one case that we treated with intensive exposure, a full blown paranoid state was instigated that required a considerable period of time to dissipate. The problem was that the patient did not appear paranoid even following a thorough assessment that had included a clinical interview, a semistructured personality disorder inventory, and a battery of psychological assessments including the Minnesota Multiphasic Personality Inventory (MMPI). We have seen a number of these patients over the past 12 years, and although we have not developed a foolproof way of identifying all of those with significant paranoid features, there are several anomalies that appear in their clinical history. First, in a number of cases, we have noted that the frank onset of social phobia appears to be later than is typical, usually well after young adulthood. Second, although the MMPI profiles of these patients do not reveal paranoia, we have found that these individuals have elevated scores on the subtle paranoid research scale of the original version of the MMPI (Hathaway & McKinley, 1940). For example, the patient described above had a T score of 76 on this research scale. Third, when placed in a behavioral performance task requiring an impromptu speech, these patients report feeling humiliated. Individuals with social phobia easily understand the purpose of this task, see it as distressing but nevertheless useful. As noted in the section on comorbidity, the number of socially phobic patients comorbid for paranoid personality disorder is about 1%. However, the problem is significant when it does occur. Those clinicians treating social phobia should be vigilant regarding this possibility in those presenting with apparent social phobia.

Schizoid Personality Disorder

Although not listed among the personality disorders commonly found, there is a critical clinical distinction between social phobia and schizoid personality disorder. Those with the latter diagnosis arrive at the clinic because someone other than the patient is not pleased with his or her level of social interaction. The differentiating factor is that those with social phobia desire to interact with others, whereas those with schizoid personality disorder prefer their own company to the necessity of social discourse. They are not necessarily anxious when in these settings, they simply prefer not to engage in social activities.

CONCLUSION

Elaine's case, described at the beginning of this chapter, shows how her social distress impacted her personal and professional functioning. Because of the severity of her distress and the resulting impairment, Elaine's clinical presentation was consistent with a diagnosis of social phobia. Existing data indicate that social phobia is a significant psychiatric disorder that affects a substantial percentage of the adult population. Over the past 15 years, data have accumulated to demonstrate that this disorder results in considerable emotional distress, social inhibition, and occupational and social maladjustment. The boundary between social phobia and shyness is not fully understood at this time, but it is likely that at least some of those referred to as shy meet diagnostic criteria for social phobia. The exact nature of the relationship, however, awaits further study.

Using *DSM-IV* criteria, there are two patterns of social phobia. The first, referred to as the specific or nongeneralized type, is characterized by social fear and avoidance of social performance situations as exemplified by fear of public speaking. The second pattern, the generalized subtype, consists of pervasive social anxiety and fear associated with most social situations and activities. The generalized subtype is far more common based on data from clinical settings, and this subtype is significantly more severe symptomatically than the specific subtype. In addition, the generalized subtype is more often associated with concurrent Axis I and II conditions, and among this group significant depression and suicidal thought are more likely to be found. Also, considerable social skill deficits appear to characterize this subtype, and preliminary treatment data suggest that treatment incorporating social skill training is needed for this group.

As noted above, social phobia, as is the case for other anxiety disorders, frequently is comorbid with other Axis I and II conditions. The relationship of social phobia to APD particularly is an issue because of the overlap in diagnostic criteria in previous and current versions of the *DSM*. Although the presence of a comorbid Axis I or II condition does not affect the use of current treatment for social phobia, the presence of a comorbid condition can affect the management of patients and the level of improvement at posttreatment. Therefore, other interventions will be needed to treat the comorbid condition, and the time required to treat the social phobia may be longer. In the next chapter we discuss issues of the clinical presentation of social phobia in children and adolescents.

2

Clinical Presentation of Social Phobia in Children and Adolescents

Lawrence is a 14-year-old African American adolescent who has been refusing to attend school. Lawrence's guidance counselor and the school principal call him a truancy problem because he has been on the school grounds after school, watching football practice. However, Lawrence does try to go to school each morning. He gets in the car and allows his mother to drive him to school. She explained that when he gets there he appears to be overcome by fear, and he cannot get out of the car. Because his mother can identify with his feelings (she experienced anxiety as a child), she brought him to the clinic for an evaluation.

Lawrence readily acknowledged his school refusal. However, he indicated that he was very interested in attending school and was worried that by missing classes he would not pass eighth grade. He reported that being around the other children made him nervous. Lawrence explained that when he was with a group of children his heart would race and he would sweat and become nauseated. On several occasions, he had vomited in the school lavatory because of his distress. He was becoming increasingly afraid that the next time he would vomit in the classroom, which would be extremely embarrassing. His mother reported that he had a long history of social fearfulness and reluctance to interact with others. On the basis of the interview, a battery of self-report inventories, and behavioral monitoring, Lawrence was diagnosed as having social phobia.

Throughout this chapter we will discuss the clinical syndrome of social phobia in children and adolescents. However, for the sake of brevity and unless otherwise noted, we will use the terms *childhood social phobia* or *children with social phobia* to include both children and adolescents. We noted in chapter 1 that research on social phobia in adults is of relatively recent vintage. Even more recent is clinical and research interest in this syndrome in children. Lawrence's case illustrates how easily children's social fears can be misinterpreted by adults, primarily because of a lack of understanding of the disorder. Because they were unfamiliar with the syndrome, the school administrators interpreted Lawrence's school refusal as a conduct problem, particularly because he was on the school grounds after school. In reality, however, Lawrence watched football practice away from the presence of others. If others approached, he would leave. Clearly, then, his fearfulness centered around social interactions with others, which is the hallmark of social phobia.

DEVELOPMENTAL CONSIDERATIONS

Now that it is clear that social phobia can be manifested in childhood, the questions are, How early in childhood does this syndrome appear? Are there precursors to social phobia that can be identified before a diagnosis can be made? and Are there other factors that may be associated with social anxiety and avoidance in children other than social phobia?

Studies of social phobia per se have not been undertaken in infants. However, developmental psychologists long have studied aspects of temperament that relate to socialization. *Sociability*, for example, is defined as the preference for affiliation and companionship rather than

34

solitude (Buss & Plomin, 1984; Thomas & Chess, 1977). Another term, *shyness* (discussed in chapter 1 in this volume), is defined as social withdrawal motivated by social–evaluative concerns, particularly in novel situations (Rubin & Asendorpf, 1993). However, the terms *sociability* and *shyness*, both describing common dimensions of temperament, are not interchangeable. Rather, the two constructs represent what appear to be distinct traits (Cheek & Buss, 1981). Social withdrawal, for example, need not be motivated by concern with negative evaluation. There are those individuals who simply prefer solitude to social interaction; social situations do not elicit distress. These individuals would be considered to have low sociability but not to be shy. Therefore, it is important to understand that social inhibition or reluctance to engage in social interactions does not necessarily mean that the child is shy or suffering from social phobia. Other factors, such as emotional distress or functional impairment that result from nonparticipation, must also be considered.

Developmental psychologists also have studied social isolation in young children, and its long-term detrimental effects have been documented clearly. In second graders, passive isolation (the type most commonly associated with social anxiety), low perceived social competence, or both, significantly predicted depression and loneliness in these students when they reached the fifth grade (Rubin & Mills, 1988). Similarly, internalizing problems (anxiety, depression) in middle childhood were significantly predicted by earlier (second grade) childhood difficulties, including poor peer acceptance and social isolation (Hymel, Rubin, Rowden, & LeMare, 1990). Among young adolescents who recently had moved to a new school district, higher social anxiety predicted less social interaction and fewer friendships even many months later (Vernberg, Abwender, Ewell, & Beery, 1992). Other studies of children identified as shy, socially isolated, and withdrawn (children who are alone and are not approached by other children), or peer-neglected (children who are ignored by other children) indicated that the characteristics of these various groups overlap considerably with the diagnostic categories of social phobia and avoidant disorder of childhood. For example, children with an anxiety disorder are more likely than other children to be classified as peer-neglected (Strauss, Lahey, Frick, Frame, & Hynd, 1988). Conversely, peer-neglected children reported the highest level of social anxiety among various groups of school children (LaGreca, Dandes, Wick, Shaw, & Stone, 1988).

Despite the interest in the constructs of sociability, shyness, and social inhibition by other psychologists, clinicians' interest in social phobia has been relatively recent. One reason may be that children's fears were believed to be transitory in nature (Barrios & O'Dell, 1989), although Achenbach (1985) noted that this axiom did not appear to apply to social fears. However, some shy children do seem to "outgrow" their shyness. Retrospective reports of adults revealed that about 50% of college students who were shy as children outgrew their fears during adolescence and early adulthood (Bruch, Giordano, & Pearl, 1986; see chapters 1 and 4 in this volume for a more extended discussion on shyness and social phobia). However, currently there are no predictors that will identify children who will outgrow social fears and those who will not. In addition, as the data in this chapter will illustrate, children with social fears suffer immediate as well as long-term consequences. Thus, attention in the form of research and clinical intervention is well-founded.

DIAGNOSIS

Although the average age of onset for social phobia has been considered to be mid-adolescence, several authors (Beidel & Turner, 1988; Last, Perrin, Hersen, & Kazdin, 1992; Strauss & Last, 1993) reported that children as young as age 8 can be diagnosed with the disorder. Also, many adults with social phobia date the onset of their social fears to childhood, reporting that they have been socially anxious "all their lives" (Stemberger, Turner, Beidel, & Calhoun, 1995). However, prior to 1994, children with social–evaluative fears could be diagnosed as having social phobia, overanxious disorder, or avoidant disorder of childhood. With the introduction of the fourth edition of the *Diagnostic and Statistical Manual of Mental Disorders* (*DSM-IV*; American Psychiatric Association, 1994), avoidant disorder was dropped and overanxious disorder radically changed. This revision has several positive features, including ensuring that all children with social fears now will be given a consistent diagnosis of social phobia (Beidel & Morris, 1995). In addition, epidemiological studies now will be able to determine more specifically the prevalence of this disorder in children. Another advantage of the revised diagnostic criteria is that specific descriptors designed to illustrate the clinical presentation in children have been added. These descriptors are presented below.

As we noted in chapter 1, social phobia is "a marked and persistent fear of one or more social performances in which the person is exposed to unfamiliar people or to possible scrutiny by others." The individual fears that he or she will act in a way (or show anxiety symptoms) that will be humiliating or embarrassing. "In children, there must be evidence for capacity for social relationships with familiar people and the anxiety must occur in peer settings, not just in interaction with adults" (American Psychiatric Association, 1994, p. 416). This statement defines two very important issues related to the diagnosis of social phobia in children. First, "the children must be capable of social interactions." This differentiates children with social phobia from those with pervasive developmental disorders such as autism, for example. In reality, determining the capacity for social interaction is a fairly easy distinction for most clinicians. Parents often describe shy children as socially engaging with siblings, cousins, or close family friends. However, outside this small family circle, the child is reclusive and socially isolative.

A second important qualifier with respect to the diagnosis of social phobia in children is that "the anxiety must occur in peer settings, not just in interactions with adults." Obviously, because of the inherent differences between children and adults (age, experience, authority), many children are somewhat reticent when interacting with adults, particularly unfamiliar adults or those in authority (such as the school principal). For a child to be diagnosed with social phobia, the child must express or demonstrate fearfulness in peer settings. Again, assessing this is not difficult. For example, these children often stand at the perimeter of other children's social activities (such as during recess). They often are reluctant to speak in class and refuse to attend pleasant events such as parties. In all of these instances, the anxiety is occurring in peer settings.

The *DSM-IV* criteria also specify that "exposure to the feared social situation almost invariably provokes anxiety, which may take the form of a situationally bound or situationally predisposed panic attack. Note: In children, the anxiety may be expressed by crying, tantrums, freezing or withdrawal from the social situation" (American Psychiatric Association, 1994, p. 417). In relatively rare cases, the anxiety may be manifested as selective mutism, when the child refuses to speak in certain social situations (see below for an extended discussion). These various expressions highlight a particularly important aspect of the diagnosis, especially in reference to younger children. Although adolescents may report having panic attacks in social settings, such a response is uncommon for young children. The most common physical symptoms reported by children between the ages of 8 and 12 with social–evaluative fears (and which differentiated them from normal controls) included choking, flushes or chills, palpitations, fainting, shaking, feeling like dying, and headaches (Beidel, Christ, & Long, 1991). These are many of the same symptoms reported by adults with social phobia. Symptoms characteristic of panic attacks (dizziness, shortness of breath, numbness, or tingling) are less common in children with social phobia.

It is important to remember that young children (less than 10 years old) often cannot describe many specific physical symptoms (although they may complain of butterflies in the stomach or headaches). Parents, however, often report that the child has crying episodes, tantrumming behaviors, freezing, or withdrawal. Importantly, some children may be mistakenly diagnosed as *oppositional*. For these children, fears are so extensive that when it comes to social engagement, they refuse to do what their parents ask but are unable to explain why. One of our young patients refused her mother's directions to wear her "nice clothing" to school. In addition, she refused to wear jewelry or allow her mother to style her hair, preferring a straight part down the middle of her long hair, with no curls, barrettes, or other accessories. Although her mother did not understand why she would not acquiesce to her desires, after analysis it seemed evident that the girl was choosing a plain appearance to decrease the likelihood of drawing attention to herself. Thus, this oppositional behavior was motivated by the child's social fear. Similarly, Lawrence's truant behavior described in the beginning of this chapter was motivated by his social fear.

Another criterion of social phobia in the *DSM-IV* states that the person recognizes that the fear is excessive and unreasonable. However, it also states "Note: In children, this feature may be absent" (American Psychiatric Association, 1994, p. 417). In our clinical practice, we have found that children as young as age 8 are able to discern that their fears are excessive, although, as has been noted with other fears, girls more readily report the presence of social fears than boys. We usually phrase this by asking children if they think they are "more nervous" or "more shy" than other children in their class or in their neighborhood. Some socially phobic children readily acknowledge that their social distress is higher than their peers' social distress (nonanxious children too can easily identify shy peers). The problem is that even if they think they are "more shy," not all children with social phobia readily acknowledge that their fear is in need of treatment.

This last point is most important. A common diagnostic rule of thumb for clinicians working with children is that when parents and children disagree on the presence of symptoms, the parent's report is given more weight for symptomatology related to externalizing disorders (e.g., conduct disorder). However, the child's report is given more weight with reference to internalizing disorders (believing that parents may not be aware of their children's fears). Although in general this clinical lore may be a good axiom to follow, it sometimes is incorrect with respect to social phobia. A number of children who come to our clinic readily admit to shyness, but some, referred by parents or guidance counselors, do not. We have interviewed children who denied the presence of any anxiety, claiming that they had several friends and were not inhibited in school activities. Their parents, however, described children who were socially reclusive, had few, if any, friends, and had a very restricted range of social interactions. Because our clinic conducts behavioral assessments of children's social skills and assessment of social performance, we have used those data to help determine whether parental or child reports are more valid. We have the children engage in a role-play assessment using a same-age peer. The children are asked to respond to several different types of social encounters: responding to requests for help, giving compliments, receiving compliments, and being assertive. In addition, we ask children to read aloud before a small group. In virtually every instance when the child in fact has social fears, the skills and performance data are more consistent with the parent's report than with the child's own self-report. That is, in the behavioral assessments, the children who denied social difficulties were unable to display behaviors that would suggest the ability to form friendships, sustain social interactions, or behave effectively in the social performance task. Thus, we strongly advise that parental reports be given sufficient weight when determining the possible presence of social phobia in children.

PHENOMENOLOGY

The situations that are stressful for children and adolescents with social phobia are much the same as they are for adults. The percentage of children with social phobia who fear particular types of social situations is presented in Table 3.

Although speaking to peers was not formally assessed, on the basis of our clinical experience, we would estimate that the percentage of children who fear speaking with peers is approximately 40% (the same percentage that fears eating or writing in public). Strauss and Last (1993) described similar categories of fear. As with adults, these fears can be classified into two broader categories: performance situations (as in reading in class) and general conversational interactions (talking with a group of children). As noted in chapter 1, there remains controversy surrounding just what behaviors are characteristic of each of these two subtypes. In fact, this distinction has received very little study in children and adolescents to date.

Daily diaries (self-monitoring) can be used to determine specific aspects of social behavior, such as the frequency and type of social interactions feared. This form of assessment usually requires the child

Table 3	
Frequently Feared Social Situations in Children With Social Phobia	

Situation	Percentage
Public speaking (giving an oral report, reading aloud)	89%
Eating in front of others (school cafeteria, a restaurant, or at home)	39%
Writing on the blackboard	28%
Going to parties	28%
Using public bathrooms	24%
Speaking to authorities	21%

Adapted from Beidel, D. C. (1991). Social Phobia and Overanxious Disorder in School-age Children. *Journal of the American Academy of Child and Adolescent Psychiatry, 30,* 545–552.

to complete a brief checklist after the occurrence of an event or at the end of the day, typically indicating the occurrence or frequency of specific events and the child's response (see chapter 5 in this volume for a discussion and examples of self-monitoring procedures). Results of studies with socially phobic children indicate that a socially distressful event occurs about every other day (Beidel, Neal, & Lederer, 1991). Because children spend a large percentage of their time at school, it should not be surprising that the majority of distressing events occur in the school setting. The most commonly occurring event is an unstructured encounter with a peer (such as having to talk or work with another child at school). Other commonly occurring events include taking tests, performing in front of others, or reading in front of others. Although most children will readily report feeling anxious when reading aloud, the more common social situation, as we noted above, is an unstructured interaction with peers. Because such encounters may not be readily identified, clinicians need to assess carefully the presence of anxiety during informal social situations.

Other authors also have described cognitive, behavioral, and physical symptoms associated with childhood social phobia on the basis of clinical presentation at a specialty anxiety clinic (Albano, DiBartolo,

Heimberg, & Barlow, 1995). In addition to the somatic behaviors noted above, behavioral manifestations can include stuttering, poor eye contact, mumbling, nailbiting, and a trembling voice. These authors reported that cognitive content included thoughts of escape from the social situation, negative evaluation, failure, humiliation, embarrassment, and inadequacy and self-criticism. Physical symptoms can include the full range of physical responses to any anxiety-producing situation, although as noted earlier, symptoms closely related to the beta-adrenergic system (heart palpitations, blushing, trembling, and sweating) are particularly common in this disorder. Finally, the play activities of children with social phobia sometimes are unusual. Albano and her colleagues (Albano et al., 1995) noted that many children with social phobia develop unusual hobbies for their given age, including collecting Civil War facts, programming computers, or tracking weather reports. In addition, many of our socially phobic children have never participated in activities such as bowling or roller skating or roller blading. Albano et al. (1995) hypothesized that the lack of more common interests may be due to limited opportunities for social interactions that result from their social fears. Thus, because they are socially isolated, these children miss out on the opportunities to participate in more traditional childhood activities.

A comparison of the clinical presentation of adults with social phobia (as presented in chapter 1 in this volume) with the data on children presented above demonstrates remarkable similarities in feared situations. Reading or speaking before a group is the most commonly reported socially distressful situation. Physical complaints common in adults (heart palpitations, shaking and trembling, blushing, sweating) also are found in children. However, children also commonly report "butterflies" in the stomach, nausea, fear of vomiting, and headaches. It is unclear whether these different physical complaints represent true differences in physical symptomatology or whether children's verbal development limits their expression. Negative cognitions, however, so frequently mentioned as characteristic of this disorder in adults, do not appear to be present in young children (although they may exist in adolescents; Albano et al., 1995). Similarly, in anxiety-producing situations, preadolescent children do not typically report the presence of negative ideation (Beidel, M. W. Turner, & Trager, 1994).

Other clinical correlates of social phobia in children include significantly higher levels of depression, higher trait anxiety, and a more rigid temperamental style when compared with children without psychological disorders (Beidel, 1991). Children with a rigid temperamental style become distressed when aspects of their normal routine are changed or interrupted. The behaviors characteristic of this rigid temperamental style are very similar to obsessive–compulsive personality disorder (OCPD), which is a relatively common comorbid condition in adults with social phobia (Turner, Beidel, Borden, et al., 1991; also see chapter 1 in this volume).

The primary coexisting disorders that are present in adults (generalized anxiety disorder, or GAD, and specific phobias) also are present in children (Beidel & Turner, 1992b; Last, Strauss, & Francis, 1987). In a recent sample, approximately 20% of 25 children with a primary diagnosis of social phobia also had specific phobias, whereas 16% had GAD (overanxious disorder), 8% had depression, 16% had attention deficit hyperactivity disorder, and 16% had learning disabilities (Beidel, Turner, & Morris, 1997).

DETRIMENTAL OUTCOMES

Empirical data on the detrimental outcomes of childhood social phobia are beginning to emerge. In one specialty clinic, 30% of children who refused to attend school did so because of social fears (Last, Perrin, Hersen, & Kazdin, 1992). In another clinic, social phobia was the most commonly diagnosed anxiety disorder (Albano, 1995). Additionally, Perrin and Last (1993) noted that among anxious children, social phobia was much more likely to precede the onset of depression rather than vice versa. Clark (1993) reported that a substantial percentage of adolescents who abused alcohol met diagnostic criteria for social phobia. Conduct problems, difficulty getting along with peers, and truancy were common behaviors found in this sample of adolescent boys comorbid for social phobia and alcohol abuse. As noted earlier, when distress reaches a certain level, children with severe social fears may refuse to engage in certain activities, thus appearing oppositional, at least on an intermittent basis. It is clear then that social phobia can be related to a host of maladaptive child behaviors.

In addition to these short-term correlates, childhood social phobia appears to have long-term detrimental effects. For example, among a sample of 194 adult panic patients, 54% were found to have a childhood history of an anxiety disorder. Most commonly this disorder was social phobia (Pollack, Otto, Sabatine, Majcher, & Rosenbaum, 1995). Adult patients with childhood anxiety disorders had a significantly higher rate of adulthood anxiety comorbidity, family history of anxiety disorders, and comorbid depression (Pollack et al., 1995). As discussed above, on the basis of ECA survey data, Davidson (1993) noted that conduct problems and truancy were part of the childhood history of adults with social phobia and that onset of social phobia prior to age 11 was predictive of nonrecovery in adulthood. Although some of these data are preliminary, and the retrospective data reported by Davidson (1993) must be regarded cautiously, these consistent findings document the pervasive negative outcome when childhood social phobia is unrecognized and untreated.

Social Skills

Few studies have specifically addressed social skill deficits in children with social anxiety, although there have been some reports in children who are described as socially isolated (see chapter 4 in this volume). To date, there are no published studies using carefully diagnosed samples of children with social phobia that have specifically examined skill deficits. However, some intervention programs have adopted social skill training as part of an overall treatment package on the basis of clinical observations that such deficits existed in individual children (see chapter 9 in this volume). Some preliminary data from our clinic document that children with social phobia do have skill deficits. We compared children with social phobia ($n = 22$) to same-aged normal controls ($n = 18$) in a series of role-play tasks and a read-aloud task described earlier in this chapter (Beidel, Turner, & Morris, 1997). The results indicated that observers unaware of diagnostic status rated children with social phobia as significantly less skilled in both role play and read-aloud tasks. In addition, children with social phobia were rated as significantly more anxious during both tasks. These data, in combination with those found in adult populations (see chapter 1 in this volume), suggest that social skill training should be considered an integral component of treatment.

RELATED CONDITIONS

Selective Mutism

There is a condition very closely related to childhood social phobia that cannot rely on children's self-report for the diagnosis. This disorder, called *selective mutism*, is characterized by refusal to speak in certain social situations. There is a correlate of this behavior in the developmental literature that describes long latencies to vocalize as characteristic of children with behavioral inhibition (i.e., a condition characterized by reluctance to approach unfamiliar people, objects, or situations and by social reticence; see chapter 4 in this volume). Children with selective mutism have the ability to converse with others and often will speak freely in the immediate family environment and perhaps with a few close family friends. However, in virtually every other situation, selectively mute children will not initiate or respond to conversations. The average age of onset for selective mutism is quite young (3.7 years).

Although there are few studies that describe the clinical presentation of this condition, there are some data to suggest that, in some cases, selective mutism may be a variant of, and perhaps an extreme form of, childhood social phobia. In a study of clinical symptomatology, Black and Uhde (1995) assessed 20 selectively mute children referred to the National Institute of Mental Health and found that 95% (19 out of 20) met diagnostic criteria for social phobia. The 20th child was described as very shy. No other diagnostic category was common among these children, but about 30% had a coexisting specific phobia (fear of a specific nonsocial situation, such as heights). This rate of comorbidity is about the same percentage as is found in children with a primary diagnosis of social phobia. Parent and teacher ratings of children with selective mutism indicated high levels of anxiety, especially social anxiety (Black & Uhde, 1995).

In the largest study to date, Dummit et al. (1997) assessed 50 children with selective mutism. All children met *DSM-III-R* criteria for social phobia or avoidant disorder. In addition, 48% had additional anxiety disorders (26% had separation anxiety disorder, 14% had overanxious disorder, and 24% had specific [simple] phobia). Parental ratings indicated substantial social distress and functional interference. Only one child was comorbid for oppositional disorder, and another was comorbid for attention deficit hyperactivity disorder. Problematic behaviors, such as conduct disorder or attention deficit hyperactivity disorder, were assessed by a one-item rating scale. Although ratings were not in the range suggesting clinically significant difficulties, a broader assessment is needed in order to determine the pervasiveness of oppositional behaviors (as opposed to oppositional defiant disorder) in this group of children. The finding of only one child in this study who met diagnostic criteria for oppositional defiant disorder is in contrast to the 10% who met criteria in Black and Udhe (1995). Data from the Dummit et al. (1997) study is consistent with previous descriptions of selectively mute children who have been noted to have higher levels of trait anxiety, fearfulness, and shyness, and have at least one shy or socially reticent parent (Brown & Lloyd, 1975).

Aside from oppositional behavior and conduct problems per se, there often are other aspects to the clinical presentation of selective mutism that are suggestive of externalizing behavioral problems in these children. However, we noted that children with social phobia can become oppositional when asked to engage in situations that make them anxious. Similarly, children with selective mutism often exhibit defiant rather than anxious behaviors when under duress. For example, we have had children with selective mutism in our lobby area, loudly talking to their parents and siblings as they play. When we appear for the session, they immediately assume a defiant posture (feet apart, arms folded across the chest, and eyes that issue the challenge "I dare you to make me talk"). Such a stance is not characteristic of typical socially anxious children, whose oppositional behavior is more likely to consist of crying, hiding, or refusing to leave the parent. Although not all children with selective mutism will meet criteria for oppositional defiant disorder, we have observed many operant features that help to maintain the condition that are not often seen in other socially phobic children. In fact, we believe that in order to effectively treat these children, additional strategies to those typically used to treat social phobia will be needed.

Although the literature is sparse, the data that do exist appear consistent with the speculation that selective mutism is a variant of social phobia, and therefore treatments developed for social phobia also may be useful for this disorder. Furthermore, it has been our clinical experience that oppositional problems in children with social phobia are sometimes the result of poor parenting skills (see chapters 6 and 9 in this volume) and that various reinforcement contingencies may serve to foster and maintain the behavior. Thus, thorough attention to all aspects of parent–child interactions are necessary.

Test Anxiety

Test anxiety is a condition commonly related to social phobia. Significant test anxiety appears to occur in approximately 40% of elementary school aged children (Beidel & Turner, 1988; B. G. Turner, Beidel, Hughes, & M. W. Turner, 1991). Like social phobia, test anxiety is a fear of negative evaluation that has cognitive, somatic, and behavioral components. Children with test anxiety fear that they will perform poorly on tests just as children with social phobia fear that they will make a mistake when performing in front of others. Heart palpitations, sweating, and blushing are common among children with test anxiety, as they are in children with social phobia (Beidel et al., 1991). Finally, children with test anxiety will "play sick" in order to avoid going to school on a test day. Thus, school refusal (at least on an intermittent basis) also occurs in this population.

In addition to the similar clinical presentation, approximately 60% of children with test anxiety meet diagnostic criteria for social phobia or overanxious disorder (Beidel & Turner, 1988). Furthermore, this percentage is consistent for White and African American children (there also is consistent similarity in the clinical presentation across these two racial groups; see chapter 3). These data suggest that test anxiety may serve as an indicator for the presence of more pervasive social fears in at least half of test-anxious children. Complaints of test anxiety in children should prompt clinicians to do a thorough evaluation for other anxiety problems, particularly social phobia.

DIFFERENTIAL DIAGNOSIS

Children with anxiety disorders rarely present with just one type of fear. Particularly when using *DSM-III-R* diagnostic criteria, comorbidity rates were quite high. Last et al. (1992) reported that 87% of socially phobic children had an additional diagnosis. It is important to note that in many of these cases, the comorbid diagnosis was overanxious disorder or avoidant disorder of childhood. This pattern of comorbidity should not exist using *DSM-IV* criteria because overanxious disorder has been revised significantly and avoidant disorder of childhood has been eliminated. Because studies using *DSM-IV* criteria are not currently available, rates of comorbidity for children with social phobia remain uncertain (see chapter 3).

Panic Disorder

As noted in chapter 1, one of the most difficult distinctions is differentiating social phobia from panic disorder. Because children are less likely to experience panic disorder, the clinician will be faced with the challenge of making this distinction less often than with adults. However, the guidelines offered in chapter 1 are still useful when identifying children and adolescents with panic disorder. To reiterate, those with panic disorder experience the constellation of symptoms that define a panic attack. Although those with social phobia fear that their physical symptoms may be observable to others, unlike those with panic disorder, they do not fear the symptoms themselves. In addition, their symptoms occur only in the presence of, or anticipation of, social situations.

School Refusal

Although the term *school phobia* no longer is used, school refusal is a behavioral symptom of anxiety (as well as other disorders). Kearny and Silverman (1990) noted four behavioral patterns that may be associated with school refusal. They included avoidance of negative-affectivity-provoking objects or situations, escape from aversive social or evaluative situations, attention-getting behavior, and positive tangible reinforcement. In fact, school refusal may be associated with either externalizing or internalizing disorders. Certainly, children with conduct disorders or oppositional disorder may refuse to attend school. For other children, staying at home is more reinforcing than going to school. Among children with internalizing disorders, those with depression may simply lack the energy or interest to attend school. Children with anxiety disorders such as separation anxiety disorder, social phobia, obsessive-compulsive disorder (OCD), or specific phobias may also refuse to attend school. Children with specific phobias may fear a particular class, a particular teacher, or a particular activity (such as jumping on a trampoline), which may result in school refusal. Children with separation anxiety disorder (see below) refuse to attend school because of their fears of separation from or harm to a caretaker. Children with OCD may refuse to attend school because the school environment might contain a contaminant they fear.

For children with social phobia, reluctance or refusal to attend school stems from their fears of social interactions. School necessitates engagement in many social and performance activities that are distressing for those with social phobia. As we have mentioned before, these include answering questions in class, reading in front of the class, writing on the blackboard, eating in the cafeteria, talking to the principal, participating in physical education classes, and performing in front of others (e.g., being in a play or a recital). With few, if any, opportunities to avoid these activities while attending school, one can understand why children with severe social fears may be reluctant to attend school. However, unlike children with conduct disorder or those who receive tangible reinforcement for non-attendance, children with social phobia are desirous of attending school. Their oppositional behavior is fueled by their fear of the social aspects of the school setting. Lawrence's case, described in the introduction to this chapter, exemplifies this distinction.

Specific Phobia

Specific phobia involves fears of objects or situations that do not involve social encounters or panic attacks (e.g., dogs, heights, and needles). Comparing clinic-referred children with social phobia and those with specific (simple) phobia, Strauss and Last (1993) reported that at the time of referral, children with social phobia were older, and on the basis of self-report instruments, were significantly more lonely, generally fearful, and depressed. Comorbid *DSM-III-R* conditions such as avoidant disorder and overanxious disorder were more likely to be present in children with social phobia than simple phobia. The presence of these latter two conditions may have resulted from the vagaries of the *DSM-III-R* diagnostic system noted earlier. Because this overlap has, to a large extent, been eliminated by the change in diagnostic criteria with the publication of *DSM-IV*, it is unclear whether the higher presence of comorbid disorders will continue to discriminate social phobia from specific phobia.

Separation Anxiety Disorder

An important distinction, and one that is not always easily accomplished, is differentiating social phobia from separation anxiety disorder (SAD). This latter condition refers to excessive concern about separation from a major attachment figure. Children with SAD fear that some harm will befall them, their parents, or someone else who serves a major caretaker role. Thus, whereas SAD involves distress over being separated from a significant other, social phobia entails distress over approach or interaction with others (Beidel & Morris, 1995). In clinical practice, this distinction often is difficult to make, particularly in young children, and children with either disorder can experience and display anxiety when in social settings. For example, the "clinging" behavior so often seen in anxious children could result from a desire to stay close to a caretaker or fear of approaching an unfamiliar social situation. As noted above, school refusal cannot differentiate these two disorders because both groups report feeling fearful in the school setting. Strauss and Last (1993) reported that fear of school was reported by 64% of a group of socially phobic children. Most, but not necessarily all, children with separation fears also reported feeling fearful in school. Because both groups are fearful in school, behavior in other settings may be more important in differentiating these disorders. For example, unlike children with SAD, socially phobic children do not exhibit inordinate distress when parents leave them at home or when they are away from their parents. Children with social phobia typically do not report nightmares or dreams of separation from parents. In contrast, children with SAD do not have significant fears when speaking, eating, or writing in front of others. Thus, clearly there are avenues by which to differentiate these two disorders. However, relying on school refusal alone will not be sufficient. Furthermore, the problem is complicated by the fact that a child can have both conditions simultaneously, and each may have to be treated separately.

Generalized Anxiety Disorder (Overanxious Disorder)

Using *DSM-III-R* diagnostic criteria, it was often difficult to differentiate children with social phobia from those with overanxious disorder as both included social–evaluative fears as part of the diagnosis. Under *DSM-IV*, children with GAD (overanxious disorder in children) express significant worry about a myriad of concerns and have somatic symptoms such as feeling keyed up, on edge, or restless, being easily fatigued, having difficulty concentrating, feeling irritable, experiencing muscle tension, and experiencing sleep disturbance. Children with this disorder worry about a broad range of situations, not just social encounters, making this diagnostic distinction easier. However, 16% of our sample of socially phobic children, consistent with the adult literature, also had a concurrent *DSM-IV* diagnosis of GAD (overanxious disorder in children), and the implications of this comorbidity for treatment are not yet clear.

Depression

Another important distinction is the differentiation of social phobia from depression. Strauss and Last (1993) reported that 10% of their socially phobic sample also met criteria for depression. In our sample, 8% had concurrent depression (Beidel, Turner, & Morris, 1997). With respect to differential diagnosis, there are no empirical data to guide the clinician in the decision-making process. Children with depression often refuse to attend social engagements and may even refuse to attend school. However, the reason for the refusal often is markedly different. Children with depression often have a low energy level and have lost interest in participating in many activities (i.e., things are not fun any more). In addition, based on research with depressed adult women, dysphoric mood can inhibit social behavior, making social interactions less rewarding and therefore less likely to occur (Hersen, Bellack, Himmelhoch, & Thase, 1984). It appears that depressed children avoid or refuse to participate in social activities because of their anergia and anhedonia; reasons similar to those of depressed adults. In contrast, those with social phobia avoid social settings not because of a lack of energy and interest but because of their fears. It should be clear, then, that in order to arrive at a proper diagnosis, the motivating factor for the inhibited social behavior must be understood fully. Of course, both patterns of social avoidance may be present in those who have both disorders concurrently.

Externalizing Disorders

Sometimes anxiety disorders co-occur with externalizing disorders. Last, Hersen, Kazdin, Finkelstein, and Strauss (1987) reported that among a sample of 91 children referred to an anxiety disorders clinic, 21% also had either conduct disorder, oppositional defiant disorder (ODD), or attention deficit hyperactivity disorder (ADHD). Other evidence for comorbidity comes from rates of anxiety disorders among relatives of children with ADHD (without a concurrent anxiety disorder) ranging from 23.5% for first degree to 11.0% for second degree relatives. Although it would appear to be quite easy to differentiate social phobia from externalizing disorders such as ADHD or ODD, such distinctions are not always so clear. Part of the difficulty is that children with ADHD often exhibit substantial distress in social settings. In some cases, children with ADHD are afraid that their impulsive actions will result in embarrassment or ridicule by others. For these children, their concerns are reality-based, unlike the mostly unfounded fears of those with social phobia. That is, children with ADHD might actually act impulsively (e.g., blurting out answers, knocking things over), thus drawing scrutiny by others. In such cases, these concerns would not meet the *DSM-IV* criteria for social phobia because the concerns are not unreasonable. These children do, intentionally or unintentionally, engage in behaviors that draw unwanted scrutiny and negative evaluation by others.

Other children with ADHD experience social anxiety for a different reason. Some children with ADHD can be bossy or intrusive; they interrupt others' conversations, are unable to wait their turn in line or during games, and often inappropriately "break in" during a group activity. Unlike children with social phobia, who often are neglected by peers, children with ADHD are actively rejected by peers. Their behavior is so negative that others openly ostracize or ignore them. Because social encounters with others often lead to such negative consequences, it is likely that children in these situations would report social anxiety in the presence of others (particularly a peer group). However, once again, this expression of anxiety is not social phobia because the social anxiety and fear of negative consequences is not unrealistic. Rather, social rejection is an unfortunate regular occurrence for some children with ADHD.

Sometimes anxious children can be misdiagnosed as having ADHD. For example, Ricardo came to our clinic because his teacher felt that he was inattentive and hyperactive. He was fidgety in the classroom (glancing out the windows, squirming in his seat) and "daydreaming." His teacher felt that he was performing below grade level on the basis of his classroom participation, although individual testing in the clinic indicated that he was functioning at grade level in all academic subjects. His parents denied any evidence of hyperactivity at home but did describe behaviors consistent with social anxiety. When in social settings (and only in social situations), his motor activity increased. He would shrink away from groups of children and was very reluctant to engage even one other child in conversation. In addition, he would refuse to answer the telephone, even if instructed by his parents to do so. In the behavioral assessment, he had adequate social skills, but he did not use them in social settings, even when he was sought out by other children.

There were several key indicators that ruled out ADHD in Ricardo. First, there was no increased motor activity except when he was in social situations (that is, motor hyperactivity appeared to be cued by the presence of others). This is inconsistent with ADHD. Furthermore, although disruptive behaviors consistent with ADHD often increase in unstructured encounters, Ricardo's behavior was cued by the social content of the situation, not the nature of its structure. Second, Ricardo was not necessarily inattentive in the school setting. Although his teacher thought that he was performing below grade level, his achievement scores indicated otherwise. To us, this suggested that his social phobia was inhibiting his ability to perform well in school (i.e., answering questions in class). Third, his social skills were adequate, although he did not use them (possibly because of inhibitory anxiety). Fourth, Ricardo sometimes was sought out by other children, even though he would consistently shrink away from social contact. That is, he did not actively seek to join other children, but he was not actively rejected by them. On the basis of this clinical presentation, Ricardo's behavior was more consistent with a diagnosis of social phobia than ADHD. Intervention using the Social Effectiveness Therapy for Children (SET-C; see chapter 9 in this volume) was effective in remediating his anxious behaviors and increasing his social interactions.

The discussion of comorbidity with ODD has received very little attention in the literature. Although some children may have both disorders (see Russo & Beidel, 1994), clinicians must be aware, as we have noted in several places throughout this chapter, that oppositional behavior and ODD are not interchangeable terms. Oppositional behaviors, for example, may occur in the context of social fears. When such fears are remediated, tantrumming and refusal behaviors should subside.

Personality Disorders

Finally, adolescents with social phobia also can present with features of Axis II personality disorders. In adults with social phobia (see chapter 1), the two most common personality disorders are avoidant personality disorder (APD) and obsessive-compulsive personality disorder (OCPD). Parents of one adolescent with social phobia and school refusal behavior presenting at our clinic described behaviors such as preoccupation with details, perfectionism, overconscientiousness and scrupulousness, and rigidity and stubbornness (all characteristic of OCPD). In addition, the patient avoided occupational activities involving interpersonal contact, had only one friend, viewed himself as personally unappealing, and was unwilling to take risks (all characteristic of APD). Although adolescents may not exhibit enough behaviors or enough consistency in these behaviors to actually receive a diagnosis, many of the core features were present in this adolescent. In addition, the presence of these personality disorders (and perhaps the personality features) may suggest the need for alterations in the administration of the intervention (see chapter 8 in this volume). Thus, careful attention to the presence of these characteristics is necessary.

CONCLUSION

The clinical presentation of social phobia in childhood and adolescence is both similar to and different from its presentation in adults. Revised criteria in *DSM-IV* acknowledged the different manifestations associated with childhood and adolescence. Consistent with the syndrome in adults, excessive and unreasonable fears are acknowledged. However, children, particularly children younger than age 12, frequently do not acknowledge that they have fewer friends or that they engage in social activities less often than their peers. Parent and teacher input is needed to help determine whether the child's social behavior is a significant problem.

Other features of the syndrome in children may differ as well, owing to their developmental stage. Children may cry or throw temper tantrums when faced with fearful events or situations, whereas this is rarely seen in adults. Adults have more "degrees of freedom" regarding how they attempt to manage their anxiety and fears. Rather than refusing to work, they seek types of employment that minimize the need to engage in behaviors they fear, and they develop subtle avoidance strategies, such as those discussed in chapter 1. Children and adolescents often do not have this flexibility. Instead, they may refuse to go to school and may complain of vague physical symptoms to avoid certain activities. In short, developmental parameters exert some influence on the manner in which the behavioral expression of the syndrome is manifested, but the motivating factors are the same.

Although Albano et al. (1995) reported that adolescents had cognitions concerning negative evaluation similar to what is seen in adults, in our clinical experience, such cognitions are not typically part of the clinical picture in children younger than age 12. This may simply be due to the level of cognitive development in young children. They may report being uncomfortable, feeling sick, or just not liking to do certain things. Furthermore, they frequently cannot report specific ideation while engaged in an anxiety arousing task. Therefore, the clinician will have to use other variables, such as report of physical symptoms, behavioral avoidance, social behavior history, and parent and teacher reports, to make a diagnosis.

The overlap in clinical features of childhood social phobia and adult social phobia are strikingly similar. For example, the types of social situations feared and avoided are virtually identical, although there are differences with respect to frequency between the two groups. Similarly, the pattern of co-occurrence of Axis I and II conditions is strikingly similar. Thus, the percentage of those with childhood social phobia with specific phobia and the percentage with generalized anxiety disorder are virtually identical. Furthermore, it is interesting to point out that children with social phobia manifest many features of behavioral rigidity and obsessionality, features that are highly prevalent among adults with social phobia. This similarity strengthens the conclusion that the syndrome in children overlaps with the clinical picture in adults.

Despite the numerous similarities in the syndrome between adults and children, there are a number of conditions sometimes associated with childhood social phobia that are not typically seen in adults. Many children apparently suffering from externalizing disorders actually may suffer from social phobia. Of course, social phobia may not be the motivating factor for externalizing problems in all cases (i.e., the disorders could coexist independently). Similarly, children with behavior problems frequently have social difficulties because other children reject them, preferring not to interact with them. Furthermore, although some oppositional and school refusal behavior is motivated by social fears, this is not true in every case. Finally, socially phobic children are sometimes fidgety and may appear overactive, particularly to teachers. This could lead to a misdiagnosis of ADHD. A careful evaluation is required to determine the correct diagnosis. Clearly, a thorough understanding of the clinical picture of social phobia in children and adolescents is required to properly diagnose the syndrome. Furthermore, the possible role of social phobia in other externalizing and internalizing disorders needs to be considered when evaluating and treating these children.

3

Prevalence of Social Phobia

I'm here because I saw the newspaper story. That woman
sounded just like me. I was so relieved to find out that
others also feel the same way. I thought I was alone.

An adult patient with social phobia during an initial
interview at our clinic.

Social phobia exists across all ages, in both genders, in various racial
and ethnic groups, and cross-nationally. In this chapter, the prevalence
of social phobia, in all its variations, will be presented.

PREVALENCE ACROSS AGE GROUPS

The most current epidemiological data available for childhood social
phobia are based on *DSM-III-R* criteria (American Psychiatric Association, 1987). Using this schema, the prevalence of social phobia appeared to be about 1% of the general child and adolescent population
in the United States. Among 11-year-olds in New Zealand, about 0.9%
of the population met criteria for social phobia (Anderson, Williams,
McGee, & Silva, 1987). When these same children were reassessed 4
years later (at age 15), the prevalence rate was 1.1% (McGee et al.,

1990). These rates most likely are an underestimate because fear of public speaking was classified as a specific phobia, not a social phobia, in this study. A cross-sectional study of children in the United States ages 8, 12, and 17 found an overall prevalence rate for social phobia of 1% (Kashani & Orvaschel, 1990). Although not stratified by the number of children at each age who met diagnostic criteria, these authors presented data on the prevalence of certain fears across these three age groups. Fear of social situations was reported by 21.4% of 8-year-olds, 45.7% of 12-year-olds, and 55.7% of 17-year-olds. Similarly, "worrying about what others think of me" was reported by 38.6% of 8-year-olds and 67.1% of 12- and 17-year-olds. Thus, consistent with the age-of-onset data derived from adult populations, it is clear that concerns about social evaluation increase as children age, and by extrapolation, the incidence of frank social phobia probably does as well.

Prevalence estimates of social phobia are only approximate because under *DSM-III-R* criteria, children with social fears could be given a diagnosis of social phobia, overanxious disorder, or avoidant disorder of childhood. If one combines prevalence rates for these three conditions, the epidemiological estimates for social fears would increase to 9.6% (Kashani & Orvaschel, 1990); a rate strikingly similar to that derived for adults from the most recent adult epidemiological study (the National Comorbidity Study, or NCS, see below).

Among children in the United States, a recent study by Shaffer et al. (1996) reported that 7.6% of children (by self-report) and 3.7% of adolescents (by self-report) met *DSM-III-R* criteria for social phobia (including impairment criteria). Prevalence on the basis of parental report (combined across all age groups) was 4.5%. It should be noted that these data are from a study assessing the psychometric characteristics of the NIMH Diagnostic Interview Schedule (DIS) for Children, Version 2.3. Therefore, as the authors noted, no attempt was made to assure that the data were representative of the U.S. population (Shaffer et al., 1996).

In specialty anxiety clinics, 15% of children seeking treatment for an anxiety disorder had a primary diagnosis of social phobia and another 3% had a primary diagnosis of avoidant disorder of childhood

(Last, Perrin, Hersen, & Kazdin, 1992). Albano and colleagues (Albano, DiBartolo, Heimberg, & Barlow, 1995) reported that 18% of children seeking treatment at an anxiety clinic received a diagnosis of social phobia. These two figures are remarkably consistent and indicate that almost one out of five children presenting to specialty anxiety clinics have severe social fears.

To some degree, even the prevalence rates among adults are dependent on the assessment methodology used to study the condition. Using a structured diagnostic interview conducted over the telephone, Pollard and Henderson (1988) reported a prevalence rate of 22.6% for irrational social fears among adult respondents. However, when *DSM-III* (American Psychiatric Association, 1980) criteria were strictly applied, the prevalence rate dropped to 2%. Using a similar telephone methodology, Stein, Walker, and Forde (1994) surveyed 500 adults in the Winnipeg, Manitoba, Canada area and reported that 33% reported feeling much more nervous than other people in one of seven social situations. However, once again, when a functional impairment or marked distress criterion was imposed, the prevalence rate dropped to 7.1%.

Among adults, the Epidemiological Catchment Area survey (ECA) provided one of the largest epidemiological samples for the study of psychopathology in the United States. On the basis of data from several different sites and the use of a structured interview schedule and in-person interviews by laypersons, the lifetime prevalence rates for social phobia (using *DSM-III* criteria) was 2.4% (Schneier, Johnson, Hornig, Liebowitz, & Weissman, 1992). This figure is consistent with international studies of lifetime prevalence rates where the DIS was used. Prevalence rates were 0.99% in Italy, 1.6% in Puerto Rico, 1.7% in Edmonton, and 3.0% in New Zealand. Rates appear to be much lower in Asian countries, ranging from 0.5% in South Korea to 0.6% in Taiwan (Chapman, Manuzza, & Fyer, 1995). It is unclear why the rates are lower in East Asian countries, but these authors discussed several possibilities. First, inconsistencies in translation, cultural differences in willingness to admit the presence of fears, or issues of cultural relevance may have limited symptom acknowledgement (i.e., the specific situations assessed may have been more culturally relevant for American or English-speaking populations). Second, as noted by the authors, the DIS does not address the existence of *taijin kyofu-sho* (discussed specifically later in this chapter). This condition, probably a variant of social phobia, is common in several East Asian countries, but because it is not assessed by the DIS, the prevalence of social phobia in Asian countries may underestimate the true rate of social fears and anxieties existing in that population.

Those who developed the DIS noted that among its limitations was that this structured interview sampled only a restricted number of potentially fearful situations (Chapman et al., 1995). This may be because at the time of the DIS's construction, social phobia was understudied, and the extent and severity of this condition was unknown. As a result, there is some suspicion that the 2.4% in the United States figure may be an underestimate. In fact, a more recent study in the United States (the NCS, using *DSM-III-R* criteria) reported a 13.3% lifetime prevalence rate and an 8% 12-month prevalence rate (Kessler et al., 1994). The NCS differed from the earlier ECA survey in several respects. The NCS used a national probability sample, *DSM-III-R* criteria, and a different diagnostic instrument. Although the variations between the two studies might account for the differences, follow-up validity checks on the study and prevalence rates reported from three large foreign studies (Lepine & Lellouch, 1995; Stein et al., 1994; Wacker, Mullejans, Klein, & Battegay, 1992) suggest that the higher figures reported in the NCS could be accurate. On the basis of all these data, it seems clear that social phobia is a highly prevalent condition. In addition, on the basis of NCS data, it is the most common of the anxiety disorders.

GENDER

Among children, girls generally are more likely to report the presence of fears than are boys. Using a sample of children recruited through a public school district, approximately 70% of those with a diagnosis of social phobia were female (Beidel & Turner, 1992b). Among clinical populations, however, the gender distribution is more equal. Last et al. (1992) reported that 44% of their treatment-seeking sample of children were female. Among adults, the gender ratio from epidemiological populations was reported as 3:2 female to male in several studies (Mannuzza, Fyer, Liebowitz, & Klein, 1990; Kessler et al., 1994; Pollard & Henderson, 1988). However, as with children, the ratio of male to female adult patients seeking treatment is reported to be equal (e.g., Turner & Beidel, 1989).

RACIAL AND ETHNIC FACTORS

Above, we noted the cross-cultural prevalence of adults with social phobia as assessed by the DIS. However, there are relatively few data examining the prevalence of social phobia by various racial and ethnic groups. Among 8-year-old to 12-year-old school children initially identified as test anxious, 55% of those who met criteria for social phobia were African American and 45% were European American (Beidel, Turner, & Trager, 1994). When rates for social phobia and overanxious disorder were combined, 59% of the children were African American and 41% were European American. In contrast, among treatment-seeking populations of children, Strauss and Last (1993) reported that 86% of the sample was European American. Similarly, 73% of our current clinic sample is European American. The differences among samples, at least in part, likely reflect the racial makeup of the community where these clinics are located. The differences also suggest that the prevalence of social phobia among these groups mimics the racial composition of the general population. Similarly, although no specific figures were given, social phobia was reported in the NCS to be about equal among White and African American adults (Kessler et al., 1994). Among European American and Hispanic children seeking treatment at an anxiety clinic, social phobia was present in 15.2% of the Hispanic children and 9.8% of the European American children, a difference that was not statistically significant (Ginsburg & Silverman, 1996).

Although the symptomatic picture across racial groups appears to be the same, racial factors can play an important role in the maintenance and treatment of these conditions. In a case study, Fink, Turner, and Beidel (1996) reported how lack of careful attention to the presence of racial factors that were part of an African American adult female's core fear did not allow for a complete understanding of the patient's disorder. Refining the case conceptualization to include attention to these cues made a substantial improvement in the effectiveness of the intervention (see chapter 8 in this volume for more specific details).

A recent study of fears in Japanese children (Ihenaga et al., 1996) found a substantial number of children with social fears. Fear of eye to eye contact was present in 40% to 50% of children between the ages of 10 and 17 (the specific percentage varied slightly by age and gender). Similarly, fear of flushing (blushing) was common among 20% to 40% of these children. In addition to their substantial prevalence, the phrasing of these fears suggests that questions used typically in Western diagnostic interviews, such as "fear of speaking" or "fears of social interaction," may not detect the presence of relevant social fears in some ethnic groups. Thus, knowledge of the verbal expressions used by a particular culture is necessary for a valid assessment.

In addition to differences in clinical symptomatology, social skills often are dictated by cultural norms. For example, among Native Americans *pause time* in a conversation is longer than among European American dyads (Renfry, 1992). Similarly, downcast eyes are an appropriate sign of respect among Native Americans rather than an indication of unassertiveness. Furthermore, silence may be a form of communication. Clinicians must also take these differences into account when assessing the presence of social anxiety in various ethnic and racial groups.

Perhaps best exemplifying the culture-specific nature of some forms of social phobia is one called *taijin kyofu-sho*, commonly found only in East Asian countries. First reported in Japan, the syndrome also is common in Korea and possibly other Asian countries (Chapman et al., 1995). Taijin kyofu-sho is a fear of causing offense or embarrassment to others by blushing, emitting body odors, or displaying unsightly body parts (Chang, 1984). As noted, these concerns, most frequently occurring in young men, appear to be unique to East Asians and may reflect a cultural emphasis on politeness. When interviewing individuals from Asian cultures, it may be important to rephrase traditional assessments of social phobia to include an assessment of this apparently important cultural variant.

SOCIOECONOMIC STATUS

Schneier et al. (1992), using the ECA data, reported that the highest rates of social phobia were found among those with the lowest socio-economic status and the poorest level of education. As noted by Rapee (1995), there may be multiple reasons for these findings. First, individuals with social phobia sometimes select specific careers, decide whether to attend college, or decide which college to attend on the basis of their fears. Patients seeking treatment at our clinic often recount personal histories of social fears dictating decisions not to attend college (thereby limiting career options) or specifically selecting a career that minimizes interpersonal contact (thereby eliminating most managerial or administrative positions). Second, impairment in social and occupational functioning as a result of social phobia may result in job loss, loss of promotion, or demotion. Similarly, because most administrative positions involve some level of interpersonal contact, individuals with limited social skills and substantial social fears may be "passed over" for promotion or may turn down promotional opportunities. One of our patients refused the vice presidency of a corporation (as well as a substantial pay raise) because of the severity of social fears. Lawyers with social phobia, for example, will work as law clerks rather than as practicing attorneys, as a way to minimize their social distress. Finally, it must be recalled that the ECA data are based on diagnostic interviews using the DIS, and some of its limitations have been discussed above. Using a community epidemiological sample, it may be that social phobia is more prevalent among lower socioeconomic groups. However, on the basis of those seeking treatment in our specialty clinic, individuals with social phobia exist across all socioeconomic strata.

CONCLUSION

Because of the recent adoption of *DSM-IV*, prevalence data based on the most recent diagnostic criteria are not yet available. This presents only minimal consequences for adult populations as changes from *DSM-III-R* to *DSM-IV* were minimal for adults. However, as was discussed above, the magnitude of the diagnostic revisions for children and adolescents renders prevalence rates in younger populations suspect. Kendall and Warman (1996) compared the rates of specific anxiety disorders when children were diagnosed using either *DSM-III-R* or *DSM-IV* criteria. Using *DSM-III-R* criteria, only 18% of a sample of children ($n = 40$) seeking treatment for anxiety disorders were diagnosed as having social phobia. However, when *DSM-IV* criteria were applied, 40% of the same sample of children were diagnosed as having social phobia. To further demonstrate the overlap between the *DSM-III-R* conditions of social phobia and avoidant disorder of childhood, children who met criteria for either of these disorders made up 43% of the entire sample (compared with 40% of *DSM-IV* social phobia). These data provide evidence that prior epidemiological studies considerably underestimated the rate of this disorder in children. Current gender ratios or racial and ethnic minority data likewise may be affected. Data addressing these issues should emerge over the next few years. Until then, clinicians should treat the current epidemiological data with appropriate skepticism.

As noted at the beginning of this chapter, social phobia exists across both genders and within various racial and ethnic groups. Different cultural norms or forms of expression may affect the specific manner of clinical presentation. Therefore, clinicians must be aware of, and sensitive to, cultural nuances that could influence determination of a diagnosis and the success of treatment outcome.

4

Etiology of Social Phobia

I played big-time college football. I was used to getting out in front of 100,000 people every Saturday. I never got nervous about the crowds. I was often asked to give speeches at football banquets and I did well. Then, one day, my note cards got mixed up. I couldn't get them straight, and I couldn't find my place in the speech. The silence was deafening, and I was horribly embarrassed. Now, I cannot even make a presentation in front of the five-member school board, let alone a large crowd.

An adult social phobia patient

I always was considered shy. I came from a big family and never needed to seek out friends. My siblings were my friends. Now I see my daughter is just like I was. Did I do something to cause this?

The parent of a child with social phobia

Professional and laypersons alike typically think of the causes of emotional disorders, including social phobia, in unidimensional terms, favoring either a biological or psychological explanation. However, in all likelihood, most disorders are due to both biological and psychological factors. In recent years, there has been a resurgence in emphasis on biological models to explain most of the major psychiatric disorders, including the anxiety disorders. In this chapter, we will review empirical research related to major biological and psychological explanations for social phobia. Specifically, we will consider evidence for a genetic hypothesis, and we will examine evidence related to direct conditioning, observational learning, and information transfer. Also, we will devote some attention to the issue of predispositional factors and discuss what we believe to be an integrated perspective on the genesis of social phobia.

PSYCHOLOGICAL FACTORS

Direct Conditioning

There is a considerable behavioral literature attesting to the fact that fear behavior often is the result of negative emotional or traumatic experiences (e.g., Watson & Rayner, 1920). Perhaps one of the more striking illustrations of the effects of trauma on human emotional behavior is revealed through studies of posttraumatic stress disorder (PTSD). In fact, although not exploited fully to date, paradigms centered on PTSD have the potential to provide unique insight into the development of fear in humans. During clinical interviews, many of those with social phobia report recalling a specific traumatic event in their past that is associated with the onset of their disorder. Sometimes, even when problems with socialization and performance existed before the specific event, patients attribute much to the traumatic episode in terms of responsibility for their current condition (i.e., the event exacerbated their fears). The following case examples will illustrate the type of events typically reported by those with social phobia as being responsible for their social fears. One of our patients recalled that while she was in her seventh grade English class, other students counted the number of times she said "uh" during a class presentation and later made fun of her. Since that time, she has had debilitating performance anxiety. Another patient recalled having to sing a solo of "Rudolph the Red Nosed Reindeer" during the school Christmas concert. Instead of singing "Then one foggy Christmas Eve," she sang "Then one *froggy* Christmas Eve," and the audience laughed. Since then, she has been afraid that she would embarrass herself again in public. A number of formal studies (discussed below) of characteristics associated with social phobia onset corroborate the importance of events such as those in these clinical vignettes.

In a survey designed to examine the acquisition of fear and anxiety, Ost (1985) reported that 58% of those with social phobia attributed the onset of the disorder to the occurrence of a traumatic conditioning experience. In a study of developmental factors associated with social phobia, Stemberger, Turner, Beidel, and Calhoun (1995) compared the prevalence of traumatic conditioning experiences in the specific and generalized subtypes of social phobia and in control subjects who had no disorders. Overall, 44% of those with social phobia recalled a conditioning experience that marked the onset or clear exacerbation of social fears. Interestingly, 20% of the controls who had no disorders also reported episodes considered to be traumatic conditioning experiences, yet they did not develop social phobia. When examined by social phobia subtype, 56% of those with the specific subtype identified a traumatic conditioning experience, compared with 40% of those with the generalized subtype who identified a traumatic conditioning experience. However, only those with the specific subtype were significantly different from those in the control group in terms of the prevalence of conditioning episodes. The data suggest that traumatic conditioning is more related to the development of the specific subtype of social phobia than the development of the generalized subtype. However, a sizable portion of those in each of the groups did not report experiencing any type of traumatic event, and a number of control subjects experienced traumatic episodes but did not develop social phobia or any other anxiety disorder. It is unclear why some controls who had experienced traumatic social events did not develop social phobia. One hypothesis is that some individuals are more prone to develop anxiety and fear than others. That is, when those with a heightened tendency to become anxious experience a traumatic event, anxiety or social phobia, perhaps as a function of their biological or psychological makeup, results (see biological etiology section in this chapter).

Although this issue remains unclear, we do know that the process of conditioning is a complex phenomenon. For example, Mineka and Zinbarg (1995) noted that conditioning experiences do not occur in a vacuum but rather are associated with a multitude of contextual variables. Also, conditioning need not occur as a result of a single extremely traumatic event. In many cases, conditioning is cumulative (e.g., Mineka & Zinbarg, 1991, 1995). That is, rather than a single traumatic event, a series of smaller conditioning events may combine to produce a fear response at some point in time. For example, in the studies reported above, some participants were unable to recall specific conditioning experiences, but small conditioning episodes could have accumulated over an extended period of time, resulting in a conditioned fear response through the process of cumulative conditioning. Also, cumulative conditioning could serve to "prime" an individual to develop a fear response. In this scenario, the results of cumulative conditioning places one in a high vulnerability state such that a traumatic event triggers the onset of a fear response.

Observational Learning

Although the potent effects of observational learning, and the variables affecting such learning, were eloquently demonstrated several decades ago by the work of Bandura and others (cf. Bandura, 1969), recent experiments by Mineka and her colleagues clearly demonstrate observational learning of fear responses in nonhuman primates. Mineka and Cook's important studies (Cook & Mineka, 1991; Mineka, 1987; Mineka & Cook, 1988) on the vicarious acquisition of snake fear in laboratory-bred rhesus monkeys provide some of the strongest evidence to date for vicarious (observational) learning of fear. Laboratory monkeys, who initially did not show any fear of snakes, observed wild-born monkeys behaving fearfully in the presence of snakes. After only 4–8 minutes of observation, the laboratory monkeys acquired a fear of snakes. Interestingly, the monkeys not only acquired the specific avoidance behavior but also behaved in a manner suggesting that they had acquired the emotional aspect of fear as well. To date, there have been no direct studies of observational learning as a mode of acquisition for social phobia.

However, Ost and Hughdahl (1981) reported that 13% of those with social phobia identified vicarious learning as instrumental in the onset of their disorder. Thus, the observation of another undergoing a traumatic social experience could lead to the emergence of social fear in the observer. Many individuals with social phobia have parents or other close relatives who have social phobia (see genetic and family studies sections), and one could speculate that observational learning as well as genetics might contribute to the greater prevalence of social phobia among their relatives. In the section on predispositional factors, evidence for the role of parents in the onset of the disorder is discussed (see below).

Information Transfer

The least studied form of learning with respect to the acquisition of fear in general, and social fears in particular, is information transfer. However, recent data from our clinic on verbal and nonverbal communication from parents to children suggest that fear may be acquired by this pathway. Parents with an anxiety disorder, normal control parents, and both groups of children were asked to interact in a setting that included traditional playground equipment such as a jungle gym. During a 15 minute interval, interactions of parent and child were observed by raters unaware of whether or not the parent had an anxiety disorder. When behaviors of anxious parents and control parents were compared, parents of anxious children used statements such as "Be careful," "Watch out," and "Don't climb so high," significantly more than their counterparts who had no disorders (Turner & Beidel, 1996). All of these statements could communicate to children that there might be something dangerous about the activity or the environment in which it occurred. If the communications of these anxious parents in this laboratory situation are characteristic of their interactions with their children in the natural environment, then one can speculate that if a parent continuously cautions "Be careful," the child could begin to believe that there is something about the stimulus or situation that should be feared. It also can be reasoned, then, that this might lead to the development of fear, although in this case the fears were not of a social nature. Although it would not be ethical to conduct studies with humans to test this hypothesis fully, there is some less direct evidence supporting the view that fears can be acquired in this fashion. We discuss these studies below.

As noted, specific data on the acquisition of fear through information transfer with social phobia is even more sparse than it is for observational conditioning, but some findings appear to be relevant. For example, Ost (1985) found that 3% of those with social phobia reported that they acquired their fear in this manner. Relatedly, although not a direct test of information transfer, Bruch and Heimberg and their colleagues (Bruch & Heimberg, 1994; Bruch, Heimberg, Berger, & Collins, 1989) assessed the role of family sociability, concern about the opinions of others, isolation of the child, and emphasis on shame in generalized and nongeneralized (specific) subtypes of social phobia. Compared with normal controls who had no disorders, patients with both types of social phobia reported significantly greater parental concern with the opinions of others and greater parental use of shame as a disciplinary procedure. However, those with the generalized subtype, in comparison with those with the nongeneralized subtype and normal controls, reported greater isolation and less family socializing. Despite finding some group differences, these data clearly do not allow one to determine how these factors might have been expressed in these families. However, in light of the data on anxious parents and their children presented above (Turner & Beidel, 1996), it is tempting to speculate that parents, for example, either verbally or nonverbally, modeled socially fearful and avoidant behavior by being socially timid and withdrawn. Similarly, expressions of concern by parents about the opinions of others or instructions that certain situations may be embarrassing, fear producing, or socially dangerous also could provide opportunities for learning to be afraid through information transfer.

GENETIC AND BIOLOGICAL FACTORS

Twin Studies

One of the strongest designs available to examine genetic influence in the etiology of a disorder is through the study of twins. Although there are relatively few twin studies of social phobia, two studies provide some insight into possible genetic factors. Monozygotic (MZ), or identical, twins share identical genetic makeup, whereas dizygotic (DZ), or fraternal, twins share no more genetic similarity than regular siblings. Therefore, if social phobia more commonly occurs in MZ twins, in comparison with DZ twins, this higher rate of occurrence (i.e., concordance rate) would be evidence of a genetic contribution to the disorder. Torgersen (1983) did not find a higher concordance rate for social phobia among MZ twins when compared with DZ twins. However, the sample of twins for any particular disorder was quite small, and the results must be interpreted cautiously. Using a very large sample of twins, Kendler and colleagues (Kendler, Neale, Kessler, Heath, & Eaves, 1992) found a concordance rate for social phobia of 24.4% for MZ twins compared with 15% for DZ twins (based on *DSM-III* criteria). However, the heritability estimate was approximately 30%, and statistical models determined that environmental factors also were important in determining the presence of social phobia. Thus, data from twin studies at this point are inconclusive. Data do suggest, however, that there likely is a genetic component in at least some cases.

Family Studies

Another method of studying the role of genetics in the genesis of disorders is to examine the clustering of disorders within families. These studies use samples ranging from first-degree adult relatives to all available adult relatives, to anxious parents and their children. Overall, the results of these studies have supported the notion that anxiety disorders "run in families" (e.g., Noyes et al., 1986; Turner, Beidel, & Costello, 1987; Weissman, Leckman, Merikangas, Gammon, & Prusoff, 1984). Basically, all of these studies reported that individuals with anxiety disorders are more likely than nonpsychiatric controls to have relatives with an anxiety disorder, although not necessarily the same disorder.

Several studies specifically have assessed familial relationships in individuals with social phobia. In an early study, Reich and Yates (1988a) assessed psychopathology in the first degree relatives of patients with social phobia or panic disorder and normal controls. This study, however, did not assess relatives directly but interviewed the patients about their relatives (i.e., the "family history" method was used). In addition, those assigning the diagnoses to the family members were aware of the patient's diagnosis. With these limitations in mind, the study found that rates of social phobia were higher in the relatives of a patient with social phobia (6.6%) than in the relatives of patients with panic disorder (2.2%) or normal controls (0.2%). In a study by Fyer, Manuzza, Chapman, Liebowitz, and Klein (1993), first degree relatives were interviewed directly (i.e., the family method was used) and the clinician was unaware of the patient's diagnosis. Their findings indicated that 16% of relatives of patients with social phobia also met criteria for this disorder. This is compared with 5% of relatives of nonphobic controls, a difference that was statistically significant.

Familial rates of social phobia and social anxiety also have been examined on the basis of social phobia subtype. Manuzza et al. (1995) reported that rates of social phobia in first degree relatives of patients with the generalized subtype (16%) were higher than rates of social phobia in relatives with the specific (nongeneralized) subtype (6%). Stemberger et al. (1995) found that there were no differences in rates of social anxiety among first degree relatives of patients with social phobia and controls who had no disorders or between the specific and the generalized subtypes. However, unlike the Manuzza et al. (1995) study, patients in this study were not assessed directly. Because those with social phobia do not openly express their fears (many have never told even their closest relatives or friends about their distress), studies that do not interview the relatives directly may underestimate the true prevalence of the disorder.

Most recently, Mancini, Van Amerigen, Szatmari, Fugere, and Boyle (1996) examined rates of psychopathology in the offspring of parents with social phobia. The results indicated that 49% of these children had at least one DSM-III-R anxiety disorder, most commonly overanxious disorder (30%), social phobia (23%), and separation anxiety disorder (19%). However, this was an uncontrolled trial and interviewers were not blind to parental diagnosis. Therefore, these data must be interpreted with appropriate skepticism. Overall, however, the results of both twin and family studies support the contention that anxiety disorders, including social phobia, are familial and that genetics likely play some role in at least some cases.

PREDISPOSITIONAL INFLUENCES AND MAINTAINING FACTORS

As illustrated by the above findings, it is well established that anxiety disorders are familial, although it is unclear whether genetic or family environment variables exert primary influence or whether they interact in some fashion to produce social phobia. Many theorists long have considered emotional disorders to result from a diathesis of biological and environmental factors (e.g., Akiskal, 1985), and this likely is the case for many of those with social phobia as well. Also as noted above, social phobia might develop through observational learning, direct conditioning, or information transfer. It also is possible, however, that even those who develop emotional disorders through these means are more likely to develop social phobia than others (i.e., they are more vulnerable). Thus, just because one develops an emotional disorder through one of the proposed psychological pathways does not mean that biological factors are not involved. Still, it is possible that different factors are responsible for the onset of the disorder in different individuals (i.e., there could be multiple pathways to the disorder). One can see from these possibilities that the precise etiology of social phobia will be difficult to unravel. In the next section, we discuss additional factors, culled primarily from the developmental and social psychology literatures, that may predispose someone to the development of social phobia. In addition, these factors also may play a role in the maintenance of the disorder, once the onset has occurred. Because most of these studies have been conducted on those who already have the disorder, or on those who have designations such as shy or socially isolated (rather than socially phobic), it is not possible to determine whether these factors actually are etiological in nature. Therefore, we use the terms *predispositional* and *maintenance* factors.

Family Environment Factors

We explored the idea that higher rates of social phobia in families of individuals with this disorder may represent a genetic contribution to the etiology of social phobia. In this section, we will discuss other familial factors that may be influential. Within the developmental literature, there is strong evidence for the relationship between parental behaviors and children's social competence (e.g., Ladd & Golter, 1988; Parke & Bhavnagri, 1989; Radke-Yarrow & Zahn-Waxler, 1986). For example, there is much support for the relationship between style of infant–parent attachment and the child's subsequent social relationships with peers (Putallaz & Heflin, 1990). Specifically, secure attachments are predictive of children who easily join social groups and establish healthy peer relationships. Other studies have found that maternal warmth and engagement also are positively related to children's prosocial engagement with other children (Attili, 1989; Hinde & Tamplin, 1983).

In addition to the influence of their own personality characteristics, other parental behaviors can affect a child's social behavior. For example, generally, opportunities for social interaction among young children are arranged by parents. In some cases (see section on behavioral inhibition below), parents who recognize their child's social reticence deliberately arrange for social encounters with peers in order to decrease social inhibition. However, if social inhibition runs in families (as it seems to), mothers who are shy or socially phobic may avoid exposing their socially inhibited children to varied social situations (to minimize the parent's own social distress), thereby increasing the likelihood of perpetuating a fear cycle (Daniels & Plomin, 1985). For example, in one of our families, both the mother and her 11-year-old daughter were extremely shy. The mother reported that although she recognized her daughter's shyness and knew she should do something about it, she was unable to do so because of the extent of her own social fears. In fact, when mother and daughter came in for the interview, they were accompanied by another relative who answered most of the interviewer's questions because the mother was too distressed by the social nature of the interview to do so.

Behavior such as that described above can affect a child in at least three ways. First, parents may pass on an *anxious predisposition* (the genetic component). Second, parents may restrict or prevent the child's ability to engage in social situations, thereby possibly setting up a pattern of social isolation and social avoidance in the child. Finally, parents may pass on their fears and anxieties to their children through modeling (observation learning) or information transfer.

Other studies also highlight the role of parental behavior in perpetuating children's social inhibition. During group play situations, mothers of peer-neglected children (those ignored socially by other children) provided fewer peer-engagement instructions and more task-oriented instructions than mothers of popular children (Finnie & Russell, 1988). Furthermore, they were less likely to facilitate their child's entry into the group. Thus, rather than instructing their children to engage other children in the activity, they were more likely to give task-oriented instructions that further perpetuated the child's neglect by peers.

Parental influence is not limited to mothers. In one study, fathers of peer-neglected boys were observed to engage in less affectively rough-housing play (i.e., physical rough and tumble play) than did fathers of popular or peer-rejected boys (MacDonald, 1987). Fathers of children with *DSM-III-R* anxiety disorders of social phobia or overanxious disorder also were found to possess a more rigid personality style, and children reported a more restrictive family environment when compared with nonphobic control children (Messer & Beidel, 1994). Because this latter study used children who already had an anxiety disorder, one cannot assume that the parental personality factors and restrictive family environment precipitated the disorder in these children. However, the consistency of these data with the others reported above (and to be discussed below) suggest that these influences at least function to help maintain the disorder.

Dadds, Barrett, and their colleagues examined the role of parental influence in children with anxiety disorders. Although not solely limited to children with social phobia, those with this disorder (as well as those with overanxious disorder) were included in the sample. The results indicated that parents of anxious children often reinforce anxious avoidance and discourage courageous behavior (Dadds, Barrett, Rapee, & Ryan, 1996). In the paradigm used in this study, an ambiguous situation is presented (e.g., you see a group of children playing one of your favorite games) and the children are asked to describe what they would do in that situation. After the children provide responses, the situation is presented again with the parents present, and the parents are invited to discuss potential responses with their child. In comparison to parents of children without any disorder, parents of anxious children actively discouraged their children's attempts to behave courageously. For example, if in response to the above situation, the child stated that he would ask the other children if he could play, parents responded "Do you think they would let you play? You are not very good at that game, you know." Additionally, they reinforced avoidance strategies such as "I guess I would not ask them." Again, because these data were collected on children who already had a disorder, it is impossible to determine whether these parent behaviors preceded or followed the onset of the child's disorder. Surely, parents who are dealing with an anxious child would want to do everything in their power to protect them from becoming distressed and anxious. However, protective behavior on the part of the parent can keep children from becoming exposed to situations that they fear, and exposure appears to be the critical element in the treatment of the disorder (Turner, Cooley-Quille, & Beidel, 1995). If these parental behaviors preceded the child's disorder, they indeed may have been contributory. However, even if they are the result of the child's disorder, they still may be problematic because they can function to help maintain the disorder or interfere with the child's treatment program (Dadds et al., 1996; Silverman & Kurtines, 1996; see chapter 6 in this volume).

Peer Relationships and Loneliness

Developmental psychologists and developmental psychopathologists assess peer relationships through the use of sociometric ratings. In this procedure, groups of children (usually classroom groups) nominate other children with whom they enjoy playing or having as friends. They also identify those children with whom they do not like to play or would not want as friends. In recent years, the procedure has become quite controversial as some lay people feel that the harm in labeling children as popular or not popular outweighs the importance of the research questions. However, these sociometric ratings have been used to assess the relationship of children's psychopathology to peer popularity. In general, as we noted in chapter 2, children without psychopathology are usually average or popular children. Those with externalizing disorders (conduct disorder, attention deficit hyperactivity disorder) are usually rejected by their peers. Finally, children with internalizing disorders (such as anxiety disorders) usually are neglected by their peers. In other words, they are not actively liked or disliked, rather they are ignored.

LaGreca and her colleagues (e.g., LaGreca, Dandes, Wick, Shaw, & Stone, 1988) reported that social anxiety is significantly higher in peer-neglected children than it is in popular children, whereas Strauss and her colleagues (Strauss, Lahey, Frick, Frame, & Hynd, 1988) reported that children with an anxiety disorder were more likely to be peer-neglected than both psychiatric and nonpsychiatric controls. Others have reported that socially anxious children are less confident about their competence in social interactions (Patterson, Kupersmidt, & Griesler, 1990). One of the most common results of social phobia in children and adolescents is that social anxiety impairs the ability to establish and maintain friendships (Rubin, LeMare, & Lollis, 1990). Retrospective reports of shy adults indicate that unpleasant experiences with peers may have contributed to the development of shyness (Ishiyama, 1984). The retrospective nature of these data means that they must be interpreted cautiously, but the reports are consistent with the findings from socially anxious children.

Cognitive Development

As noted in chapters 1 and 2, social phobia is characterized by the fear that results in humiliation or embarrassment. Embedded in this definition is the idea that children must be able to take on the perspective of another person; that is, for children to be socially fearful, they must be able to imagine how another person perceives their behavior. Darby and Schlenker (1986) assessed the ability of second, fourth, and seventh graders to determine social anxiety in their peers. The results indicated that children in second grade can recognize signs of worry, uneasiness, and lack of confidence in others. By fourth grade, children can associate social anxiety with high motivation to make a positive impression, and this ability increases with age. All children, even those in second grade, expect less socially competent children to fidget, act clumsy, avoid making eye contact or smiling, and to communicate less. These data clearly indicate that an understanding of the experience of anxiety occurs at an early age, and the ability to recognize these fears increases with age. At this time, it is unclear whether children less than age 7 possess these cognitive abilities.

Temperament (Behavioral Inhibition)

One early-developing predisposition that appears most strongly linked to shyness and social unease, and perhaps ultimately to social phobia, is the temperamental variable of behavioral inhibition (BI). Perhaps the most researched sample of children with this characteristic is the Harvard cohort studied by Kagan and his colleagues. According to these authors, BI is an early-appearing behavioral characteristic that is expressed as shyness, social withdrawal and avoidance, social uneasiness, and fear of unfamiliar situations, people, objects and events (Garcia-Coll, Kagan, & Reznick, 1984). This behavioral style is found in 10% to 20% of White children. Toddlers (14–31 months) with BI, when placed in unfamiliar or novel settings, cry, fret, emit distressful vocalizations or display distressful facial expressions, withdraw socially, and show an absence of initiation or interaction with the experimenter. Also, when in these challenging situations, those with BI show a characteristic physiological response of higher heart rate and minimal heart rate variability (Garcia-Coll et al., 1984). At later ages, children with BI have larger pupillary dilation during testing periods and higher salivary cortisol levels in laboratory and home environments (Reznick et al., 1986). Finally, the correlation between epinephrine activity and BI was found to be modest but statistically significant, suggesting that higher epinephrine activity level was more characteristic of children with BI (Kagan, Reznick, & Snidman, 1987). At this time, the true extent of the stability of the BI construct remains unclear. However, from these early-appearing behaviors, a subset of these children continued to manifest this pattern during early childhood and pre-adolescence (e.g., Reznick et al., 1986).

Other researchers also have studied BI. Like social phobia, BI appears to be a cross-cultural phenomenon. Behaviors consistent with BI have been documented in Swedish (Bromberg, 1993) and German children (Asendorpf, 1990, 1993). However, precursors to BI (high-motor, high-crying activity found in 4-month-old toddlers; Kagan et al., 1994) show some differences across cultures. American children are more motorically active than Irish infants, who are in turn more motorically active than Chinese infants. Although the relationship of this initial reactivity to later expressions of BI remains unclear, these data suggest that this initial temperamental reactivity may be more common in American, or perhaps among White, children than in other racial and ethnic groups. For a more extensive review of the construct of behavioral inhibition and its relation to anxiety, see Turner, Beidel, and Wolff (1996).

For the purposes of this chapter, studies that have examined the relationship of BI to the development of anxiety disorders are most relevant. These studies consist of three types: family studies assessing the presence of BI in the children of anxious parents, family studies assessing anxiety in the parents of BI children, and studies assessing psychiatric disorders in children with BI. The findings of these studies will be reviewed below. However, as with any research, these investigations are not without limitations. Because a close critique of all of these studies is beyond the scope of this chapter, the reader is referred to Turner, Beidel, and Wolff (1996) for the details.

In an initial publication of BI's relationship to anxiety disorders, Rosenbaum et al. (1988) reported that rates of BI were 85% for children of parents with panic disorder (PD) only, 70% for children with PD and major depressive disorder (MDD), 50% for MDD only, and 15% for controls. In a reversal of this research paradigm, Rosenbaum, Biederman, Hirshfeld, Bolduc, and Chaloff (1991) found that parents of children with BI were more likely than parents of children without BI to have histories of two or more anxiety disorders, a childhood history of anxiety disorders, higher risk for a current anxiety disorder (specifically social phobia), and higher risk for the childhood disorders of avoidant disorder of childhood and overanxious disorder. Using a larger sample, Rosenbaum et al. (1992) reported that the prevalence of social phobia in the parents of children with BI (10%) was higher than in the parents of children without BI (0%). Although the prevalence rates were small, these data suggest a relationship between BI and social phobia. One hypothesis is that if social phobia runs in families, and does so because of genetic transmission, BI may be the manifestation of the biological substrate from which social phobia develops.

In the first study to determine the presence of anxiety disorders in children with BI, Biederman et al. (1990) reported that children with BI were significantly more likely to have four or more disorders per child and two or more anxiety disorders per child. A greater number of diagnosable disorders is considered by these investigators to be an index of severity. In addition, these children particularly were more likely to have overanxious disorder when compared with uninhibited or normal control children who had no disorders. Because *DSM-III-R* criteria for overanxious disorder included social–evaluative concerns, this finding is consistent with the data presented above attesting to the relationship between BI and social anxiety or phobia. In a second sample reported in the same study, children with BI were more likely to have a phobic disorder, including fear of public speaking (56%), fear of strangers (44%), fear of being called on in class (33%), and fear of crowds (33%). Two of these fears were clear examples of social fears; stranger fear probably could be included as a social fear, as could fear of crowds (although it also could be considered a symptom of agoraphobia).

As we noted earlier, not all children remain behaviorally inhibited throughout childhood. This stability factor may be an important mediating variable in determining those children who will develop anxiety disorders and those who will not. Hirschfeld et al. (1992) found that children who consistently received inhibited ratings throughout childhood (stable inhibited) were significantly more likely to have two or more anxiety disorders, and specifically more likely to have phobic disorders, than the nonstable comparison group or an uninhibited group. Also, parents of these stable inhibited children were more likely to have a childhood history of two or more anxiety disorders, and specifically avoidant disorder of childhood. Thus, like the data presented previously, these findings suggest that although BI may be one possible precursor to the development of anxiety disorders, including social phobia, it alone does not appear to be sufficient for its development, and as we shall see below, neither does it appear necessary (Turner, Beidel, & Wolff, 1996).

Shyness

As we noted in chapter 1, it is unclear how shyness and social phobia are related. However, it is clear that not all those who are shy meet criteria for social phobia. Yet, there is much overlap in behaviors displayed by those who are shy and those who are socially phobic. For example, Turner, Beidel, and Townsley (1990) examined the relationship between shyness and social phobia on six different dimensions. Somatic responses of both groups were similar (heart palpitations, sweating, trembling, and blushing), as were the type of negative cognitions (fear of negative evaluation or of doing something humiliating or embarrassing). However, the groups differed with respect to occupational and social functioning, behavioral characteristics, age of onset, and course of disorder. Individuals with social phobia were more likely to be occupationally and socially impaired, more likely to avoid social encounters, had an earlier age of onset, and a more chronic course. About 40% of college students describe themselves as shy, although a much lower percentage of the general population meets diagnostic criteria for social phobia (approximately 2% to 8%, depending on the data used). Turner, Beidel, and Townsley (1990) concluded that although there was overlap between the constructs of shyness and social phobia, there were important differences as well.

Stemberger et al. (1995) assessed differences in rates of childhood shyness among those with either the specific or generalized subtypes of social phobia or normal control subjects. The results indicated that 76% of those with the generalized subtype reported a history of childhood shyness, compared with 56% of those with the specific subtype and 52% of the controls who had no disorders. Only those with the generalized subtype were different from the controls who had no disorders, indicating that childhood shyness may be more characteristic of those with the generalized subtype.

There also exists a separate body of literature on childhood shyness emerging from the developmental literature. Early-appearing shyness appears to have implications for later psychopathology. For example, second graders who were shy and passively isolated and had low perceived social competence reported high levels of depression and loneliness when they were in fifth grade (Rubin & Mills, 1988). Similarly, Hymel, Rubin, Rowden, and LeMare (1990) found that lower perceptions of social competence, poor peer acceptance, and social isolation in second grade predicted anxiety and depression in fifth grade. Although supporting a relationship between shyness and psychopathology, these data do not indicate a specific relationship between shyness and social phobia. Rather, they illustrated the limitations of attempting to extrapolate from developmental data to the clinical condition of social phobia. *Shy* is a term used to describe a pattern of reticence associated with social situations. However, as we have noted, there are many reasons for social reticence. Thus, although reports of extreme shyness should alert the clinician to assess carefully for the presence of psychopathology, it cannot be used as a de facto indicator of social phobia.

Early Attachment

Recently, a 20-year prospective study examined the relationship between an anxious–resistant attachment style in infancy and the presence of anxiety disorders in childhood and adolescents (Warren, Huston, Egeland, & Sroufe, 1997). The results indicated a significant relationship between these variables. Of those who were anxiously–resistantly attached as infants, 28% had a lifetime history of anxiety disorders compared with 13% of children who were not anxiously–resistantly attached. This represents a twofold increase in the presence of anxiety disorders, which were primarily separation anxiety disorder, overanxious disorder, or social phobia. Although this study does not indicate a specific relationship between early attachment and social phobia, it does suggest that an anxious–resistant attachment style is a risk factor for the development of anxiety disorders, including social phobia.

Social Skill

From reviews of studies of socially phobic children and adults, shy children and adults, and children who are neglected by their peers, a picture of a child who is not only socially reticent but also appears to lack the necessary social behaviors for engaging in effective interpersonal discourse emerges. How do these social skill deficits develop? Children who fit any of these descriptors seem ideal candidates for maladjustment in social functioning. Those who are shy or socially phobic tend to avoid social interactions and do not have the typical developmental learning experiences as their non-shy and non-socially phobic peers. At least for those who are socially phobic, the presence of high social anxiety likely interferes even when these children attempt to engage in social interaction. Because social phobia is an early-onset disorder, a lifelong history of avoidance and social reticence develops. Thus, it is easy to see how deficiencies in social behavior would develop.

Social learning theorists view impairment in social functioning as the result of a lack of effective social skills, performance inhibition due to anxiety, or a combination of both factors (Arkowitz, 1981). In the case of socially phobic children, their learning history could well put them in a situation where both of these explanations apply. The presence of either or both of these factors could lead to further withdrawal behavior, restricted peer interaction, and then further impairment in social skills and interpersonal relationships (cf. Rubin, LeMare, & Lollis, 1990; Vernberg, Abwender, Ewell, & Beery, 1992). The majority of behavioral programs designed to remediate social withdrawal have assumed that socially isolated children lack social skills. In most cases, social skills training (SST) has proved effective in increasing social interactions in children with mild to moderate levels of social withdrawal (e.g., Finch & Hops, 1982; Jupp & Griffiths, 1990; Ladd, 1981; Paine et al., 1982; Schneider & Byrne, 1987; Sheridan, Kratochwill, & Elliott, 1990; Whitehill, Hersen, & Bellack, 1980; see chapter 9 in this volume for a more complete discussion of these treatment studies), although it is unclear whether the skills training or the exposure to group social interactions in which the skills training occurs is the active therapeutic ingredient. Nevertheless, although providing indirect confirmation, these data on skills training support the contention that skill deficiencies are an important part of the clinical picture. Similarly, among adults, it remains unresolved whether patients with social phobia are deficient in the skills necessary to engage in successful interpersonal discourse. As we noted in chapter 1, few studies have directly addressed the question of skill deficits in those with social phobia, and the results from those that have are mixed. Yet, when both child and adult studies are considered, the evidence is rather strong that social skill deficiencies are an important part of the clinical picture for at least some individuals with this disorder.

CONCLUSION

In this chapter, we discussed the various theories of how social phobia develops. Not surprisingly, there is no one unified theory, but rather there are data to support a number of different hypotheses regarding etiology. On the basis of the available data, we concluded that there are multiple pathways to the development of social phobia. This is not a new concept, as others have speculated that other disorders also have multiple pathways, but in the case of social phobia, there are sufficient data to begin to hypothesize more specifically about some of these pathways.

One possible pathway is through genetic transmission. Based on extant data, there is support for the position that social phobia runs in families, and this typically is interpreted as the direct genetic transmission of the disorder to the offspring. Not all individuals with social phobia, however, have a parent or other relative who is socially phobic. The available evidence from the best family study to date indicates that 16% of the relatives of socially phobic patients meet diagnostic criteria for social phobia (Fyer et al., 1993). Additionally, even the concordance rates for MZ twins is only about 24% versus 15% for DZ twins. Thus, it seems very clear that the majority of social phobia cases cannot be explained by genes alone. Furthermore, the results of the large Kendler et al. (1992) study revealed that nongenetic factors accounted for a significant portion of the variance in the model that was used, although the nature of these nongenetic factors was not discussed. This should not be surprising because genetic researchers long have recognized that the presence of a gene does not indicate that a disorder will develop, but rather that some type of Gene X Environment interaction seems to be necessary (e.g., Scarr, 1969). Therefore, as noted, it is unlikely that those with social phobia acquire their conditions solely through genetic transmission. A more reasonable hypothesis, we think, is that one acquires vulnerability through genetic inheritance and that for the disorder to develop, other factors are necessary. We discussed a number of these factors in this chapter.

With respect to psychological theories of social phobia, we outlined three theories for which there is some empirical evidence: direct conditioning, observational learning, and information transfer. By far, it appears that direct conditioning or traumatic conditioning is most important among the three in the etiology of social phobia. Traumatic conditioning is followed in importance by observational learning and then information transfer.

Each of these psychological mechanisms may be a viable avenue for the development of social phobia, at least in some cases. If we assume that the available data are correct, as many as 71% of those with social phobia report experiences consistent with direct conditioning or observational learning (Ost, 1987). It must be pointed out, however, that just because someone has experienced what might be considered a traumatic episode (either through direct conditioning or indirectly through observation), or has been exposed to information transfer, the development of social phobia is not inevitable. Recall that Stemberger et al. (1995) reported that some individuals experience traumatic events but nevertheless do not develop social phobia. In that study, 20% of individuals without psychiatric disorders reported histories of traumatic conditioning, and many of us can recall embarrassing social faux pas, but not many of us go on to develop social phobia. Clearly, just as genetic transmission alone probably cannot account for the development of social phobia, conditioning, observational learning, or information transfer cannot fully explain etiology either. As might be expected, then, the precise causal factor for social phobia is difficult to pinpoint, even though we appear to have various pieces of the puzzle.

Another plausible explanation (pathway) for the etiology of social phobia is that it results from some combination of the factors discussed above. For example, those who are genetically predisposed might be more susceptible to traumatic conditioning, observational learning, or information transfer. In other words, these modes of acquisitions may be more likely in individuals with certain predispositions. To date there have been no studies to directly test the hypothesis that those who are considered more vulnerable (due to genetic inheritance) are more susceptible to direct conditioning, observational learning, or information transfer. However, there is a small amount of data to suggest that the offspring of a group of parents with mixed anxiety disorders are more responsive to various types of stimuli than the offspring of parents without anxiety disorders (Turner, Beidel, & Epstein, 1991).

Additional factors also may predispose one to the onset of social phobia or function to help maintain social phobia after it emerges. As noted, family environment variables, including parental personality factors and behaviors, and parenting skill, may combine with a biological predisposition or specific traumatic events to contribute to the onset of anxiety disorders, and in this case, social phobia. To illustrate the powerful impact of family interaction style, Barrett et al. (1996) demonstrated how protective parental behaviors may serve to maintain avoidance behaviors in anxious children. Also, findings with behaviorally inhibited children show that even if they initially were inhibited temperamentally, they became less so when their parents deliberately engaged them in social interactions with others. These findings suggest that parental behavior plays a significant role in the manifestation of social fears despite one's genetic makeup.

Behaviors such as social reticence, behavioral inhibition, shyness, or social isolation clearly are related to poor peer relationships and lone-liness, although to date conclusions are limited by the correlational nature of the data. Nevertheless, it is likely that a vicious cycle can develop. For example, children who are socially isolated have limited opportunities for interaction and thus do not acquire the social skills necessary to develop friendships. As a result, they feel lonely and iso-lated, which further limits their interactions with peers and further retards their skill development. As Davidson (1993) noted, it is those with the earliest onset of social phobia who probably have the most chronic course.

To reiterate there is no definitive answer for how social phobia develops. Yet, the current clinical, social, and developmental literature all address what appear to be relevant factors likely associated with onset and maintenance. We think in most cases a combination of fac-tors are present, including a biological vulnerability to become anxious. Clearly, some cases can develop through direct as well as indirect con-ditioning. However, even here biological vulnerability could be impor-tant. We envision that the next decade will lead to further clarification of how these many factors interact to contribute to development of social phobia.

5

Assessment

My life is perfect except for this fear of giving speeches.

**The introductory statement from a patient who, after assessment,
was determined to have the generalized form of social phobia.**

The proper assessment of social phobia, as with any disorder, involves a careful and multifaceted inquiry into the presenting problem as well as into the individual's overall emotional and social functioning. In this chapter, we discuss the assessment of social phobia in children and adults, review various assessment methods and procedures, discuss issues particularly relevant to the diagnosis of social phobia, and provide a number of practical suggestions for facilitating the assessment process. Finally, we will highlight the methods used to explicate those specific variables that are critical to the conceptualization and treatment of social phobia in each individual (i.e., the core fear; see chapters 8 and 9). We will begin by discussing the initial interview.

THE INITIAL INTERVIEW

Several factors need to be considered when interviewing those with social phobia, no matter whether the individual is a child, adolescent, or adult. It is important to remember that individuals with social phobia suffer substantial anxiety when interacting with others, and, throughout their lives, they often have attempted to hide their distress. Therefore, although a patient may be motivated to enter treatment, discussing fears and social anxiety with a stranger can be very distressful. One of the clinician's initial tasks is to create an atmosphere such that individuals with social phobia feel calm and secure discussing their fears and anxieties.

As noted above, those with social phobia often are somewhat secretive about their distress. This is sometimes due to embarrassment about their inability to control what they, as well as others, believe they should be able to control. Many patients report that when they have tried to discuss their anxieties with others in the past, they have been told, "Well, everyone feels that way when they make a speech," or, "don't worry you'll get over it." Of course, neither of these statements is quite true. Although most people do experience some anxiety in social performance situations, as we noted in chapter 1, everyone does not have an identical physiological response during public speaking presentations (Beidel, Turner, & Dancu, 1985). Although those with social phobia and those without social phobia show arousal as indicated by elevated blood pressure and pulse rate when in a public speaking situation, those without social phobia quickly adjust to the situation and their blood pressure and pulse rate return to baseline levels. This indicates that they become relatively comfortable in the setting. On the other hand, the blood pressure and pulse rate of those with social phobia remains elevated throughout the task. Thus, socially phobic individuals never adjust to the setting.

The therapist's ability to communicate understanding has a particularly important effect for people with social phobia. Because for so many years this disorder was not studied by researchers and there was little information in the popular media about the condition or its treatment, those with social phobia have been described as "suffering in silence." As recently as 6 years ago, a number of patients who sought treatment in our clinic remarked that they "feel 50% better just knowing it (social phobia) has a name and somebody knows how to treat it." Of course, this good feeling is only temporary, and in itself is not an intervention. However, it does illustrate the relief that those with social phobia experience when they finally talk to someone who understands that everyone does not feel the way individuals with social phobia do when engaging in social interactions.

It also should be noted that some with social phobia (primarily adults) present initially as only having a "public speaking problem." However, only about 30% of adults with social phobia have the specific subtype, and even then, it rarely involves just one particular situation. Rather, there often is distress in several related settings, although at the time of the initial interview the patient may be unaware of the significance of these additional situations. It also has been our observation that some patients are committed to the idea that their problem is centered on one specific situation, usually speech anxiety or some other specific performance situation. In some cases, the patient has had the disorder for so long that they have constructed their environment to provide maximum protection from threatening situations. This extensive pattern of avoidance becomes their lifestyle, and they may no longer be aware of the motivating factor for why they engage or do not engage in certain behaviors. In other cases, personality features (e.g., OCPD, see chapter 1) also may play a role. We have discussed elsewhere the fact that those with social phobia often are very perfectionistic and rigid in their thinking style. In a number of cases, this appears to be related to the need to see the condition as a unidimensional problem. Typically, when this scenario is applicable, other factors reveal themselves as treatment progresses.

We have referred to this lack of awareness of the severely restricted lifestyle of those with social phobia as the *social phobia cocoon* (Turner, Beidel, & Cooley, 1994). Given the chronic nature of this disorder, and its relatively early onset, patients with social phobia often exist within a very limited social environment and in some cases often are unaware of the extensive nature of their behavioral avoidance. Their avoidance of social encounters functions to minimize their distress (i.e., because they are not engaging in social encounters, they are not anxious). Conversely, if they were to engage in these interactions, they would become extremely anxious. The *cocoon* alleviates distress but also limits any opportunities for social interactions. Therefore, although individuals with social phobia initially may present as having merely speech phobia, careful assessment often reveals a more extensive pattern of fear and avoidance.

There is another issue to consider during the initial interview when treating children and adolescents. As we noted, children rarely seek treatment on their own volition. Thus, the task of forming a positive relationship is made more difficult because the child often does not want to participate in treatment, even when the impairing consequences of the fears are clear. One exception may be children whose fears result in school refusal. Some of these children are motivated for treatment so they can return to school, but others remain reluctant, preferring homebound instruction. In any case, when treating children and adolescents the clinician can be faced with a formidable task. Therapeutic relationships must be forged not only with the child but also with the primary caregiver (usually the parent).

One approach that seems to be very successful in "breaking the ice" with patients of any age with social phobia is to begin by explaining the parameters of the initial meeting. By speaking first, the therapist allows the patient a few moments to adjust to the office setting and perhaps to become slightly more comfortable prior to discussing his or her social distress. Once we have explained the purpose and structure of the initial interview, we allow the patient (or parent) to begin wherever he or she wants by saying something like "What brought you in today?" Griest and colleagues (Griest, Kobak, Jefferson, Katzelnick, & Chene, 1995) recommended a similar approach, suggesting opening questions such as "What is the nature of your difficulty? What problems are you having? How can I help?" Details of the situation can be addressed once the big picture has been established. These details should include all of the salient aspects of the disorder, including negative cognitions, overt behaviors, physiological responses, range of social situations affected, and any coping strategies currently used to deal with the distress.

The importance of a general diagnostic interview in these situations cannot be overemphasized. As we noted in chapters 1 and 2, like all of the anxiety disorders, social phobia has a high prevalence of co-occurring conditions (other anxiety as well as nonanxiety disorders). The presence of these other conditions could affect how treatment is conceptualized and implemented. In addition, as noted in chapters 1 and 2, other disorders may mimic social phobia. Thus, a clear differential diagnosis of social phobia and knowledge of co-occurring conditions is critical for the treatment planning process. Because the assessment of psychopathology is so crucial to patient diagnosis, management, and treatment planning, we recommend using a general semistructured interview schedule in addition to the typical open clinical interview. Use of such an instrument ensures a thorough diagnostic evaluation. Below, we discuss the nature of structured and semistructured interviews and a number of specific instruments and procedures for conducting a semistructured interview.

STRUCTURED AND SEMISTRUCTURED DIAGNOSTIC INTERVIEWS

In chapter 3, we introduced the Diagnostic Interview Schedule (DIS), which was developed for use by lay interviewers in the large-scale Epidemiological Catchment Area survey (Robins et al., 1984). Because nonprofessional personnel were used to conduct the interviews, the DIS was constructed so that reliance on clinical judgment was minimized and diagnostic decisions were made with the use of a computer algorithm (Robins et al., 1984). Thus, the DIS is a structured interview schedule. Although the very structured nature of the DIS was appropriate for the context of this epidemiological study, most clinicians find it far too constraining for general clinical use.

In contrast, semistructured interview schedules guide the clinician through the diagnostic decision making process yet allow for the exercise of clinical judgment. It is important that clinicians understand that these interview schedules do not determine an individual's diagnosis. Rather, by following the interview schedule, clinicians will be certain that they have asked all of the questions necessary to determine the proper diagnosis. Unlike the DIS computer algorithm method of assigning a diagnosis, semistructured interview schedules leave the determination of the diagnosis in the hands of the clinician. Therefore, these schedules require some training to be administered properly, and they also require extensive knowledge of psychopathological states. The clinician's level of experience will determine the extensiveness of the training required to learn to administer the interview properly. However, these schedules cannot be used effectively by lay interviewers.

Because semistructured interview schedules usually take anywhere from $1^1/_2$ to $2^1/_2$ hours to complete, we recommend conducting this interview in a second session (following the initial interview). There are several semistructured clinical interview schedules available, each having advantages and disadvantages. In addition, many of these interview schedules have a child version for administration to children and adolescents (and their parents). Each of the available relevant interview instruments will be discussed below. At the time of the writing of this volume, few interview schedules had been adapted to *DSM-IV* criteria (see below). For adults, the differences between the *DSM-III-R* (American Psychiatric Association, 1994) and *DSM-IV* diagnostic criteria for social phobia are minor and should not affect the use of extant interview schedules to assist in diagnosis. However, this is not the case for some of the other anxiety disorders or for social phobia in children (where more substantial changes occurred). Therefore, these limitations must be acknowledged when selecting a semistructured interview schedule.

The *Schedule for Affective Disorders and Schizophrenia* (SADS; Endicott & Spitzer, 1978) was one of the initial semistructured diagnostic interviews. Its purpose was to increase the reliability of diagnostic evaluations (Griest et al., 1995). Because it was developed prior to 1980 (before *DSM-III*, American Psychiatric Association, 1980, was published), the SADS is keyed to Research Diagnostic Criteria (RDC; Spitzer, Endicott, & Robins, 1978). Thus, the SADS is not based on current *DSM* or *International Classification of Diseases* (*ICD*) diagnostic criteria, the diagnostic schemas most commonly used by insurance and managed care companies. Its test–retest reliability of $r = .67$ is adequate, and its inter rater reliability of $r = .94$ (for Anxiety Summary scale scores, not for a particular anxiety diagnosis) is acceptable (Endicott & Spitzer, 1978). However, reliability for specific anxiety diagnoses were not reported. Furthermore, the SADS, as its name implies, emphasizes the assessment of schizophrenia and affective disorders. Thus, it does not provide sufficient attention to the differential diagnosis of anxiety disorders (DiNardo, O'Brien, Barlow, Waddell, & Blanchard, 1983). Although the SADS is a well-accepted semistructured interview, its utility for the assessment of anxiety disorders is limited, and for this reason other schedules probably are more appropriate for the anxiety disorders.

Perhaps in response to this limitation, Manuzza, Fyer, Klein, and Endicott (1986) developed the SADS-LA (Lifetime Anxiety), a modification of the SADS specifically designed to assess the lifetime presence of anxiety disorders. The SADS-LA allows a diagnosis to be made on the basis of RDC, *DSM-III*, or *DSM-III-R* criteria. As indicated by the SADS-LA, the emphasis is on assessing the presence of lifetime anxiety disorders, and it does provide an opportunity for rating anxiety in 10 social situations. Kappa coefficients for inter rater agreement for the presence of social phobia was .68 for current diagnosis and .71 for lifetime diagnoses (Manuzza et al., 1986). These kappa coefficients represent acceptable, although not particularly high, reliability for the diagnosis of social phobia.

The child version of the SADS, the *Schedule for Affective Disorders and Schizophrenia for Children*, is commonly known as the Kiddie-SADS (Chambers et al., 1985). Last (1986) adapted this schedule to assess *DSM-III* childhood anxiety disorders more effectively. The reliability coefficients for inter rater agreement for any specific anxiety disorder was $k = .88$. The Kiddie-SADS requires separate administration to the child and the primary caregiver. Thus, the time of the diagnostic interview can be lengthier than when interviewing an adult patient. Although the Last (1986) adaptation has made the Kiddie-SADS more useful for the assessment of childhood anxiety disorders, its primary focus remains the assessment of affective disorders. It has been our clinical experience that children (and sometimes their caregivers) find many of the initial questions (which focus on depression) irrelevant, and this could lower their cooperation with the interview.

The *Structured Clinical Interview for DSM-III-R* (SCID) and the *Structured Clinical Interview for DSM-III-R Axis II* (SCID-II) were developed specifically as a diagnostic interview using *DSM-III-R* criteria. The interview schedules assess the entire range of Axis I and II psychopathology and are presented in a modular format. These modules allow the clinician to selectively assess certain aspects of psychopathology. However, we would discourage selecting only specific modules for the interview inasmuch as social distress can result from many different disorders (see chapter 1 in this volume). Deleting the assessment of certain modules (perhaps with the exception of the psychosis module) may result in the neglect of information significant for case formulation and treatment planning. An advantage of the SCID and SCID-II is that they use a branching logic structure (Griest et al., 1995), thus allowing the clinician to skip-out of sections when it is clear that the patient is not endorsing psychopathology consistent with the diagnosis. However, kappa coefficients for interrater agreement for social phobia were $k = .47$ for current diagnosis and $k = .57$ for lifetime diagnosis (Spitzer, Williams, Gibbons, & First, 1992; Williams et al., 1992). These coefficients indicate only fair diagnostic agreement, and in our view are too low to recommend the SCID for assessing social phobia. One reason for the only fair diagnostic agreement may be that the social phobia module consists of only one screening question. Additional interviewing probably is necessary to make this interview schedule useful in the detection of social phobia. A *DSM-IV* version is in the final stages of development.

Developed as a semistructured interview specifically for the diagnosis of anxiety disorders, the *Anxiety Disorders Interview Schedule for DSM-IV* (ADIS-IV; DiNardo, Brown, & Barlow, 1995) allows for the diagnosis of all anxiety disorders and selected affective and other disorders. The ADIS-IV has added use for the clinician's assessment of anxiety disorders. In addition to the diagnostic criteria and an impairment severity rating, the ADIS-IV assesses clinical history, cognitive, physiological, and behavioral components, situational parameters that may affect symptomatic expression, ratings of fear intensity, and avoidance of anxiety-producing situations. In addition, the Hamilton Rating Scale for Anxiety (Hamilton, 1959) and the Hamilton Rating Scale for Depression (Hamilton, 1960) are included, thus allowing for clinician ratings of general anxiety and depression. Reliability coefficients are not yet available for the ADIS-IV; however, the kappa coefficient for a diagnosis of social phobia (using *DSM-III-R* criteria) was .79 (DiNardo et al., 1993). The social phobia section allows for fear intensity and avoidance ratings across 13 different settings, thereby allowing the clinician basic data on the extent of the individual's social fears. This is a good interview schedule for the anxiety disorders. However, the limited coverage of other disorders means that it needs to be used in conjunction with an instrument that provides coverage of those disorders not covered by the ADIS.

The child version of the ADIS-IV, the *ADIS-IV (Child)* and *ADIS-IV (Parent;* Silverman & Albano, 1995), assesses all *DSM-IV* anxiety disorders as well as affective disorders, externalizing disorders (conduct disorder is only assessed on the Parent version), and the presence of substance abuse. The structure of the ADIS-C and ADIS-P appear to be more "child-friendly" than other semistructured interview schedules. It begins with questions about the child's functioning in the school setting. This is an area that most children are accustomed to discussing (particularly with adults), and thus it allows the child time to adjust to the interview setting prior to embarking upon a more detailed discussion of his or her fears and clinical status. Additionally, the ADIS-C and ADIS-P ask specific questions about the child's friendships and socialization patterns, areas that are particularly appropriate for the assessment of childhood social phobia. With respect to semistructured interviews for children and adolescents, the K-SADS (Last's version) and the ADIS-C and ADIS-P (*DSM-III-R* version) have the highest published inter rater reliability for categories of anxiety disorders, possibly because they were developed specifically for determining anxiety disorders diagnoses. There are no inter rater or test–retest reliability data yet reported for the recently revised ADIS-C and ADIS-P for *DSM-IV*. However, we would expect, given the extent of the revisions, relia-

Table 4

Semistructured Interview Schedules

Group	Instrument
Adults	Diagnostic Interview Schedule
	Schedule for Affective Disorders and Schizophrenia-Lifetime Anxiety
	Structured Clinical Interview for DSM-III-R
	Anxiety Disorders Interview Schedule for DSM-IV
Children	Diagnostic Interview Schedule for Children
	Schedule for Affective Disorders and Schizophrenia for Children
	Anxiety Disorders Interview Schedule for Children—DSM-IV

bility will be similar to that for the *DSM-III-R* version. Thus, the use of these two interviews for children can be recommended.

Table 4 lists the semistructured interview schedules commonly used in diagnostic evaluations. When administering any semistructured interviews, the clinician should remember that the interview situation is very artificial for children (and perhaps even adolescents). Thus, they often do not respond well to structured or semistructured interview formats. This means that sometimes they will not answer the interviewer's questions or will answer every question by saying "no." Particularly if they notice that by saying no the interviewer skips several pages, they may come to realize that continuing to say no will quickly end their ordeal. Clinicians can counteract this tendency in several ways. First, prior establishment of good rapport will enlist cooperation. Second, an interview schedule such as the ADIS-C begins with a conversation about school and friends. Thus, rather than initially discussing specific fears or problems, topics with which children are much more comfortable are discussed first. Third, we find it easier to interview the parents first, usually because they are the ones who initiated the clinic contact. Then after discussing the situation with the parent, the interview with the child is more productive. Finally, asking the child if he or she would like a break during the interview may assist in keeping the child's cooperation.

Whether interviewing a child, adolescent, or adult, we must emphasize the need for training to administer these diagnostic interviews. Most are accompanied by manuals that provide many of the necessary guidelines. In addition, many of these interviews have instructions regarding when the therapist ceases administration of one line of questioning and where to proceed next. However, in some cases, these instructions are not well-marked and during the course of an actual interview can be easily overlooked. In order to become proficient, one should practice administering the interview on several occasions prior to conducting actual patient interviews.

Also, there is the temptation to treat the diagnostic interview as a self-report instrument. It is tempting to ask the questions and just record the patient's answer verbatim. However, as noted above, the purpose of semistructured interview schedules is to guide the clinician through the diagnostic process. Many of these schedules require the clinician to rate the behavior as mild, moderate, or severe. Although tempting to ask the patient to provide symptom ratings along this dimension, it is really the clinician's judgment (on the basis of experience) that is relevant for the rating and the final diagnostic decision.

Using these interview schedules with children requires conducting separate interviews with parent and child. Most interviews developed for use with children actually consist of two parallel interview schedules: one for children and a second for parents. For most, the major difference is a change in pronoun; that is, for the child version a question is phrased "Do you get nervous when . . . ," whereas for the parent version the question is phrased "Does your child get nervous when . . ." In a few cases, certain disorders, such as conduct disorder, are only found in the parent's schedule (Silverman & Albano, 1995). We have found the use of separate interview forms for parents and children somewhat cumbersome. When using separate schedules, notes that we might have written on the schedule itself in response to what a child said are not readily available when interviewing the parent (using a separate form). Our solution is to use one schedule (usually the parent schedule) and score both the parent and child responses using two different colors of ink, such as red and black. In this way, notes conducted during the first part of the interview are readily available when conducting the second half. With respect to the change in pronouns, we do not find it difficult to remember to say "you" when interviewing a child or "your child" when interviewing a parent.

CLINICIAN RATING SCALES

Currently, there are no clinician rating scales developed specifically for the quantification of social fears in children and adolescents. However, several clinician rating scales designed to rate various dimensions of social phobia in adults are available. The first was the Liebowitz Social Anxiety Scale (LSAS; Liebowitz, 1987), which consists of 24 situations, 13 performance situations, and 11 social interaction situations. Each is rated on two 4-point scales: the first gauges fear and the second gauges avoidance. Inter rater reliability data are not published. However, Heimberg and his colleagues reported that the LSAS has good clinical use (Holt, Heimberg, & Hope, 1992) and good criterion validity (Brown, Heimberg, & Juster, 1995; Holt, Heimberg, Hope, & Liebowitz, 1992) and is sensitive to treatment outcome (e.g., Davidson et al., 1993; Liebowitz et al., 1992). In addition, the scale is fairly easy to administer and score.

An even more brief rating scale (11 items), appropriately named the Brief Social Phobia Rating Scale (BSPRS), was developed by Davidson, Potts, et al. (1991). This scale also allows for separate ratings of fear and avoidance (on a 5-point scale) in seven situations. In addition, there is a four-item physiological scale that allows for assessment of the four most common physical symptoms (blushing, palpitations, trembling, and sweating). The BSPRS is to be scored after completion of a clinical interview. This rating scale has good test–retest reliability ($r = .99$) and inter rater reliability ($r = .99$; Davidson, Potts et al., 1991). It also has good concurrent validity as measured by correlations with the LSAS ($r = .76$) and the Social Phobia and Anxiety Inventory (SPAI; Turner, Beidel, Dancu, & Stanley, 1989; $r = .86$). Finally, the scale is sensitive to treatment effects (Davidson et al., 1993).

Rating scales can be very useful as a quick quantification of the extent of an individual's fear and avoidance. Like semistructured interviews, however, they were designed to be administered by qualified clinicians who have some experience with the disorder. Although Griest et al. (1995) noted that the LSAS has been used as a self-report instrument and that the BSPRS also might be used in this way, we believe that this would be a misuse of these scales because they were not developed for that purpose. Furthermore, no psychometric properties exist to support their use in this fashion. The scales are used correctly when they are rated by the clinician, either during or after the completion of a clinical interview.

SELF-REPORT INVENTORIES FOR ADULTS

In their review of self-report inventories for the assessment of social phobia, McNeil, Ries, and Turk (1995) noted that there are a number of instruments available to assess social anxiety. However, many of these were developed prior to the publication of social phobia as a separate diagnosis in the *DSM* nomenclature. Therefore, although these instruments may assess anxiety in social settings, as we noted in chapter 1, this does not automatically indicate they are appropriate to assess social phobia. Therefore, our review will be restricted primarily to those instruments that were developed specifically to assess the construct of social phobia as defined by *DSM-III* (or *DSM-III-R* or *DSM-IV*). However, two scales that were developed previously but are still in common use will be discussed first.

The Social Avoidance and Distress (SAD) scale and the Fear of Negative Evaluation (FNE) scale (Watson & Friend, 1969) are among the most commonly used self-report instruments for social anxiety. The SAD contains 28 items and the FNE contains 30 items rated as true or false. Initially, the SAD and FNE were developed to assess social anxiety in schizophrenic populations. However, the face validity of the items fostered their adoption by social phobia researchers. Initial reports of reliability and validity for the SAD and FNE based on socially anxious (not necessarily socially phobic) populations indicated adequate to good psychometric properties (see McNeil, Reis, Taylor, et al., 1995, for a review). However, the validity of the SAD and FNE for social phobia has been a subject of debate. In an initial report, the SAD and FNE failed to differentiate patients with social phobia from those with other types of anxiety disorders (with the exception of simple phobia; Turner, McCanna, & Beidel, 1987). Furthermore, the measures were significantly correlated with general measures of distress, indicating that they did not specifically assess social phobia. In a reply, Heimberg, Hope, Rapee, and Bruch (1988) reasoned that the scales would not necessarily differentiate social phobia from other anxiety disorders because (a) substantial social anxiety exists across all anxiety disorders, (b) those with social phobia were heterogeneous with respect to the range of social fears and need not necessarily all score high on the inventory, and (c) social anxiety may be a component of other emotions such as depression and trait anxiety.

The points raised by Heimberg and his colleagues may have some validity. As we noted in chapter 1, social anxiety and social phobia are not synonymous terms. However, these points did not address the central question. That is, do the FNE and SAD assess the unique condition of social phobia? The results of a discriminant function analysis indicated that they do not (Turner, McCanna, & Beidel, 1987). Scores on these instruments did not differentiate a patient with social phobia from someone with panic disorder or agoraphobia. Therefore, their use as specific measures of social phobia are not recommended. In recent years, self-report instruments designed for the specific purpose of assessing social phobia have been developed.

The Social Phobia Scale (SPS) and the Social Interaction Anxiety Scale (SIAS) were developed by Mattick and Clarke (1989; as cited in McNeil, Reis, Taylor, et al., 1995) as an attempt to assess two dimensions of social phobia: social performance and social interaction. The SPS and the SIAS each contain 20 items rated on a 5-point Likert scale. Although the initial data remain unpublished (McNeil, Reis, Taylor, et al., 1995), Heimberg and his colleagues (Heimberg, Mueller, Holt, Hope, & Liebowitz, 1992) reported that the scales have good test–retest reliability ($r > .90$ for intervals up to 13 weeks). The SPS and the SIAS are correlated significantly with other measures of social anxiety (Mattick & Clark, 1989). The SIAS appears capable of differentiating patients with social phobia from those with other anxiety disorders (Rapee, Brown, Antony, & Barlow, 1992), except for patients with panic disorder and agoraphobia (Brown et al., 1997). In addition, the SIAS can, to some extent, differentiate the generalized from the nongeneralized subtype (Heimberg et al., 1992). Although these instruments have some established psychometric properties, one troubling aspect is that the SPS and the SIAS, which are supposed to measure different aspects of social phobia, actually are highly correlated ($r = .72$; Brown et al., 1997). This high correlation suggests that (a) the scales do not address different components of the clinical presentation of social phobia, or (b) these two dimensions of social phobia are not as independent as suggested by these scales.

A final self-report instrument for the assessment of social phobia in adults is the Social Phobia and Anxiety Inventory (SPAI; Turner, Beidel, Dancu, & Stanley, 1989). The SPAI was developed to specifically address various components of social phobia, including overt behaviors, cognitions, and physiological response. The Social Phobia subscale has 32 items that are rated using a 7-point Likert scale format. The SPAI also allows for separate ratings of anxiety based on audience characteristics (e.g., opposite gender, authority figures). In addition, there is a 13-item Agoraphobia scale that assists in differentiating those with social phobia from those with panic disorder and agoraphobia. Scores on the Agoraphobia subscale are subtracted from the Social Anxiety subscale, resulting in a difference score, which has been validated as a "purer" measure of social phobia (Turner, Stanley, Beidel, & Bond, 1989).

Herbert, Bellack, & Hope (1991) suggested that the social phobia subscale was a slightly better measure of social phobia symptoms. This interpretation was based primarily on the pattern of correlations between the SPAI Social Phobia subscale, the difference score, and scores on various instruments used to determine the SPAI's concurrent validity. Although at first glance such an interpretation seems to have some merit, there are several factors that mitigate against accepting such a conclusion (Beidel & Turner, 1992a). A brief synopsis is presented here.

The interested reader is referred to the original articles for more detail. First, it is important to note that the conclusion drawn in the study by Herbert et al. (1991) (that the correlations between the Social Phobia subscale and various measures are larger than the correlations between the difference score and the various measures) was not reached on the basis of a statistical test. In addition, some of the correlation coefficients were "larger" by a mere point or two, making it highly unlikely that they were statistically or clinically significant. Second, the SPAI was developed as a specific measure of social phobia, and the original discriminant function analysis indicated that only the difference score could differentiate patients with social phobia from those with agoraphobia. This is a very important distinction for diagnosis and treatment planning. Third, the concern in Herbert et al. (1991) that the subtraction of the Agoraphobia subscale from the Social Phobia subscale (in order to derive the difference score) would artificially deflate the scores of those who are comorbid for both social phobia and panic disorder is not based on any empirical data. Therefore, we strongly feel that the original scoring and decision-making procedures, which were empirically derived over the course of a 4-year period, should be retained. In short, the SPAI difference score is the score that should be used to assist in diagnosis and treatment outcome evaluation.

The psychometric properties of the SPAI have been studied extensively, and the inventory has been translated into at least 10 different languages. The SPAI has good test–retest reliability and concurrent, external, and discriminative validity (Beidel, Bordon, Turner, & Jacob, 1989; Beidel, Turner, Stanley, & Dancu, 1989; Turner, Beidel, et al., 1989; Turner, Stanley, et al., 1989). It successfully discriminates patients with social phobia from those with other anxiety disorders and from controls without any disorders. In addition, the SPAI is the only self-report instrument that has been tested to determine its ability to reflect clinically significant change. The results indicated that change assessed by the SPAI as a result of treatment represents reliable and clinically significant improvement (Beidel, Turner, & Cooley, 1993). Finally, although developed as an adult instrument, the SPAI is the only self-report measure that has been validated for use with an adolescent population (Clark et al., 1994). A child version is available for pre-adolescent children[1] (see below).

SELF-REPORT OF SOCIAL PHOBIA IN CHILDREN

Two instruments have been developed specifically to assess social anxiety and social phobia in children. The earliest instrument was the Social Anxiety Scale for Children—Revised (SASC-R; LaGreca & Stone, 1993). This children's scale is modeled on the adult SAD and the FNE scales discussed above. There are 22 items that comprise three factors: fear of negative evaluation, social avoidance and distress in new situations, and social avoidance and distress in general. The SASC-R has good internal consistency and test—retest reliability. It correlates moderately with general anxiety, social competence, self-worth, and conduct (deportment). To date, studies addressing its ability to discriminate socially anxious children from other diagnostic groups have not been reported.

The Social Phobia and Anxiety Inventory for Children (SPAI-C; Beidel, Turner, & Morris, 1995) is a 26-item empirically derived inventory that assesses distress in a variety of social settings and includes separate items measuring cognitive, somatic, and behavioral components of the disorder using a 3-point Likert scale. It has high internal consistency, and good to excellent test—retest reliability over short (2 week) and long-term (10 month) intervals. It is moderately correlated with general anxiety, fear of criticism, and parental ratings of internalizing behaviors and social competence (Beidel et al., 1995). Additionally, the scale has been demonstrated to correlate with children's daily social behaviors (as measured by a daily diary) and to differentiate children with social phobia from controls without a disorder, from those with externalizing disorders (primarily attention deficit disorder; Beidel, Turner, & Fink, 1996), and from children with other types of anxiety disorders (Beidel, Turner, & Hamlin, 1997). There also is a parent version of the SPAI-C that is currently under development. A score of 18

---

[1]The Social Phobia and Anxiety Inventory (Turner, Stanley, et al., 1989) and the Social Phobia and Anxiety Inventory for Children (Beidel, Turner, & Morris, 1995) are available from Multi-Health Systems, Inc., 65 Overlea Boulevard, Suite 210, Toronto, Ontario M4H 1P1 Canada, (800) 456-3003.

on the SPAI-C appears to be a good indicator of the need to conduct a diagnostic interview for the presence of social phobia. The scale is most useful for children between the ages of 8 and 14. Below that age, the parent SPAI-C alone may be determined to be most useful. Over age 14, the adult SPAI is recommended.

On the basis of the available literature and our own clinical experience, we have some recommendations concerning the use of self-report inventories. Table 5 summarizes the available self-report inventories for children, adolescents, and adults with social phobia. Self-report inventories are useful to assist in the quantification of symptoms, and several (including the SPAI and the SPAI-C) provide scores that have been empirically validated as a cut-off score indicating someone who may have the disorder. However, these inventories cannot take the place of a clinical interview for the purposes of making a diagnosis, and we do not recommend that they be the sole means by which to assign a diagnosis. On the other hand, they can be used to survey the range of experiences and, in the case of the SPAI and SPAI-C, also allow for an assessment across different interpersonal partners. Finally, an important advantage for the administration of these inventories is that items on the self-report instruments can trigger recall of additional

Table 5

Self-Report Instruments for Social Phobia in Children, Adolescents, and Adults

Group	Instrument
Adolescents and Adults	Social Avoidance and Distress Scale
	Fear of Negative Evaluation Scale
	Social Phobia Scale
	Social Interaction Anxiety Scale
	Social Phobia and Anxiety Inventory
Children	Social Anxiety Scale for Children—Revised
	Social Phobia and Anxiety Inventory for Children

aspects of the disorder in the patients. This can be extremely helpful in final diagnostic decision making and treatment planning.

SELF-MONITORING PROCEDURES

Self-monitoring (daily diary) can play a very important role in the assessment of social phobia, both prior to and during treatment. Self-monitoring forms can be developed to assess various dimensions of the clinical presentation. Commonly assessed aspects include entry into or avoidance of social encounters, ratings of distress and cognitions associated with events, associated somatic responses, and behavioral responses to distressing events. This information can be used (a) to assist in the diagnosis (e.g., does the patient actually experience as much or as little distress on a daily basis as was described during the diagnostic interview?), (b) to generate appropriate behavioral practice situations (e.g., exposure to the feared situations), (c) to determine fear-producing situations or avoidance patterns, and (d) to determine treatment outcome (e.g., are ratings lower at posttreatment than they are at pretreatment?). Therapists can request that patients monitor as the events occur (event basis) or provide a summary at the end of the day (daily basis). There are no empirical data attesting to the advantages of an event-based versus a daily-based monitoring system. However, it is our clinical impression that the closer the recording occurs to the actual event, the more valid the record will be. This would argue for an event-based record.

What probably is more important than when the recording occurs, however, is the amount of material that the patient is expected to record. Again, although few empirical data are available, it is our impression that patient compliance is inversely correlated with the length of the self-monitoring forms. Forms that require 5 minutes or less to complete are most likely to be completed consistently and conscientiously. Figure 1 illustrates a self-monitoring form successfully used by adults with social phobia. For some patients, expanding the monitoring to include a description of the actual thoughts or events that elicited the event may be helpful. For others, simple frequency counts are all that is necessary.

Date: _____   Place: _____

Check which occurred

_____   Occurrence of a Distressful Thought

_____   Occurrence of a Distressful Event

_____   Avoidance of a Distressful Event

Rate how anxious you were when the above occurred:

1	2	3	4	5	6	7
Not at All Anxious			Moderately Anxious			Extremely Anxious

Figure 1

Self-monitoring form used with adults

As an example of how self-monitoring can be useful in the treatment-planning process, consider the statement that we used to open this chapter ("My life is perfect except for this fear of giving speeches"). The clinical interview and the self-report measures hinted at the presence of a more pervasive condition, but the patient could not (or would not) identify any additional distressful situations. However, he was asked to complete the self-monitoring form depicted in Figure 1 for a 2-week period. The self-report data indicated that the patient experienced at least moderate distress anytime that he had to speak to three or more people, even if it was an informal conversation at the water cooler. Therefore, self-monitoring revealed a more pervasive pattern of distress than that expressed by the patient at the initial interview.

Self-monitoring is less commonly used with children and adolescents, but it can nonetheless be valuable. Because adolescents and children usually do not come into treatment entirely voluntarily, they may be less motivated to participate in self-monitoring strategies. In addition, written forms such as in Figure 2 may be very unappealing to young children, thereby limiting their cooperation. In a study of the feasibility of daily diary procedures, Beidel, Neal, and Lederer (1991) reported that children as young as age 8 were able to use a daily diary to monitor distressing activities for a 2-week period of time. However,

Daily Record

Date _____

Circle the number that describes how nervous you were today

1	2	3	4	5
Not nervous at all		Medium nervous		Very nervous

Today I worried about:

_____ Something bad happening to my family

What was the thought? _____

How many times did you have it? _____

_____ Something bad happening to me

What was the thought? _____

How many times did you have it? _____

_____ Doing something to embarrass myself

What was the thought? _____

How many times did you have it? _____

_____ Other _____

What was the thought? _____

How many times did you have it? _____

Figure 2

Self-monitoring form used with children

younger children (ages 8–10) were more likely to complete the monitoring if the diary was presented in a picture, rather than a written, format. There was no difference in rate of compliance for children aged 10 or older, although some of the older children did confide to us that they found the pictures "childish." Nevertheless, this study demonstrated that children (even as young as age 8) can use self-monitoring procedures effectively if the child's stage of development is taken into consideration. Figures 2 and 3 illustrate some self-monitoring forms used successfully with children. Forms developed for adults tend to be more appropriate for use with adolescents.

When using self-monitoring procedures, we have found that issues of compliance probably are most important. Completing these forms is something that most individuals do not expect to be part of their treatment. However, the data collected through this method can provide important adjunct data to that collected via other assessment methods. Unlike self-report instruments that collect the same information for every patient, self-monitoring forms can be modified to address the unique aspects of the patient's fears. Thus, they provide for a highly personalized assessment that may more clearly reflect the patient's clinical status both before and after treatment when compared with any standardized measure. Therefore, a careful explanation of the importance and necessity of these data will help ensure the patient's cooperation. We explain the necessity to patients and inform them that in order for therapy to continue in an orderly fashion, they need to complete the monitoring sheets as directed. To reinforce their importance, the forms are checked promptly at the beginning of each session. Of course, it is up to the therapist to make the forms easy to complete. In addition, we have found that asking for the forms at the beginning of every session and graphing the data for the patient's inspection at various points in therapy also increases compliance.

The situation is more difficult with children. Telling them that therapy may not continue if they do not complete the forms may be just what they want to hear and could actually encourage noncompliance. In addition, clinicians must be cautious about using parents to ensure children's compliance. One would not want to be in the position of

Daily Diary

Date _____ Morning _____ Afternoon _____ Evening _____

Where were you? School - Which Class _____ Home _____ Outside _____

Cafeteria _____ with Friends _____ Other - Where? _____

What Happened?

_____ A popular kid spoke to me
_____ The teacher called on me to answer a question
_____ I had to work with a popular kid in class
_____ I had to talk to someone on the telephone
_____ I had to perform in front of others (sing, dance, play a sport or instrument)
_____ I had to eat in a public place
_____ I had to use a public restroom
_____ Other- What? _____

What did you do?

_____ Pretended I didn't hear the person talking to me
_____ Hid my eyes so I was not called on
_____ Pretended I was sick, so I would not have to go
_____ Told myself not to be nervous, it would be okay
_____ Refused to do what was asked
_____ Did not go to the place (baseball game, school, recital) so I would not have to do it
_____ Waited to go to the bathroom until I got home
_____ Got a stomachache or headache
_____ Cried
_____ Did what I was supposed to do
_____ Other - What? _____

PUT AN X UNDER THE PICTURE THAT SHOWS HOW NERVOUS YOU WERE WHEN THIS HAPPENED

Today I did not feel nervous

Figure 3

Self-monitoring form used with children

setting up a power struggle between the child and parents regarding the completion of the monitoring forms. On the other hand, the offer of a small reward (by either the parent or the therapist) for the completion of the forms may be effective. These rewards may take the form of a later bed time, a special snack food, stickers from the therapist, and so forth. The receipt of a small token emphasizes the importance of the forms and acknowledges the child's effort in completing them.

Adults usually are asked to complete monitoring forms during the entire time that they are in treatment. It is unlikely that children will be able to accomplish such a task and to do so validly. Therefore, it is recommended that with children, self-monitoring be completed on an intermittent basis, perhaps 1 week of every month.

BEHAVIORAL ASSESSMENT TESTS

Behavioral Assessment Tests (BATs) represent a useful strategy to determine the extent of an individual's fear. BATs have a long history in the assessment of other anxiety disorders, but more recently have been used in the assessment of social phobia. As we noted in chapter 2, children who verbally denied any difficulties making friends were unable to demonstrate friendship-making skills in a behavioral test. In addition, BATs can differentiate treatment responders from nonresponders even when other outcome measures do not. For example, in a study of atenolol and flooding treatment for adults with social phobia, there were no differences between the two active interventions when assessed by self-report or clinician ratings (Turner, Beidel, & Jacob, 1994). However, when asked to give an impromptu speech, those treated with flooding were significantly more likely to complete the impromptu speech than were those treated with atenolol. Without this assessment, inaccurate conclusions regarding the efficacy of these interventions may have been drawn. Similarly, as noted earlier in this chapter, BATs can be very useful in helping to define the nature of social fears and determining if, in fact, the patient has significant social fears. For social phobia, behavioral assessments may consist of several types. Some have addressed the presence of social skills by using role-play tests and asking the patient to engage in a simulated social interaction with a confederate. Others have focused more on the ability to perform certain activities in front of others, such as giving a speech.

Initially, BATs for social anxiety were primarily role-play tests of social skills. In this paradigm, the patient is asked to imagine a social encounter with another individual. A trained confederate plays the role of the interpersonal partner. The patient's behavior is either audiotaped or videotaped and is scored for various indicators of skill or anxiety (e.g., eye contact, appropriate verbal content). The results of social skill assessments for social phobia are mixed. Early studies suggested that those with *DSM-III* social phobia had significantly better social skills than those with *DSM-III* avoidant personality disorder (Turner, Beidel, Dancu, & Keys, 1986). However, changes in the diagnostic criteria since that time have clouded these results. To date, no study has definitively established the existence of social skill deficits in adults with social phobia when compared with controls with no disorders, or skill differences between the specific and generalized subtypes, although there are some data that suggest that some differences might exist (Turner, Beidel, Cooley, Woody, & Messer, 1994). However, recent results from the assessment of social skills in children with social phobia did reveal significant differences when compared with a peer group with no disorders (Beidel, Turner, & Morris, 1996). One problem may be that the variables currently used to assess social skills are based on deficits noted in conditions other than social phobia. It may be that a set of measures developed specifically to address the behaviors of patients with social phobia would identify deficits heretofore undetected.

More recently, BATs have focused on the patient's behavior in a performance situation, primarily an impromptu speech task. Although all patients present with a unique fear pattern, virtually all patients endorse at least moderate anxiety during a speech. Thus, the impromptu speech is an "all-purpose" task that can be used for all patients with this disorder (Beidel, Turner, Jacob, & Cooley, 1989). In one paradigm, patients are asked to give a speech in front of a small live audience. They are given several topics and are asked to speak for 10 minutes. However, they may end the task prematurely (i.e., escape) if they become too distressed. The length of time that the patient is able to speak is the primary dependent variable (Beidel, Turner, Jacob, et al., 1989). Other variations include using a camera instead of a live audience, varying the length of time the patient is required to speak, and rating social skill during the speech. Some researchers have used individualized assessment tasks rather than one standard task (Heimberg, Hope, Dodge, & Becker, 1990). Each approach has advantages and disadvantages, and there are no data to suggest the superiority of one approach over another.

As with any assessment tool there are procedures and issues to consider when using a BAT. The behavioral assessments described in this section require the use of analogue situations and confederates to play the role of the interpersonal partner. However, information obtained from BATs can be very important in determining diagnosis and treatment outcome, making the effort worthwhile. For example, in the Turner, Beidel, and Jacob (1994) treatment study for social phobia (see chapters 7 and 8 in this volume), there were no differences in outcome across groups of patients treated with either behavior therapy, atenolol (a beta-blocking drug), or pill placebo when ratings of improvement by an independent evaluator were examined. In contrast, there were clear differences (favoring behavior therapy) when patients were asked to give an impromptu speech; those treated with behavior therapy could speak for a significantly longer period of time with less subjective distress than those patients treated with either atenolol or pill placebo. Restricting outcome measures solely to clinician ratings would have resulted in a biased judgment of treatment outcome. Thus, BATs can provide substantial information about the actual behavior of a patient when in a social setting, although they are not easily adapted for use by most clinicians. However, even if the assessment cannot be standardized as it is in most outcome studies, asking the patient to briefly interact with the therapist in a role-play situation, or asking the patient to make a short impromptu speech that is videotaped (even without an audience), can provide the therapist with important clinical information about a patient's skill and comfort in these types of settings. The tests also can be adapted to many different types of situations to allow therapists to test various hypotheses. Thus, the importance of this form of assessment cannot be discounted. Familiarity with BATs will allow the clinician to better evaluate the treatment literature and make a decision regarding the effectiveness of intervention options, and will provide a valuable tool in treatment planning and outcome determination for any individual patient.

PSYCHOPHYSIOLOGICAL ASSESSMENT

The study of the somatic component of social phobia has indicated that those with social phobia have many of the same physiological responses as do those with other anxiety disorders. However, those with social phobia particularly have a set of symptoms that appear to be mediated by the beta-adrenergic system. Activation of this system results in heart palpitations, trembling, shaking, sweating, and blushing. During BATs, physiological measures often are included as part of the assessment protocol. The autonomic nervous system, particularly heart rate and blood pressure, has been the most commonly studied (Heimberg, Dodge, et al., 1990; Turner, Beidel, & Larkin, 1986). Other variables that have been assessed include electrodermal activity (Lader, 1967) and respiration rate (Rapee et al., 1992). All of these variables have shown differences between individuals with social phobia and normal controls, and in one case, between the specific and generalized subtypes of social phobia (Heimberg, Dodge, et al., 1990). To summarize the outcome of these studies, those with social phobia show increased physiological response when in anxiety-producing situations. Increased physiological response is important not only for its theoretical relevance but also because these responses can serve as an important indicator of arousal during imaginal and in vivo exposure sessions. Most clinicians will not have the luxury of conducting psychophysiological assessments of patients with social phobia, thus we will not elaborate further on this method of assessment here.

CONCLUSION

In discussing the assessment of social phobia, we have emphasized the necessity of conducting a thorough clinical evaluation of individuals presenting with a complaint of social anxiety. Table 6 provides our recommendation for conducting an assessment of social phobia. The general clinical interview is important for determining the patient's

Table 6	
Recommended Assessment Strategy for the Assessment of Social Phobia	
Session	Assessment Strategy
Initial session:	Conduct clinical interview
	Provide self-monitoring forms and instruction
Second session:	Administer structured clinical interview
	Complete clinician rating scales
	Administer self-report instruments
	Check on validity of self-monitoring and instruct patient to continue for another week
Third session:	Review self-monitoring data
	Discuss results of evaluation with patient and present treatment plan
	Begin intervention

overall clinical status as well as determining that the presenting complaint satisfies the criteria for social phobia. We noted, in particular, the need to differentiate social phobia from other similar conditions that were elaborated on in chapters 1 and 2. To assist in the diagnostic process, the clinical interview, the use of self-report clinical rating scales, and semistructured interviews were highlighted. The core of any assessment in the clinical setting is an open interview, for it is here where patients get the opportunity to describe the condition in their own words. Similarly, the therapist has the latitude to search and discover areas of importance that could be critical to the diagnosis and subsequent treatment.

To supplement the general clinical interview, we recommended the use of semistructured interview schedules and discussed the advantages and disadvantages of a number of instruments available for this purpose. These interview schedules ensure that a wide range of questions are posed so that relevant information needed for a wide range of diagnoses are revealed. The use of these instruments reduces the likelihood that an improper diagnosis will be made or that co-occurring conditions will be missed. In addition, self-report inventories and clinical rating scales can be used to assess the magnitude of the disturbance and, in the case of the SPAI, can be used to help ascertain the pervasiveness of the disorder.

An important assessment component in social phobia is the use of self-monitoring strategies. We pointed out the ways in which this strategy can aid in the diagnostic process and assist in elucidating the parameters associated with social anxiety. We also discussed how self-monitoring strategies might be used to help gauge treatment progress and outcome.

The use of overt analogue behavioral assessment strategies also was discussed. Behavioral tasks can be constructed to meet virtually any purpose, but in the case of social phobia, they primarily have been used to assess anxiety during performance situations and to measure social skills. For example, behavioral tasks have proved useful in helping to determine whether patient fears are limited to performance situations or whether the difficulty extends to casual social interactions as well. In treatment outcome studies, this type of task frequently provides a stringent test of the overall efficacy of a given treatment and serves as an overt indicator of what the patient can or cannot do.

Finally, assessment of psychophysiological response can prove helpful in clinical decision making, particularly within the context of BATs. Highly reactive autonomic responses reassure the clinician that proper fear cues were selected. Conversely, decreased autonomic responsiveness when confronted with these cues helps to confirm that treatment progress has been made. Fancy equipment is not necessary to conduct this type of assessment. Simple heart rate or pulse readings can be used. Together these strategies represent a comprehensive approach to the assessment of social phobia by assisting in the establishment of the diagnosis, delineating associated conditions, elucidating the relevant parameters associated with the disorder, and providing evidence of treatment progress and outcome.

6

Patient (and Parent) Management

Dr. Turner: Mr. Brown called to cancel his appointment for today.
He said he is uncertain of whether he will be able to do the
homework assignments as discussed in his last session.

A telephone message from a patient.

Dr. Beidel: Mrs. Smith called. She won't be bringing Bobby (her
8-year-old son) in for his session. She says he doesn't want to come,
and she cannot make him get into the car.

Another telephone message regarding a patient's appointment.

The problems described in the two examples above do not concern the technical aspects of treatment implementation. Rather, they can best be described as patient management issues because they are related to difficulties experienced by the patient or the patient's parent that have the potential to derail the treatment process. The manner in which such problems are managed can determine whether a patient remains in treatment and whether the outcome will be positive. Patient management is as important as any other factor in the overall care of those with social phobia, and the therapist should do as much as possible to prevent problems from occurring and to address the problems directly when they do occur. In this chapter, we elaborate on patient management issues that we alluded to above, pointing out particular difficulties associated with the management of children.

EDUCATION

Adult Educational Sessions

One important factor that can significantly affect the likelihood of a management problem arising during the course of treatment is whether time is taken to educate the patient. By education we mean a formal program in which the patient (including the patient's family when appropriate) is informed about the nature of the condition (including any co-occurring disorders) and what is known about the disorder. Thus, we always spend a session educating the patient about the phenomenology, epidemiology, clinical correlates, and course of the disorder. This is a detailed discussion, and time is taken to answer questions from the patient and family members. In addition to informing the patient about the nature of the disorder, available treatment options are explored in detail, including the advantages and disadvantages of each. A synthesis of the treatment outcome literature is provided because we feel that if the patients understand that they will be receiving a treatment known to produce positive results, their willingness to engage in behaviors typically avoided increases. Finally, the nature and requirements for the treatment are spelled out clearly, and patients are informed about their responsibilities in the treatment process (e.g., maintaining self-monitoring data, attending regular sessions, completing homework assignments as directed). The patient agrees to a treatment plan in which the therapist explains what treatment involves and what will be required of the patient (see Table 7 for an example of a successful education session).

Parent and Child Educational Session

Educational sessions also are conducted for children with social phobia and their parents (see Table 8). The presentation is geared toward the

Table 7

Patient Educational Session Content

1. The educational session begins with a presentation of what is known about the disorder (in this case, social phobia). Included in this discussion is the disorder's etiology, clinical syndrome, and demographics. The material presented to the patient is similar to that found throughout these chapters but without some of the more advanced statistical concepts. We also discuss potential developmental pathways and variations in the clinical presentation.

2. After presenting information about the clinical aspects of the disorder, the most current available data on treatment outcome are presented. Pharmacological and psychological interventions are discussed. This is an empirically based presentation, and the advantages and disadvantages of each intervention are discussed. The presentation is continuously updated so that the information remains current.

3. An overview of the treatment package used in our clinic, including outcome data, is presented. This includes the rationale for why we developed (or why a clinician selected) the treatment program, the purpose of each individual treatment component, and the effectiveness of the intervention. We try to set positive but realistic expectations for treatment outcome. We emphasize that we cannot guarantee treatment effectiveness for any particular patient. In the case of behavioral treatments, it would be important to emphasize the active nature of the intervention and the patient's need to be an active partner in the treatment process. Similarly, pharmacological interventions require a commitment on the part of the patient to take the medication as prescribed by the physician.

4. The details of the treatment program, including specific procedures and time commitment, are presented. We present the individual treatment components and the methods used for each component. In addition, a substantial amount of time is spent discussing the time commitment involved in treatment: the length of the sessions, the number of sessions per week, the average treatment duration, and the necessity of completing homework assignments. In the case of pharmacological treatments, a description of the dosage schedule, potential

Table continues

123

Table 7 (*Continued*)

side effects, drug interaction effects, and of course the expected positive effects (and when they can be expected to occur) are discussed.

5. Finally, it is important to assess the motivation of the patient (and significant others) for participating in the presented intervention. Patients who express uncertainty about their ability to commit to the treatment or who try to bargain for a reduced number of sessions or for a more limited intervention should be encouraged to take some time to consider whether they want to participate in the intervention. In each case, the clinician must decide what is reasonable while maintaining the integrity of the treatment. If the patient cannot commit to what is viewed as minimally acceptable, referral should be considered.

child's understanding but covers all of the areas included in the adult presentation above. The presentation is organized in terms of questions that parents and children might ask.

Such an educational process does not prevent difficulties from arising in treatment, but it significantly reduces the occurrence of such problems as well as decreases the likelihood that there will be discongruent treatment expectancies on the part of therapist and patient. Suc-

Table 8

Educational Outline for Children and Parents

1. How many children have social phobia?
2. What kinds of situations make boys and girls feel shy?
3. What happens to my body when I feel shy?
4. What do I think about when I feel shy?
5. What do I do when I feel shy?
6. Why do I feel shy and how did I get this way?
7. Can I get better?
8. How do I get better?

cessful treatment of social phobia involves more than mere application of a specific intervention strategy. It includes managing all aspects of the patient's clinical state. Furthermore, management of childrens' clinical status must be expanded to include potential management of parents' clinical status. Finally, comprehensive treatment of the child may involve consideration of the parent's child management skills.

PATIENT MANAGEMENT

In some cases, managing the patient is just a matter of setting reasonable expectations regarding therapy and expected treatment outcome. Complicated clinical conditions, however, often require an active and ongoing clinical management program. Below, some of the problems encountered in treating patients with social phobia are discussed.

Setting Appropriate Treatment Expectations

Treatment expectations will vary with respect to the type of intervention that will be provided. For example, patients receiving pharmacological intervention will have a different therapeutic regimen than those receiving psychological interventions, although in some cases both modes of treatment might be used concurrently. In the case of children, parents may not initially understand that they may be called upon to play an active role in treatment.

Sometimes, patients enter treatment at a time of crisis. For example, they have an impending major presentation, meeting, or social event in the next week, or a child has begun to refuse going to school. Some adults feel that their heterosocial relationships may be in imminent danger because of their reluctance to accompany a partner to social events. Children often are brought to the clinic because the school is threatening immediate expulsion or there is a truancy hearing due to school refusal. Unless the patient is going to receive a short-acting beta-blocker or benzodiazepine (see chapter 7), therapeutic effects will not be immediate enough to provide quick relief. A decision will need to be made regarding how to best handle the immediate crisis, which may entail temporary interventions prior to implementation of the full behavioral treatment program.

Some patients attribute their social fears to a lack of self-esteem. That is, they believe that if they just had more confidence in themselves (had higher self-esteem), then they would not feel so distressed and anxious in social encounters. Certainly, some patients with social phobia have low self-esteem, and some interventions specifically focus on improving this aspect of personality. However, other approaches to treatment (such as those based on behavioral and cognitive–behavioral theory) address this problem more indirectly and assume that patients gain confidence and self-esteem through the behaviors in which they engage. Successful and rewarding experiences in social interactions change the way one thinks about oneself and one's abilities (e.g., Turner, Beidel, & Jacob, 1994). Therefore, behavioral interventions focus on changing behavior, and improvement in self-esteem naturally results when the change from maladaptive social behavior to more functional social behavior occurs. We explain to patients that the way they feel about themselves probably is a function of their life experiences, which in this case have not been very positive. The way that they feel about themselves results from what they have learned through previous experiences (or lack of such). Therefore, the task is to focus on improving skills and helping them develop the abilities and confidence to interact with others in a manner that will be productive and positive. Once they begin to be successful in their interactions, patient concerns that their poor self-esteem is not being addressed tend to subside.

Most of the cognitive–behavioral or behavioral treatments and many of the pharmacological treatments for social phobia include some form of exposure to the feared setting or situation. In the case of behavioral or cognitive–behavioral treatment, exposure assignments may be quite structured. In the case of pharmacological treatment, exposure instructions may be less specific, encouraging the patient to "try out" new behaviors to see whether the medicine is effective. Therapists may have to deal with patient reluctance to put themselves in the anxiety-producing settings and the resulting noncompliance with exposure instructions. Below we discuss several ways to address this issue.

To begin, the therapist needs to be certain that the patient understands the rationale for the homework assignments. Asking the patient to reiterate his or her understanding of the rationale may reveal misunderstandings that may affect compliance. It also may reveal the patient's motivation to participate in treatment. The therapist also needs to be assured that the assignment is not too difficult for the patient. Devising initial assignments so that they are successful will build patient confidence. For example, an individual who has trouble interacting with others even on an informal basis may be given a first assignment to enter a crowded store (such as at a mall) but not be required to speak to anyone. When the patient becomes comfortable completing this assignment, more advanced assignments can be given.

For patients with a severe form of the disorder, the clinician may need to accompany the patient on the first few exposure assignments. We have found that patients' anticipatory anxiety often is more severe than the distress they experience once they are engaged in the task. Patients often remark to us afterward that worrying about doing the assignment was more distressful than actually completing it. Therefore, accompanying patients on the first assignment and allowing them to see that their distress is not as severe as they imagined may increase compliance with future tasks. If it is impossible to accompany a patient, a significant other may be engaged for this assignment.

Although in vivo exposure exercises can be planned, the behaviors of other individuals in most social interactions cannot be scripted. Interactions with the general public often will not go as planned (or sometimes not even as desired). Clinicians must be aware of and plan for these contingencies when conducting in vivo exposure sessions (i.e., have an alternate plan ready for use). In planning the exposure session, careful consideration needs to be given to the likelihood that the assignment can be completed successfully. Also, there is a need to deliberately arrange opportunities for engagement in various types of social encounters, thus allowing patients to interact with a broad range of individuals, groups, and situations. This is because one significant feature of social phobia is that those with the disorder often fear uncertainty. Even after they have had success with one person or one situation, new persons or situations still generate apprehension. Part of the treatment goals for those with social phobia is to ensure that they learn to accept some uncertainty regarding the actions of others when they engage in social encounters. This necessitates experiences with multiple persons and situations.

Other Associated Clinical and Personality Issues

Additional Axis II Disorders

Social phobia involves fear of doing something that is humiliating or embarrassing. It is our clinical impression, supported by a small amount of empirical data, that those with social phobia often have a tendency to see the world in a rigid and perfectionistic fashion; either they do things perfectly or they have failed miserably. Such behavior also is characteristic of those with obsessive–compulsive personality disorder (OCPD), which is characterized by a pervasive pattern of orderliness, perfectionism, and mental and interpersonal control at the expense of flexibility, openness, and efficiency (American Psychiatric Association, 1994, p. 672). As we noted in chapter 2, 13.2% of those with social phobia in one sample also met criteria for OCPD, and another 48.5% had traits characteristic of the disorder. This latter group is considered to have a subclinical form of the disorder (Turner, Beidel, Bordon, Stanley, & Jacob, 1991). Among children, those with social phobia score higher on temperamental scales assessing rigidity and inflexibility, behavioral characteristics that are similar to those found in adults with OCPD. Because these behaviors exist in individuals who already have a disorder, it is unclear what role they might play in etiology. It is clear, however, that this behavior can have an impact on the process of treatment.

Our clinical experience indicates that the presence of OCPD can impact patient management considerably. First, clinicians will need to be particularly attuned to issues of control. Second, as noted above, those with this syndrome might present more difficulties with imaginal exposure due to the perfectionistic manner in which they approach the material, often attending to minute details rather than the overall scenes. For example, one of our patients told us he was having difficulty imagining a scene because he could not decide whether the woman he was imagining should be wearing earrings. Verbalization of the scene is one method used to get around these perfectionistic tendencies. Third, those with OCPD have greater difficulty interpersonally, and it is particularly difficult to get them to engage in novel social interactions. Finally, even when frank OCPD is not present, if subclinical features exist, they may impact the therapeutic process. Therefore, careful clinical assessment is required to prepare an adequate treatment plan and to structure sessions appropriately.

Among adults with social phobia, about 22% also meet criteria for avoidant personality disorder (APD; Turner, Beidel, Borden, et al., 1991). In our sample discussed earlier, another 53% had behavioral traits characteristic of this disorder, although they did not meet full diagnostic criteria (Turner, Beidel, Borden, et al., 1991). Even those with subclinical features of APD are extremely sensitive to criticism, particularly when they are under a great deal of stress. Patients with the APD diagnosis or characteristics often exhibit a "paranoid-like" quality to their thinking, again usually when they are under duress. Such distressful situations might include interventions (pharmacological or psychological) that require the patient to try out the medicine or their new found skills learned through social skills training. For example, for a homework assignment, one of our patients was asked to go to the bank and greet a bank teller who in the past had always been friendly toward the patient. However, on this occasion, the teller was polite, but cold and distant. The patient immediately interpreted the teller's behavior as persecutory toward him and berated us for forcing him to "embarrass himself in public." Obviously, there were many other reasons why the teller might have behaved as she did on that particular occasion. In such cases, a cognitive strategy, such as generating alternative explanations, might be helpful, although currently no empirical data on such a strategy are available.

Clinicians must be prepared to deal with the unusual interpretations of a patient with comorbid APD, particularly if treatment involves exposing the patient to fearful situations. There are several actions that the clinician can consider to address this situation. First, careful explanations of the role of exposure in the treatment of social phobia (as is done in our education session) may help the patient understand its purpose. Most adult patients intuitively understand that in order to reduce their anxiety, they ultimately must "face their fears." Children, particularly younger children, are less likely to understand this necessity, and age might dictate how much effort is expended toward helping the patient understand the rationale. Similarly, the intensity of the patient's fear and clinical sensitivity in general might be such that a high intensity strategy should be avoided. This is a decision that must be made by the clinician. Second, a clear statement to the patient (and if necessary, the parents) that the purpose of exposure to socially feared situations is not to humiliate but to assist in overcoming fears may be effective in setting appropriate expectations. Third, if these explanations are ineffective and paranoid-like interpretations regarding social interactions or the therapist's motives continue, changing strategies to use a low intensity (rather than a high intensity) exposure paradigm (see chapter 8) may avoid this type of problem. Finally, we noted in the Turner, Beidel, Cooley, et al. (1994) study of social effectiveness therapy (SET) treatment that individual sessions particularly are useful to help establish a trusting relationship. Each patient will need to be evaluated to determine the most appropriate method of exposure.

One particularly critical disorder to discriminate is paranoid personality disorder. Although this condition has been detected in only a small number of cases among reported samples (e.g., Turner, Beidel, Borden, et al. 1991), we have seen a number of such patients in our clinic who seek treatment because of difficulty in social interactions. Although typically recognizable, in a small minority of cases the condition can be difficult to detect. In our experience, paranoid patients do not respond very well to behavioral treatments used for social phobia, and in fact, exposure treatment often results in increased anxiety and exacerbation of paranoid thinking. In other words, the patient's condition worsens. These patients typically view the exposure sessions involved in treatment as humiliating. Careful diagnostic practice is necessary to detect the presence of these features. One clue for the clinician that might serve as a trigger to suspect an atypical case is late onset (i.e., after young adulthood) of social distress. Social phobia is an early onset disorder, and it is among those who claim to have onset later in life that we have found some patients with paranoid personality disorder (threshold or subthreshold) as well as some who have significant paranoid features.

Additional Axis I Diagnoses

In addition to the presence of Axis II disorders, comorbid Axis I conditions also require attention and clinical management. Although few data are available on treatment outcome for patients with comorbid conditions, those that do exist indicate that patients with comorbid disorders improve as a result of treatment designed for social phobia (Brown, Heimberg, & Juster, 1995; Hofmann, Newman, Becker, Taylor, & Roth, 1995; Mersch, Jansen, & Arntz, 1995; Turner, Beidel, Cooley, Woody, et al., 1994; Turner, Beidel, Wolff, Spaulding, & Jacob, 1996; see chapter 8 in this volume for a review). One study (Turner, Beidel, Wolff, et al., 1996) reported that although both groups made equivalent improvements over the course of treatment, there was a trend for patients without a comorbid diagnosis to have a higher end-state functioning status at posttreatment than those with comorbid disorders. This means that their status was more similar to the status of those with no disorder than to that of those who had a comorbid condition. Additionally, at posttreatment, those with comorbid disorders had higher scores on several measures of general anxiety and ratings of clinical severity. Mersch et al. (1995) reported a similar outcome. When taken together, these findings indicate that the clinical status of those patients with a comorbid condition was worse than the clinical status of those who did not have a comorbid condition, despite equivalent improvement over the course of treatment. Most recently, and consistent with prior studies, Chambless, Tran, and Glass (1997) assessed depression, personality disorders, and treatment outcome expectancy as predictors of improvement for cognitive–behavior therapy. No predictor was related to outcome across all domains of functioning, but a higher level of pretreatment depression was associated with less reduction in anxious apprehension, social interaction anxiety, and skill. In summary, these data indicate that those with comorbid Axis I conditions may be successfully treated, although the extent of improvement may be less than that expected to occur in patients without comorbid conditions.

In a minority of cases, such as when panic disorder is intimately intertwined with social phobia, treatment for social phobia may result in considerable improvement of panic symptoms. Yet, here too, additional treatment directed at panic disorder likely will be needed to achieve an optimal outcome. Individual patient needs must be determined on a case by case basis. Data on treatment effects for socially phobic children with comorbid conditions do not exist, although data from adult studies and our clinical experience suggest that the outcome probably would be similar.

These results indicate that the presence of Axis I comorbid conditions need not preclude treatment for social phobia in the usual manner. However, the social phobia treatment likely will not significantly affect an existing comorbid condition, such as GAD or panic disorder. Although there are few data at this time, our experience is that these conditions will require an additional specific intervention.

For those who have comorbid severe depression, and for whom suicidal behavior is an issue, immediate treatment with antidepressants or other treatments specifically directed toward depressive symptomatology might well be necessary. Even in those cases where depression is severe but the patient is not necessarily suicidal, symptoms such as sleeplessness, lethargy, and loss of interest in activities may prevent the individual from being able to engage fully in exposure and social skill training activities, thereby limiting their effectiveness. In these cases, patients will need to be treated for their depression prior to beginning behavioral treatment for social phobia.

Patient Education Session

As noted above, it is our position that one of the most important aspects of clinical management for all patients is their familiarity with their disorder and its prognosis. If a patient understands what to expect from the disorder and the intervention, it is more likely that they (and in the case of children and adolescents, their parents) can actively and fully participate in the treatment process. Patient and parent expectations can sometimes be unrealistic. Some expect that psychological treatment follows the medical tradition; that is, a patient sees the doctor once, receives a prescription, and usually does not return for some time for an additional visit. Patients need to understand that psychological treatments, even short-term treatments, do not operate according to a traditional medical model. Also, lay perceptions of psychological treatments still largely are shaped by the media, which depict psychological treatment as a verbal enterprise where the goal is to uncover hidden motives "deep" in the patient's psyche that are responsible for the patient's difficulties. Although verbal therapies may well help develop insight into one's functioning, current empirically supported therapies do not rely on insight as the primary mechanism of therapeutic change. Similarly, most pharmacological treatments require a series of visits during which medication is titrated to a therapeutic dose and side-effects are monitored. Thus, the educational process should address this issue specifically to fully ensure that the patient understands the treatment process.

PARENT MANAGEMENT

As noted throughout this volume, clinicians face a special challenge when treating children with social phobia. Not only must they forge a therapeutic relationship with the patient, but also with the patient's parents or primary caregiver. Throughout this chapter, the term *parent* will be used to refer to either the child's parent or primary caregiver. When considering issues of general clinical management, there are two primary aspects of parental behavior that merit consideration: (a) parental psychopathology and (b) child management skills. Each is discussed below.

Parental Psychopathology

As was discussed in chapter 4, studies indicate that rates of anxiety disorders are higher in families of an individual with an identified anxiety disorder. Because the presence of anxiety disorders in parents may play a role in the etiology or maintenance of anxiety disorders in children (see chapter 4), a closer understanding of psychopathology in the parents of anxious children is necessary. In a study of school-refusing children, Last and Strauss (1990) reported that 42% of these children had mothers who also had episodes of school refusal, suggesting that they themselves might have suffered (or suffer) from an anxiety disorder. When examined by the specific diagnosis of the child, 75% of children with separation anxiety disorder had mothers with a history of school refusal. Of children with a phobic disorder, 18% had mothers with a history of school refusal. Last, Hersen, Kazdin, Finkelstein, and Strauss (1991) reported that among children with an anxiety disorder (any type), 40% of parents had a lifetime history of an anxiety disorder. The term *lifetime* indicates that the parent did not necessarily have an anxiety disorder at the time of the interview (i.e., when the child had a disorder), and it is unclear how many of these parental disorders actually were current disorders.

Last et al. (1991) also examined the lifetime prevalence of anxiety disorders separately for separation anxiety disorder, overanxious disorder, and other types of anxiety disorders (e.g., phobias, panic disorder). Across these three groups, rates of anxiety disorders among first degree relatives were highest in children with overanxious disorder (50%), followed by children with separation anxiety disorder (31.5%), then children with other anxiety disorders (27%). The most commonly occurring anxiety disorder in the first degree relatives was overanxious disorder, followed by separation anxiety disorder, then panic disorder and generalized anxiety disorder. Because these studies used *DSM-III* criteria, it is possible that some diagnoses of overanxious disorder actually might have been cases of social phobia. In any case, the data indicate that many parents of children with anxiety disorders also have a proclivity toward anxiety. Although it may not currently be manifested as a disorder, it is likely that these parents have an anxious predisposition.

Why is knowledge of the presence of anxiety disorders in the parent important when treating a child with social phobia? There are several reasons. First, parents with the disorder may be reluctant to have their child enter treatment. For example, one of our child patients with social phobia had a father who suffered from panic disorder. He had never been in formal therapy but managed his disorder with a mixture of tranquilizers and alcohol. His response to the results of his daughter's evaluation was that his daughter did not need behavior therapy but could just take a tranquilizer when necessary. Further education of the parent (particularly an examination of the outcome data for childhood social phobia) convinced him to allow his daughter to undergo a trial of behavior therapy.

In other instances, even if the anxious parent agrees that treatment is needed, the parent's own fears may limit his or her ability to assist in conducting necessary exposure sessions. For example, socially phobic parents may be unable to arrange for their children to play or interact with other children (i.e., expose the child to a social encounter) if they themselves are so anxious that they are reluctant to speak to other parents and suggest an activity. Parents with severe agoraphobia may not be able to drive their children to another child's house in order for the children to play together. Also parents who refused school themselves might be more sympathetic to their child's distress to the degree that they are reluctant to reintroduce the child to school. In such cases, the parents' own fears may have to be managed before effective treatment can be implemented.

Other Parental Behaviors That May Affect Treatment Outcome

In addition to anxiety, other factors that merit consideration when treating anxious children are the expectations and attitudes of parents with respect to treatment outcome. Kendall's (1994) study of cognitive–behavior therapy for anxious (but not necessarily socially phobic) children indicated that parents' participation in therapy was variable across the child participants. However, degree of parental involvement (based on therapist ratings) was modestly related to treatment outcome. Thus, parental participation in treatment may enhance outcome, and although not consistent for every child, our experience is that when behavior problems are an issue, it is a critical one. Additionally, parent behaviors outside the therapeutic setting also may affect outcome. As we noted in chapter 4 in this volume, Barrett and Dadds and their colleagues (Barrett, Dadds, Rapee, & Ryan, 1996; Dadds, Barrett, Rapee, & Ryan, 1996) analyzed the verbal communications between anxious children and their parents and found that family processes more often serve to enhance, rather than eliminate, avoidant responses in anxious children. Furthermore, Dadds et al. (1996) identified this family interaction pattern as playing a major role in the development and treatment of such disorders. Thus, the family's mode of interacting may serve to reinforce maladaptive behavioral patterns, and the family interactional style may need to be altered in order for treatment to be successful.

Silverman (e.g., Silverman & Kurtines, 1996) described problematic parental behavior similar to Barrett and Dadd's findings. She termed these behaviors *The Protection Trap*, the tendency of parents to protect their children, even during therapy, from exposure to objects or situations that create anxiety or distress. In such cases, the parents misdirected efforts at protecting their child from discomfort serve to foster the maintenance of the maladaptive behaviors. When present to a significant degree, this problem will need to be controlled before progress with the child can be expected. The Protection Trap is not unique to psychological interventions. Most psychopharmacologists usually provide some form of exposure instructions to the feared situation as part of the treatment program. Even though exposure can be accomplished in several different ways (see chapter 8 and 9) and need not be delivered in a high intensity fashion, parents may be reluctant to "get the child upset" or allow the therapist to put the child in a situation that may cause emotional distress. Additionally, patients and parents sometimes have unreasonable expectations about what therapy (particularly behavior therapy and drug therapy) will entail. They sometimes envision unusual (and sometimes cruel) exposure situations coupled with uncontrollable distress reactions or terrible side-effects from medication. Therapists must be certain to dispel these notions.

A final consideration when treating children is that although some parents may allow their child to participate in exposure sessions conducted by the therapist, they may be unwilling to assist the child with homework sessions because (a) they do not want the child to become distressed or (b) they do not have the time to conduct the session. Homework is an integral part of the exposure and social skills intervention, thus both of these negative parental behaviors can negatively affect treatment outcome.

Clinicians must address these disruptive parental behaviors. Because exposure to the feared situations is the core of all the empirically supported psychosocial treatments for social phobia, and also frequently is used with drug therapy, therapists must be assured that parents understand the importance of exposure for the child's successful treatment. For example, parents might observe an exposure session conducted by the therapist to view first-hand the child's "distress." Our experience is that when parents understand what happens during an exposure session, they are more likely to allow their child's participation and to assist their child in conducting the homework assignments.

Child Management Skills

As noted, parents may (either purposefully or accidentally) encourage avoidant behaviors in their anxious children. Some parents, however, are lacking in even more basic parenting behaviors, such as basic reinforcement skills. Parents will not be able to learn to reward courageous behavior and discourage avoidance until they can understand and implement differential reinforcement. When such skills are found to be lacking, child management training (e.g., Hembree-Kigin & McNeil, 1995) should be an integral part of the treatment program. Our experience is that child management training works best when conducted prior to treatment for social phobia.

ASSESSMENT OF PARENTAL INFLUENCE ON TREATMENT OUTCOME

We recommend a four-step assessment plan to determine the potential influence of parental behavior on treatment outcome for children with social phobia (see Table 9). This plan includes the assessment of parental pathology as well as parenting skills. However, because the child is the

Table 9
Assessment of Parental Influences

1. Assessment of the potential presence of parental psychopathology.
2. Assessment of parental child management skills.
3. Assessment of parental understanding of the child's disorder and the parameters of the proposed intervention.
4. Assessment of the parent's motivation for the child's participation in the treatment program.

identified patient, clinicians are cautioned that conducting full diagnostic interviews with the parent at the initial assessment would be inappropriate. We think it would be appropriate, however, to question parents about others in the family, including the parents, who may suffer from anxiety disorders now or who may have suffered from them in the past. This line of questioning could yield information regarding familial factors that may be important in understanding and treating the child's disorder.

RECOMMENDATIONS FOR GENERAL CLINICAL MANAGEMENT OF PARENTS

In Table 10, we offer suggestions for the clinical management of parents when children and adolescents are involved in treatment for social phobia. One of the clinician's first decisions is whether the parent's anxiety is severe enough to impact the child's treatment. In such cases, it might be necessary to refer the parent for treatment. In severe cases, child treatment might even need to be deferred until the parent's disorder has been controlled.

In addition, the clinician will need to consider whether part of the child's difficulty is due to poor parenting skills and if formal intervention is needed. In many instances a simple discussion coupled with one of the many available parent training manuals may be all that is required. In other cases, a more formal and prolonged training program is necessary. It is critical that parents understand reinforcement prin-

---

Table 10

Clinical Management for Parents of Anxious Children

---

1. Advise impaired parent to seek treatment.
2. If assessment reveals poor child management skills, provide for improved skills with specific skill training. This may take the form of bibliotherapy or direct intervention.
3. Provide an explanation and allow for discussion of the *Protection Trap*.
4. Include the parents in the education session about the nature of the disorder (see outline for parent and child education session noted above).

---

ciples and are able to apply them correctly inasmuch as rewarding the child for completion of various tasks is an important treatment component. Therefore, clinicians need to be assured that parents understand the basic concepts and use them appropriately.

Furthermore, the behaviors of all parents must be examined to make certain that they are not reinforcing the child's avoidance strategies. In addition, the clinician should assess the willingness of parents to help the child, when necessary, complete homework assignments. This usually can be accomplished as part of the diagnostic interview. If the parent demonstrates protective behaviors that will interfere with treatment, this should be addressed during the initial phase of treatment. Parents should be advised that treatment is not likely to be effective until this issued is resolved.

CONCLUSION

This chapter was devoted to a discussion of the many issues that have the potential to mitigate against a successful treatment outcome with socially phobic children and adults. We have dubbed one set of potential problems as patient management issues. Grouped under this rubric are all of the nondiagnostic- and nonsyndrome-specific issues that can interfere with effective treatment. In addition, we delineated a number of examples of patient management problems with children and adults.

The most effective step that can be taken to prevent management problems is to educate the patient and the family about the nature of the disorder, treatment options, the specific treatment plan that will be implemented, and patient and therapist responsibilities. If patient management issues still arise, they must be addressed in a straightforward fashion, or treatment might be stalled or even derailed.

There are two sets of issues with respect to Axis I and II disorders and patient management. One potential problematic area that could affect the process of treatment as well as treatment outcome is the existence of Axis II disorders (i.e., personality disorders) concurrent with the social phobia. The most commonly occurring disorders of this type will be APD and OCPD. Although the available evidence is that the presence of these conditions does not preclude the use of current behavioral treatments for social phobia, there is evidence that when present, the overall improvement rate is lower when an Axis II condition is present (Feske, Perry, Chambless, Renneberg, & Goldstein, 1996). It is unclear at this juncture what strategy should be used to enhance outcome. Although a longer treatment period likely would help to some extent, specific interventions aimed at the personality dysfunction will probably be necessary to obtain overall optimal results. The situation essentially is the same when Axis I conditions are present. Current treatments are effective for social phobia, but other strategies likely will be necessary for the co-occurring condition.

In addition, the effects of comorbid Axis I and II conditions also can affect the manner in which patients must be managed. The available research indicates that comorbid Axis I and II conditions do affect the level of improvement in treatment outcome studies where time limited protocols are used. Although the treatments remain efficacious, the level of improvement for those who have concurrent conditions is not as great as for those who do not have a concurrent condition. For the former patients, other interventions in most cases will be necessary.

Finally, in the case of Axis II conditions, which in most cases will be OCPD and APD, the manner in which treatment is conducted can be affected. For example, imaginal exposure may be more difficult with patients who have OCPD. Also, because of their rigidity, it may be more difficult to gain these patients' cooperation for the range of exposure needed. For those with APD, a more gradual approach to exposure rather than an intensive one may be needed.

The potential patient management problems with children are even more problematic for a number of reasons. Children typically do not seek treatment voluntarily and may not wish to cooperate. It has been our experience that there are several ways to increase cooperation and interest in these children. First, establishing a contract with adolescents for a certain number of sessions, during which improvement can be evaluated and a decision made about whether to continue or not, is effective. Second, the provision of small reinforcers (stickers, fast food coupons) will increase compliance, particularly among younger children. Third, additional reinforcers, provided by the parents, also can increase compliance for any age youngster. For example, one of our parents would buy her child an ice cream cone immediately after the session as a reward for compliance and hard work during the session.

Parenting skill and parent–child interaction is another patient management issue when children are the patients. We do not wish to imply that the parent–child relationship or parenting skill always is a problem because we see many families where they are not. However, when they are, it must be recognized and handled in an appropriate manner. In some cases, parent training in child management might be required before treatment can be carried out effectively. Patient and parent management issues are an integral part of successful treatment for patients with social phobia. Ignoring or downplaying their importance could result in attenuated outcomes, discouraged patients, and frustrated clinicians.

7

Pharmacological Treatment of Social Phobia

I've noticed that my heart does not beat fast since I have been on the medication. Because my heart is not beating fast, I don't worry so much about the blushing. In general, I am less worried about the physical symptoms and whether or not others might perceive them. But I have not felt the urge to go out and make new friends.

Elaine (from chapter 1) after 4 weeks on atenolol.

Various classes of pharmacological agents have been used to treat social phobia, including tricyclic antidepressants (TCAs), selective serotonin reuptake inhibitors (SSRIs), monoamine oxidase inhibitors (MAOIs), beta-blockers, high-potency benzodiazepines, and the atypical anxiolytic agent azaspirone (see Delgado & Gelenberg, 1996; Liebowitz & Marshall, 1995; Schneier, 1995; and Sutherland & Davidson, 1995, for a discussion of these agents, their neurochemical action, and their clinical usage). In this chapter, we will review the empirical literature describing the use of these medications for social phobia. Also, we will discuss the practical implementation of pharmacological treatment for social phobia in children and adults. Because the use of social phobia as a diagnosis in children and adolescents is only recent, few pharmacological studies are available that address the disorder as currently defined. However, we will include related and relevant literatures examining the effects of these medications on avoidant disorder and selective mutism, two conditions that symptomatically overlap with social phobia. In addition to the empirical review, we will present information pertinent to clinicians working with adults and children who may be taking these medications, including typical medication dosages and common side-effects.

EMPIRICAL STUDIES OF PHARMACOLOGICAL INTERVENTIONS

Tricyclic Antidepressants

Tricylic antidepressants, or TCAs, are medications that have been used widely in the treatment of depressive and anxious states for the past three to four decades. These medications modulate neurotransmitter activity by their action at the neurosynapse, where they influence the metabolism or reuptake of the neurotransmitters acetylcholine, norepinephrine, and serotonin (Viesselman, Yaylayan, Weller, & Weller, 1993). The degree to which the different TCAs affect each of these neurotransmitters varies with the particular medication. This class of medications includes drugs such as imipramine (Tofranil), which was among the first medications used to treat panic disorder and agoraphobia (e.g., Klein, 1964).

Research examining the efficacy of TCAs in the treatment of social phobia in adults is quite limited, and in the case of children, there are no controlled studies in the literature. Perhaps one reason there are so few studies is that initial results were not very promising. Early studies assessing the efficacy of imipramine for complaints of social anxiety among depressed patients found this drug to be less effective than the monamine oxidase inhibitor (MAOI) phenelzine (Liebowitz et al., 1984). Although an open trial of imipramine in two adult socially phobic patients who had panic attacks and mitral valve prolapse suggested rapid improvement (Benca, Matuzas, & Al-Sadir, 1986), one of the few controlled trials specifically treating patients with social phobia reported no difference between those treated with imipramine or placebo (Zitrin, Klein, Woerner, & Ross, 1983). TCAs rarely were used in the treatment of social phobia in 1983, and that appears to be the case currently as well.

Selective Serotonin Reuptake Inhibitors

The selective serotonin reuptake inhibitors (SSRIs) are relatively new and represent a different class of antidepressants from the TCAs. Rather than simultaneously affecting the metabolism or reuptake of several different neurotransmitters, the mechanism of action for the SSRIs is to selectively (more or less, depending upon the specific compound) block the reuptake of serotonin at the neural synapse. One major advantage of the SSRIs over the TCAs or the MAOIs (to be discussed below) is their more benign side-effect profile. SSRIs do not require restrictive diets (as do currently available MAOIs) and are much less likely than the TCAs to produce side-effects such as weight gain, dry mouth, and sedation. Over the past several years, a number of SSRI compounds have been developed. Two SSRIs, fluoxetine (Prozac) and fluvoxamine (Luvox) have been reported to be efficacious in the treatment of social phobia. Controlled trials of sertraline (Zoloft) and paroxetine (Paxil) have been conducted, but results are not available as of this writing.

Fluoxetine has been the most often investigated SSRI to date, although currently there are no published controlled trials for social phobia. Furthermore, the number of patients in open trials has been quite small. For example, Black, Uhde, and Tancer (1992) administered fluoxetine to 14 patients with generalized social phobia. Using clinician rating scales, 71% were judged to be moderately or markedly improved. Similarly, Schneier, Chin, Hollander, and Liebowitz (1992) reported that 9 of 12 patients (67%) treated with fluoxetine were judged as much or very much improved on the clinician-rated Clinical Global Improvement Scale (CGI). Some patients in this study had been treated with other medications in the past, and in several cases patients felt that fluoxetine was as effective as phenelzine (an MAOI) but had fewer side-effects. However, because this was not a designed comparative trial, this finding remains speculative. In one other clinical trial, Van Amerigen, Mancini, and Streiner (1993) used fluoxetine to treat 16 patients with social phobia. Although the scale used to measure patient improvement was not one in general use by researchers in social phobia, the results indicated that 77% of the patients were judged to be treatment responders.

As noted in chapter 2 in this volume, children with selective mutism tend to have many social fears, and available data suggest this condition might represent a severe variant of social phobia. In the early 1990s, two case reports suggested that medication might be useful in the treatment of children with selective mutism (Black & Uhde, 1992; Golwyn & Weinstock, 1990). These initial positive results led to the initiation of a randomized, placebo-controlled trial of fluoxetine for the treatment of selective mutism (Black & Uhde, 1994). Fifteen selectively mute children received either placebo or fluoxetine for 12 weeks. Those treated with fluoxetine were rated by their parents as significantly better on two out of nine parental ratings of improvement (mutism change and global change). However, none of the clinician ratings or teacher ratings showed any difference between the two groups. Furthermore, the authors noted that most children remained very symptomatic at the end of treatment.

Birmaher et al. (1994) reviewed the case records of 21 patients with overanxious disorder, social phobia, or separation anxiety disorder who were judged unresponsive to previous psychological or pharmacological treatment. Children were treated in an open trial with fluoxetine for up to 10 months. Outcome was judged using the CGI scales of improvement and severity. Child psychiatrists rated treatment response retrospectively on the basis of chart notes. Prospective assessments were made (using the same scales) by the treating nurses and the child's parent. Of the children, 81% were judged as moderately to markedly improved, and anxiety symptoms decreased from marked to mild. Furthermore, fluoxetine was judged to be equally efficacious across all three disorders. The outcome reported from this open trial is promising. Yet, as is evident from other studies reported in this review, promising open trials often are followed by disappointing results in placebo-controlled trials. Thus, conclusions regarding the efficacy of this medication for children with social fears must await the results of controlled trials.

There has been one placebo-controlled trial of fluvoxamine in adult patients meeting criteria for social phobia (den Boer, van Vliet, & Westenberg, 1994). Across all measures used in the study, those treated with fluvoxamine for 12 weeks were significantly more improved compared with those who received placebo. After an additional 12 weeks of maintenance, there was further improvement on general anxiety and specific social phobia symptoms as rated by treating clinicians.

Although the efficacy of SSRIs in social phobia is not well established, they are in widespread use for adults with social phobia and to a lesser extent for children and adolescents with the disorder. A major advantage of these drugs is their relatively benign side-effect profile and the ease with which they can be withdrawn safely. One potential drawback with the SSRIs in comparison to some other drugs is that it typically takes several weeks before the drug reaches a therapeutic level, meaning that there is a considerable wait before improvement can be expected.

Monoamine Oxidase Inhibitors

There actually are two kinds of monoamine oxidase inhibitors (MAOIs), "nonreversible" (nonselective) and reversible (selective) types. The labels refer to whether or not the drug binds "irreversibly" to the monoamine oxidase enzyme and whether the compound is selective for both the A and B forms of the enzyme (Potts & Davidson, 1995). Because the effects of the selective form can be reversed much more rapidly, the dietary restrictions necessitated by the older, nonreversible type are not necessary. However, much of the research has been conducted with the nonreversible type phenelzine (Nardil) and to a lesser extent, tranylcypromine (Parnate). Although several studies have been conducted with the reversible types (see below), currently these compounds are not marketed in the United States. Only the nonreversible type is available.

As noted above, an early study of depressed patients first found that the MAOI phenelzine ameliorated associated symptoms of social anxiety (Liebowitz et al., 1984). This prompted Liebowitz and his colleagues to conduct an open trial of phenelzine in 11 patients who met criteria for social phobia (Liebowitz et al., 1985). Of these 11 patients, 7 (64%) were rated as markedly improved and the other 4 (36%) were rated as improved. In a subsequent, randomized, placebo-controlled trial (Liebowitz et al., 1992), the effects of phenelzine were compared with placebo and atenolol. The latter is a beta-adrenergic blocker hypothesized to be potentially effective in the treatment of social phobia on the basis of prior research with musicians and other performing artists (see section on beta-blockers below). After 8 weeks of treatment, 64% of those treated with phenelzine improved, as did 30% of those treated with atenolol and 23% of those who received placebo. As noted by Potts and Davidson (1995), improvement was greater on clinician rating scales than on patient self-report measures. During the discontinuation phase, 33% of the patients successfully treated with phenelzine relapsed when switched to placebo, as did 33% of those initially successfully treated with atenolol. Among those who remained on phenelzine, none relapsed, but 50% of those who remained on atenolol did so. These rates indicate that a percentage of patients treated with phenelzine relapse when the medication is discontinued. The same percentage relapse when discontinued from atenolol. Furthermore, 50% of those who continue to be treated with atenolol experienced a reoccurrence of symptoms after some time. However, the number of patients who participated in the phenelzine discontinuation phase was quite small ($n = 11$). Therefore, these data must be interpreted cautiously.

An important contribution of the Liebowitz et al. (1992) study was the attempt to analyze separately outcome for those with the specific and generalized subtypes of social phobia. Among those with the generalized subtype, the improvement rate was 68% for phenelzine, 28% for atenolol, and 21% for placebo. Thus, atenolol was no more effective than placebo and both were substantially less efficacious than phenelzine. Among the specific subtype, response rates were 50% for phenelzine, 40% for atenolol, and 29% for placebo, but the number of specific subtype subjects in each of these treatment groups was quite small. Thus, although the findings are suggestive, additional studies with larger samples need to be conducted.

Heimberg et al. (1994) reported the results of a comparative study of phenelzine and Cognitive–Behavioral Group Therapy (CBGT; see chapter 8 in this volume). Although final published results are not yet available, several preliminary findings were highlighted (e.g., Heimberg et al., 1994). After 6 weeks of treatment, phenelzine produced a more rapid response than CBGT, but this effect disappeared after 12 weeks of treatment. Both interventions were superior to placebo. Phenelzine was superior to CBGT on some outcome measures at posttreatment. However, after an untreated follow-up period, those treated with CBGT maintained their treatment gains, whereas a number of patients treated with phenelzine relapsed. A full interpretation of the findings of this study await publication of the final results.

Gelernter et al. (1991) also examined the effects of phenelzine, alprazolam, placebo, or cognitive–behavioral (CBGT) therapy for the treatment of social phobia. It is important to note that all patients treated with medications also received exposure instructions. Therefore, although the inclusion of these instructions probably replicates standard clinical practice, it does not allow for a strict comparison of pharmacological and cognitive–behavioral interventions. After 12 weeks of treatment, there were no differences across groups on self-report or clinician-rating scales. Using scores in the "normal" range on the Fear Questionnaire as the "responder" criterion, 69% of those treated with phenelzine were judged to be responders, as were 38% of those treated with alprazolam, 24% of those treated with CBGT, and 20% of those who received placebo. These findings, particularly with regard to the outcome for CBGT, stand in stark contrast to the CBGT–phenelzine comparison cited above. It is beyond the scope of this chapter to discuss why these differences might have occurred, although variations in CBGT administration or a different measurement strategy are among obvious possibilities.

Finally, Versiani et al. (1992) reported a double-blind evaluation of phenelzine, moclobemide (a reversible MAOI), and placebo. After 8 weeks of treatment, both phenelzine and moclobemide were superior to placebo, and phenelzine was superior to moclobemide on one measure. However, after 16 weeks, both drug treatments remained superior to placebo, but there were no differences between the two active treatments. Improvement rates were 91% for phenelzine, 82% for moclobemide, and 43% for placebo.

Several clinical trials have been conducted with the reversible MAOIs moclobemide and brofaramine. In an open trial of moclobemide (Bisserbe, Lepine, & GRP Group, 1994), 94% of patients were rated as much improved or very much improved after 12 weeks of treatment. Using a double-blind placebo-controlled design (van Vliet, den Boer, & Westenberg, 1992), 79% of those treated with brofaramine were rated as much improved or very much improved on the basis of CGI ratings, compared with 26% of those treated with placebo. Versiani et al. (1992) found that moclobemide was significantly better than placebo on several self-report and clinician ratings. As noted by Potts and Davidson (1995), three additional studies with moclobemide have been completed. An international multicenter trial reported moclobemide to be more effective than placebo, whereas a U.S. multicenter clinical trial did not. Finally, Schneier (as cited in Potts & Davidson, 1995) reported a drug response rate of 22% for moclobemide versus a 10% response rate for placebo. Although there are some positive results for these drugs and they have the advantage of not requiring severe dietary restrictions, reversible MAOIs have been reported to have significant side-effects, including several deaths, and currently are not available in the United States (Turner, Cooley-Quille, & Beidel, 1995).

Of the available MAOIs, phenelzine has produced considerable improvement in social phobia symptoms among adults. However, there is a sizable percentage of patients who relapse once the drug is discontinued. Also, a significant deterrent to the use of the MAOIs, including phenelzine, is the need for a strict dietary regimen. To date, other than one case description of a child with selective mutism (Golwyn & Weinstock, 1990), we know of no reports of the use of MAOIs with children who have an anxiety disorder.

Beta-Blockers

Interest in this group of drugs as a possible treatment for social phobia stems at least in part from early studies indicating their ability to reduce anxiety associated with public speaking and musical performance in study participants who had no disorders (e.g., Gossard, Dennis, & DeBush, 1984; Neftel et al., 1982). Outcome of the majority of studies with these drugs indicated that they were effective in decreasing subjective distress and ameliorating physical symptoms of anxiety. However, other dimensions of anxiety tended not to improve (see Potts & Davidson, 1995). On a theoretical level, social phobia was known to be characterized by physiological reactivity of the beta-adrenergic system, thus producing a characteristic physiological response including increased heart rate, sweating, trembling, and blushing (Gorman & Gorman, 1987). Therefore, it seemed reasonable to hypothesize that drugs that blocked this system should eliminate the physiological response of patients with social phobia that occurs in anxious situations.

Despite this promising empirical database and the strong theoretical underpinnings, the efficacy of beta-blockers in the treatment of social phobia has not been impressive (Falloon, Lloyd, & Harpin, 1981). Although Falloon et al. reported that the combination of propranolol and social skills training was no more effective than placebo and social skills training in the treatment of social phobia, during the mid-1980s there was particular interest in examining the effects of a newer beta-blocker, atenolol (Tenormin), because unlike the older medications (e.g., propranolol), atenolol had only minimal effects on the brain or central nervous system (i.e., it only minimally crosses the blood–brain barrier). Thus, its primary mechanism of action was thought to be on the peripheral nervous system. This was considered a significant advantage for patients using these medications because the use of propranolol sometimes resulted in patient reports of impaired cognitive functioning.

In an open trial of atenolol with *DSM-III* (American Psychiatric Association, 1980) diagnosed social phobias (Gorman, Liebowitz, Fyer, Campeas, & Klein, 1985), 10 patients were treated with atenolol. Of these 10 patients, 50% were judged to have a marked reduction and

40% were judged to have a moderate reduction in social phobia symptoms at posttreatment. As noted in our discussion of the MAOIs, although atenolol may have had some effect in a subset of patients with social phobia, it was not as efficacious as phenelzine (and in many cases not more so than placebo). Turner, Beidel, and Jacob (1994) used composite indexes of improvement and endstate functioning to evaluate the efficacy of flooding (exposure), atenolol, and placebo. Whereas 89% of the patients treated with flooding were moderately or significantly improved, rates for the patients treated with atenolol and placebo were 47% and 44%, respectively. Using endstate functioning status (which evaluates outcome by comparing the behavior of individuals with social phobia at posttreatment with that of nonsocially phobic patients), 75% of those treated with flooding achieved moderate or high endstate status, whereas 44% of the atenolol patients and 59% of the placebo patients did so. Thus, two independent research groups using different measurement strategies have failed to confirm the superiority of atenolol to a placebo control group.

As a group, the beta-blockers have not been found to be efficacious in the treatment of other anxiety states, and available data suggest that results are relatively poor with social phobia as well. This particularly is the case for the generalized subtype of social phobia for which atenolol has not proved to be superior to placebo. Also, we were unable to find any reports in the literature describing the use of beta-blockers with children. Thus, except in unusual circumstances, the beta-blockers do not appear to be the drug of choice in treating social phobia.

High Potency Benzodiazepines

The efficacy of two high potency benzodiazepines, alprazolam and clonazepam, for the treatment of social phobia has been assessed. Although two open trials of alprazolam in adults with social phobia (Lydiard, Larraia, Howell, & Ballenger, 1988; Reich & Yates, 1988a) and one trial with children with avoidant disorder (Simeon & Ferguson, 1987) showed initial promise, subsequent controlled trials with both populations did not support the initial positive results. Among adults with social phobia, Gelernter et al. (1991) reported a 38% response rate for alprazolam plus self-exposure instructions, a rate that was not significantly different from placebo. Furthermore, 2 months following drug discontinuation, social phobia symptomatology returned for all patients treated with alprazolam. Similarly, in a controlled trial of alprazolam that included children with avoidant disorder (Simeon et al., 1992), the results did not indicate any differences in treatment outcome when alprazolam was compared with placebo.

There have been several open trials of clonazepam (Davidson, Ford, 'Smith, & Potts, 1991; Ontiveros & Fontaine, 1990; Reiter, Pollack, Rosenbaum, & Cohen, 1990). All reported substantial improvement for most patients on clinician ratings of symptoms and social phobia severity. Subsequently, there have been two controlled trials. In the first, Munjack and his colleagues (Munjack, Baltazar, Bohn, Cabe, & Appleton, 1990) compared a clonazepam group with a no-treatment control group. Using the clinician-rated CGI, 60% of those treated with clonazepam were judged to be much or very much improved compared with 20% of those in the no-treatment group. Finally, in a 10-week placebo-controlled trial of clonazepam, Davidson et al. (1993) reported that those treated with clonazepam improved on various clinician-rated and self-report instruments. Overall, 78% of patients treated with clonazepam were judged responders compared with only 20% of patients treated with placebo.

Currently, then, the results of controlled trials with alprazolam and clonazepam in adult populations have been mixed, and not enough data are available to draw firm conclusions regarding their use in children. However, clonazepam appears to be more promising than alprazolam. Other than a lack of unambiguous evidence of efficacy, a particular problem for these drugs is that, according to the extant literature, patients treated with these compounds relapse at a high rate once the drug is discontinued. In addition, although major advantages of these drugs include their quick action and relatively benign side-effect profile, there are a number of major drawbacks as well. Dependence on these drugs can develop, and withdrawal can be difficult. Among potential withdrawal difficulties are seizures and rebound anxiety (reappearance of anxiety at a higher intensity than before the drug was started). These difficulties particularly are associated with alprazolam, and there is a necessity to follow a strict withdrawal regimen to avoid their occurrence. Because of the questionable efficacy, potential for abuse and dependence, withdrawal difficulties, and because there are better choices, in our view, these drugs probably are not well suited for the treatment of chronic anxiety states, despite their widespread use.

Buspirone

A fairly unique medication, buspirone is an azaspirone (nonbenzodiazepine) anxiolytic that has been the subject of two open trials and one placebo-controlled trial. When introduced, this drug was thought to have the major benefits of the benzodiazepines without their negative features. In one open trial (Munjack et al. 1991), the positive response rate for patients with social phobia was 53%, although this was tempered by the fact that 35% of the patients dropped out of treatment. Schneier et al. (1993) also treated socially phobic patients in an open trial with buspirone. At posttreatment, 47% of patients were judged as much or very much improved on the CGI. In the only controlled trial, Clark and Agras (1991) compared buspirone, placebo, cognitive–behavior therapy (CBT), or psychotherapy in the treatment of musicians with stage fright. The outcome indicated that buspirone was not significantly different from placebo and was worse than CBT, although the narrowly defined nature of the social fear (musicians with stage fright) means that one must be cautious about extrapolating these findings to other samples of socially phobic patients. Yet, to our knowledge, this drug has not proved to be consistently efficacious in the treatment of any of the anxiety states. Thus, at this juncture it does not appear to be a reasonable choice for treatment.

Summary of Empirical Literature on the Pharmacological Treatment of Social Phobia

There are a number of pharmacological agents that may have some efficacy in the treatment of social phobia. The preponderance of evidence, particularly when limited to controlled comparative trials, supports the efficacy of the MAOIs, primarily the nonreversible type phenelzine. Improvement rates for phenelzine range from 60% to 90% across all studies. However, dietary restrictions and the side-effect profile may preclude administration of these medications for some patients. These dietary restrictions (see side-effects section below) may be particularly problematic for children and adolescents, who may not understand (or be willing to accept) the limitations (e.g., no pizza). Currently, there are no controlled trials of MAOIs with anxious children. Also, there are two controlled outcome studies with clonazepam indicating that it also is efficacious. In addition, one study with clonazepam reported a responder rate equal to that of phenelzine.

Placebo-controlled studies examining the efficacy of beta-blockers have not met the initial positive expectations. Response rates ranged from 30% (Liebowitz et al., 1992) to 33% (when the Liebowitz et al., 1992, responder criteria were applied in Turner et al., 1994). Although not meeting initial expectations, some investigators believe that there still may be a role for beta-blockers in a select group of those patients with the specific subtype (such as Elaine). However, the exact characteristics of this subgroup have yet to be established.

One limitation of the current pharmacological treatments is that relapse rates for medications are quite high, although somewhat variable depending upon the specific compound. This suggests that the effects last only as long as the individual continues to take the drug. As noted by Turner, Beidel, Wolff, Spaulding, and Jacob (1996), it is unclear whether alternative methods of discontinuation or longer treatment periods, or both, would enhance maintenance for the pharmacological interventions. This question has yet to be addressed. With respect to children, the data are so limited that it is difficult to offer any guidelines.

GUIDELINES TO THE USE OF MEDICATION IN SOCIAL PHOBIA

Several researchers have provided clinical guidelines for the evaluation and clinical management of the treatment of social phobia with pharmacotherapy (e.g., Liebowitz & Marshall, 1995; Kutcher, Reiter, & Gardner, 1995). Factors to consider include the diagnostic and medical evaluation, education and the presentation of the rationale for the medication, assurance of adequate dosage, evaluation of side-effects, evaluation of clinical response, medication withdrawal, and treatment nonresponders. Each of these factors will be discussed in turn below.

Diagnostic and Medical Evaluation

In previous chapters (chapters 1, 2, and 5 in this volume), we presented a general outline for the diagnostic assessment of patients with social phobia. As part of the diagnostic process, an evaluation of the patient's physical status is necessary. We always encourage those who have not had a recent physical examination to do so prior to initiation of any intervention, but such an evaluation is absolutely essential when medication is to be used. This will rule out medical conditions that might be contributing to the patient's emotional difficulty or may preclude the use of certain pharmacological or behavioral procedures. Prescribing physicians need to know (a) if there are physical conditions that may be aggravated by administration of the medication; (b) if the patient is taking other medications that might attenuate, potentiate, or interfere with the effects of the prescribed medication; or (c) if the patient has a previous history of difficulty using this medication (such as severe side-effects, allergic reactions, or physical or psychological addiction). Cardiovascular effects from taking TCAs have been known to occur (see side-effects section) and represent one of the most important medical considerations in the administration of this particular class of drugs, especially for children and adolescents.

Education and Presentation of the Rationale

In chapter 6, we presented a general outline for patient education and approaches to treatment. Liebowitz and Marshall (1995) offer three rationales when presenting the potential use of a pharmacological treatment to patients: citing the treatment literature; proposing that if anxiety drives the phobic avoidance, then ameliorating the anxiety may eliminate interpersonal difficulties and perhaps phobic avoidance; and in the case of generalized social phobia, discussing the effects of medication on the key symptom of hypersensitivity to criticism or rejection. Obviously, the first two rationales are not limited to pharmacological interventions and could be used when proposing psychological treatments as well. Kutcher et al. (1995) recommended a similar pharmacological educational strategy for children and adolescents, including (a) education about expected outcome with and without treatment, (b) a balanced discussion of the various treatment options available (including risks and benefits), and (c) a discussion of the potential role of medications in treating the disorder and the expected length of treatment.

Assurance of Adequate Dosage

Once the decision is made to use medication, the particular class of drug is selected and the patient is given a prescription. Obviously, medication will not be effective if it is not taken at a therapeutic level, taken as directed, or taken for a sufficient length of time. Because much of the data regarding pharmacological treatment is based on open clinical trials (this is particularly true for children and adolescents), therapeutic dose ranges for all medications have not been established. In particular, dose–response studies such as those conducted with panic disorder and agoraphobia (e.g., Mavissakalian, 1996) are not available for social phobia. In Table 11, we present recommended dosages culled from the available treatment literature.

Evaluation of Side-Effects

All medications include the possibility of producing adverse effects in addition to their therapeutic effects. The task of the prescribing physician is to inform the patient about these side-effects and to monitor him or her. However, any clinician who is treating a patient taking medication needs to be aware of the medication's possible side-effects to recognize their presence. Below (see Table 12), we present the most common side-effects for medications used in the treatment of social phobia. These side-effects represent those reported in the social phobia treatment literature, but not necessarily all those reported for the particular class of medication. It is important to remember that many side-effects are temporary (i.e., they subside as the patient continues to take the medication). There-

Table 11

Recommended Dosages for Pharmacological Treatment of Social Phobia on the Basis of the Current Literature

Medication	Adults	Children
Tricyclic antidepressants		
Imipramine (Tofranil)		3 mg/kg/day
Selective serotonin reuptake inhibitors		
Fluoxetine (Prozac)	20–80 mg	21.4–25.7 mg/day
Fluvoxamine (Luvox)	50–150 mg	
Monamine oxidase inhibitors		
Phenelzine (Nardil)	15–90 mg	52.5 mg/day
Benzodiazepines		
Alprazolam (Xanax)	2.1–6.3 mg	1.57 mg/day
Clonazepam (Klonapin)	0.75–6.0 mg	
Buspirone (Buspar)	15–60 mg	30 mg/day
Beta-blockers		
Propanolol (Inderal)	10–20 mg	
Atenolol (Tenormin)	50–100 mg	

fore, in addition to monitoring the occurrence of side-effects, their severity and their impact upon patient daily functioning should be considered in determining patient tolerance to medication as well. Finally, issues of race and ethnicity need to be considered when determining drug efficacy and side-effects. African Americans, Hispanics, and Asian Americans treated with antidepressants have been reported to achieve positive effects from lower dosages than those needed for European Americans and to have more side-effects from the TCAs than do European Americans (e.g., Turner, Cooley-Quille, & Beidel, 1995).

Cardiotoxicity With Tricyclic Antidepressants

Cardiac abnormalities as a result of TCA administration appear to occur more frequently in children and adolescents than in adults (Kutcher et

Table 12

Common Side-Effects for Medications Used to Treat Social Phobia on the Basis of Current Literature

Medication	Adults	Children
Tricyclic Antidepressants		
Imipramine	Dry mouth, constipation, nausea, dizziness, sedation, insomnia, weight gain	In addition to those found in adults, cardiac conduction abnormalities may exist, including sinus tachycardia, sudden death, and imipramine hypertension.
Selective Serotonin Reuptake Inhibitors		
Fluoxetine	Akathesia, diarrhea, precipitation of mania, nausea, insomnia, anorexia, stomach aches, headaches	Psychomotor restlessness, headaches, stomach aches in adolescents, disordered sexual functioning
Fluvoxamine	None reported in social phobia literature	None reported in social phobia literature
Monamine Oxidase Inhibitors		
Phenelzine	Postural hypotension, sedation, sexual dysfunction, weight gain, dietary restrictions	Same as adults

Table continues

Table 12 (*Continued*)

Medication	Adults	Children
Benzodiazepines		
Alprazolam	Addictive potential, sedation when used intermittently	Paradoxical or dyscontrol reactions such as disinhibition or aggression
Clonazepam	In addition to above, anorgasmia, unsteadiness, forgetfulness, impaired concentration	
Buspirone	Dizziness, headaches, gastric upset, sedation	Gastric upset, dizziness, headaches, insomnia
Beta-blockers		
Propranolol	Orthostatic hypertension	
Atenolol	Orthostatic hypotension	

Note. This list should not be regarded as comprehensive.

al., 1995). In addition, sudden death in a small number of depressed children being treated with the TCA desipramine (Norpramin) has been reported (Biederman, 1991), although the exact relationship of these medications to the deaths is unclear. Several researchers (Biederman et al., 1989; Ryan et al.,1987) have reported that clinically significant conduction abnormalities noted after administration of TCAs actually may be the result of preexisting cardiac conditions. Thus, if these medications are prescribed, a pretreatment electrocardiogram is a necessity to detect the presence of preexisting abnormalities. An alternative strategy is to administer an SSRI.

Dietary Restrictions With MAOIs

Perhaps the greatest drawback of nonreversible MAOIs such as phenelzine is the dietary restrictions they place on the patient. When taking these medications, patients need to follow a diet low in tyramine. Failure to do so can result in a hypertensive reaction that requires immediate treatment and could prove fatal. Dietary restrictions for MAOIs include avoiding most forms of cheese, alcohol (particularly red wine), aged meats, chocolate, cocoa, tomato sauce, ketchup, chili sauce, eggplant, yogurt, oranges, bananas, pineapples, raisins, and many others, including some other medications. Thus, although efficacious, clinicians may want to consider an alternative medication or nonpharmacological treatment before initiating treatment with a nonreversible MAOI.

Evaluation of Clinical Response

Liebowitz and Marshall (1995) listed five criteria that can be used to determine the efficacy of a medication to treat social phobia. First, there should be decreased anxiety during a social or performance event and perhaps improvement in the quality of the performance. Second, there should be a decrease in anticipatory anxiety. Third, there should be a decrease in social avoidance. Fourth, there should be a change in coexisting conditions, such as alcohol abuse, depression, or generalized anxiety, that may be secondary to the social phobia. Fifth, there should be a decrease in functional impairment. In other words, judgment of successful treatment should entail not only a decrease in specific symp-tomatology but also an improvement in daily functioning.

Combination of Pharmacological and Psychological Interventions

To date, only three studies (Clark & Agras, 1991; Falloon et al., 1981; Gelernter et.al., 1991) have combined pharmacological and psycholog-ical (behavioral or cognitive–behavioral) treatments for social phobia. In one study (Clark & Agras, 1991), the combination of drug and cognitive–behavioral treatment was less efficacious than was cognitive–behavioral therapy plus placebo. In the other two studies (Falloon et al., 1981; Gelernter et al., 1991), the combination of medication and behavioral or cognitive–behavioral treatment was no better than be-havioral or cognitive–behavioral treatment alone. Interestingly, various classes of medications (high potency benzodiazepines, MAOI, beta-blocker, and azaspirone) were included in these studies, and none ap-peared statistically superior to behavioral or cognitive–behavioral treat-ments alone. The small number of studies makes it difficult to draw firm conclusions. However, at this juncture, there does not appear to be any synergistic effects for the combination of pharmacological and behavioral or cognitive–behavioral treatments. Although the results from studies appear to be consistent, our own clinical experience, as well as other clinicians' reports, indicate that there are times when the combined use of medication and behavioral interventions are useful in facilitating a positive outcome. There are at least two scenarios where this applies. First, if the patient (adult or child) is depressed signifi-cantly, use of an antidepressant medication could play an important role in recovery. The medication could help to alleviate the depression, which, in our experience, increases the likelihood that the patient will comply with an active behavioral treatment program. These programs require considerable energy and commitment, and it also has been our experience that if depression is severe, the ability of a patient to par-ticipate fully might be impaired. Second, when general and social anx-iety is extremely high, reduction of anxiety symptoms through use of medication can help facilitate the patient's ability to engage in exposure (particularly in vivo exposure) assignments. Thus, the final decision on the issue of drug and behavioral treatments should be based on the clinical status of each patient.

Medication Discontinuation

If a patient improves as a result of pharmacological intervention, the next questions to arise are (a) how long must the patient continue to take the medication, (b) when can it be discontinued, and (c) can it be discontinued safely? As noted, Gelernter et al. (1991) found that all patients with social phobia treated with alprazolam relapsed within 8 weeks of medication discontinuation. Similarly, Liebowitz and Heimberg (as cited in Liebowitz & Marshall, 1995) found that 50% of those with social phobia who responded to treatment with phenelzine relapsed during a drug-free discontinuation phase. Thus, issues of discontinuation merit thoughtful consideration.

For children and adolescents, SSRIs should be discontinued gradually. Kutcher et al. (1995) recommended a gradual taper over a 1-week period, but noted that fluoxetine could be discontinued abruptly. Similarly, buspirone can be discontinued over a 4-day period. Patients (either adults or children) usually do not report difficulty with withdrawal from either class of medication if they follow the prescribed regimen. The situation is somewhat different for benzodiazepines, including the high potency variety. First, short-term discontinuation cannot occur. Although reports of benzodiazepine withdrawal in children or adolescents have not been reported (Kutcher et al., 1995), clinicians need to monitor patients of all ages for the presence of withdrawal symptoms. Most important, patients must be cautioned not to discontinue these medications abruptly. Abrupt discontinuation can result in withdrawal symptoms ranging from seizures, psychosis, and delirium to gastrointestinal distress, anxiety, concentration and memory disturbances, and ataxia. Seizures are most likely to occur when high potency benzodiazepines, such as alprazolam, are discontinued abruptly (e.g., Breier, Charney, & Nelson, 1984). Others (e.g., Liebowitz & Marshall, 1995) reported that because the withdrawal symptoms are usually considered more manageable, clonazepam is easier to taper than alprazolam. However, eliminating the last 1 mg of clonazepam also has been reported to be difficult. Potts and Davidson (1995) reported that their clinical impressions suggest that the rate and time of medication taper may have important implications for the effectiveness of medication withdrawal, but sufficient empirical data are not yet available. A complicating factor is that benzodiazepine withdrawal symptoms include anxiety, concentration difficulties, and memory disturbances. Because these behaviors also are characteristic of anxiety states, the clinician must determine whether such behaviors represent medication withdrawal or return of previous symptomatology. One method for determining this may be to track symptomatology over time. That is, withdrawal symptoms may dissipate, whereas a return of previous symptomatology likely will remain. It is clear, then, that the withdrawal of medication, and particularly benzodiazepines, must be carried out with considerable care.

Treatment of Non-Responders

Currently, there are no studies that definitively predict which patients will respond to which medication. Overall, phenelzine has the most empirical support, and one study indicated that phenelzine may be more efficacious than atenolol for the generalized subtype. However, predicting patient response is difficult at best. When patients do not respond to a particular medication, the first question that must be answered is whether the patient has had an adequate dose of the medication for a sufficient period of time. If so, then another class of medication may be considered. Currently, there also are no data indicating which patients will respond to a second class of medication if the first is ineffective. Liebowitz and Marshall (1995) suggested that, based on their clinical experience, when MAOIs or SSRIs are only partially effective, partial responders may be treated with augmentation strategies such as the addition of benzodiazepines or beta-blockers. However, currently there are no data available on the efficacy of such strategies. Finally, psychological treatment may be effective as either an augmentation or alternative strategy for treatment of non-responders. The use of behavioral intervention strategies may prove to be a more efficacious alternative than the use of augmentation strategies, but this too needs to be examined empirically.

CONCLUSION

The empirical treatment outcome literature involving the use of drugs for social phobia was reviewed in this chapter. Many of the compounds currently in use have not been fully evaluated in controlled trials, and this particularly is so for children. However, on the basis of the studies that do exist, phenelzine (Nardil, a monamine oxidase inhibitor) appears to be the most efficacious drug treatment for social phobia in adults, and the most studied drug for social phobia among the pharmacotherapeutic agents in current use. The use of other medications, particularly the high potency benzodiazepines and the SSRI antidepressants, have been reported in the literature. Yet, at this time, it is difficult to draw conclusions from existing studies because most have not been controlled. As a tentative conclusion, among the high potency benzodiazepines, current outcome data favor the use of clonazepam over alprazolam.

Currently, SSRIs (e.g., Prozac, Luvox) are in widespread use in the treatment of children and adults with social phobia. Although these drugs appear to have a more benign side-effect profile than other antidepressants, their efficacy in the treatment of social phobia has not been firmly established through empirical study. Finally, two classes of drugs, azaspirone (Buspirone) and beta-blockers (e.g., Tenormin, Propranolol) do not appear to be efficacious in the treatment of social phobia.

Although there is evidence that drug therapies can be helpful in reducing the symptoms of social phobia, one major problem is that the positive effects of the drug tend to dissipate rather rapidly once the medication is discontinued. This seems to be true, with some differences in rate, for all of the medications discussed here. Because the question has not been researched fully at this time, it is unclear whether this means that the patient must remain on medication forever or that there are critical time phases during which the medication can be withdrawn without symptom return.

Side-effects are another issue to consider when using medication for treating social phobia. The severe dietary restrictions required for the MAOI phenelzine might be an argument against its use, particularly in the case of children and adolescents. Unfortunately, the reversible MAOIs (e.g., moclobemide) have not proved safe and have been withdrawn from the U.S. market. Although the high potency benzodiazepines have shown some degree of efficacy (particularly clonazepam), and despite the fact that they are well tolerated by patients, there are a number of significant potential side-effects to these medications that suggest they should be used very carefully, if at all. In our opinion, these compounds probably are not good choices for the treatment of social phobia or any chronic maladaptive anxiety state. Among the most problematic difficulties include the potential for dependence and significant withdrawal symptoms. The SSRIs enjoy a relatively benign profile in comparison to other antidepressants and do not have the same drawbacks as the other drugs in current use. This particularly appears to be the case for children. Thus, the SSRIs might be a good place to start when considering a drug for children with social phobia despite the relative absence of data from controlled trials. One always can switch to another medication should the initial one prove not to be efficacious.

One question frequently posed is whether there is a synergistic effect from combining behavioral and drug treatment. There are few unambiguous data to make this determination in social phobia at this time. Yet, the data that do exist suggest that there is nothing to be gained from combining the two treatments, at least in the case of adults. However, we noted that in our clinical experience, there are those instances in which use of the two treatments in combination appears to facilitate a positive treatment outcome. In particular, we noted this to be the case when severe depression or very high anxiety was present. This needs to be confirmed by empirical studies, and if confirmed, the exact features of those who benefit from such a strategy need to be delineated.

8

Behavioral and Cognitive–Behavioral Treatment of Social Phobia in Adults

Dear Drs. Turner and Beidel:

Enclosed please find a copy of my wedding announcement, which recently appeared in the local newspaper. As you may remember, one of the final homework assignments that you gave me was to invite a female coworker to lunch. Well, I completed that task successfully. In fact, I began dating the person I invited to lunch, and last month we married. Thank you for all of your help.

Sincerely,

John Doe

This is a most gratifying letter (changed to protect confidentiality), received from a patient who participated in our behavioral treatment program for social phobia. Most outcomes are not quite this dramatic but are no less gratifying. As we noted in chapter 1, although described as early as 1966 by Marks and Gelder and 1970 by Marks, social phobia was introduced into the official psychiatric nomenclature only with the publication of the third edition of the *Diagnostic and Statistical Manual of Mental Disorders* (*DSM-III*; American Psychiatric Association, 1980). Yet, just a decade and a half since social phobia was recognized as a specific disorder, there have been many studies evaluating the efficacy of various behavioral and cognitive–behavioral treatments. In fact, the literature has yielded sufficient data to allow some rather firm conclusions about current treatment strategies and their short- and long-term effects. The behavioral and cognitive–behavioral treatments have been administered alone or as combinations using individual, group, or combination individual and group format. The primary interventions include exposure, social skill training, and various methods of cognitive restructuring. We will limit our discussion here to those studies involving the use of patients with a *DSM-III, DSM-III-R,* or *DSM-IV* diagnosis, and only to those treatments that have been studied empirically. For the sake of conceptual clarity, we have divided our review into two sections: those studies using traditional behavioral interventions (e.g., exposure, social skills training) and those involving the addition of a cognitive component. We will review the empirical evidence for behavioral and cognitive–behavioral treatments for social phobia, describe the major treatment strategies currently in use, discuss the manner in which treatment strategies are implemented, and explore variables that might affect outcome.

REVIEW OF EMPIRICAL LITERATURE

Traditional Behavioral Treatments

In a large study using classic behavioral treatments, Wlazlo et al. (1990) treated 78 patients with social phobia (some with concurrent avoidant personality disorder, APD) either with a form of social skills training (SST) known as *personal effectiveness training* (Liberman, King, DeRisi, & McCann, 1975), group exposure, or individual exposure. All patients improved significantly from pre- to posttreatment, but there were no between-group differences. After 3 months, patients maintained their treatment gains or made further improvements. In some cases gains were maintained for up to 2½ years. Although providing strongest support for these treatments, interpretation of outcome is complicated because the various groups received different amounts of treatment (see Turner, Cooley-Quille, & Beidel, 1995, for a more extensive discussion of this study).

In a study examining the effects of an intensive exposure paradigm, Turner, Beidel, and Jacob (1994) treated 72 *DSM-III-R* patients with social phobia using either flooding (imaginal and in vivo), atenolol (dose range = 25 to 100 mg per day) plus clinical support, or pill placebo plus clinical support. In addition to a primary diagnosis of social phobia, approximately 39% of the sample had a comorbid Axis I disorder (primarily GAD or dysthymia), and 35% had a comorbid Axis II disorder (primarily APD or OCPD). For atenolol and placebo groups, treatment was administered over a 3-month period, twice weekly for the first month and weekly thereafter (16 sessions). The exposure group was treated twice weekly for the first 2 months and weekly thereafter, for a total of 20 sessions. Overall, the total amount of treatment time was judged to be approximately equal for the groups. Although findings were not statistically significant on every single measure, in general the flooding group achieved the best results. Flooding consistently was superior to atenolol, whereas atenolol rarely was superior to placebo. On a composite index of improvement, 89% of flooding patients were moderately or significantly improved, as were 27% of atenolol patients and 44% of placebo patients. In addition to traditional outcome measures, this study evaluated outcome using an endstate functioning index on the basis of data derived from a sample that had no disorder. At posttreatment, 75% of flooding patients were judged to have moderate or high endstate functioning as assessed by this index, as were 44% of atenolol patients and 58% of the placebo group, differences that were significant. Using the SPAI difference score, the effect size was .94 for flooding, .40 for atenolol, and .01 for placebo. For the CGI rating, the effect size was 1.77 for flooding, 1.33 for atenolol, and .75 for placebo. On speech length, the effect size was 1.04 for flooding, .34 for atenolol, and .43 for placebo. These results provide compelling evidence for the efficacy of flooding in treating social phobia. In general, at the 6-month follow-up, those patients who were improved at posttreatment maintained their treatment gains regardless of which treatment they received. This study is noteworthy because it was the first to use a flooding paradigm for social phobia and because it used a normative-based endstate functioning index.

In a study designed to assess variations in exposure therapy format, Al-Kubaisy et al. (1992) examined whether exposure sessions during which the clinician accompanied the patient enhanced the effectiveness of a self-administered exposure program. Those with social phobia were included in the sample along with several other phobic groups. Treatment time was equivalent across the groups and consisted of daily 90-minute self-exposure assignments and six sessions with the clinician. Compared with a self-relaxation group, which served as a control, both exposure groups were significantly more improved at posttreatment. Across phobic conditions, there were few differences between the two modalities. However, when the groups were examined separately on the basis of phobia type, there was less support for the hypothesis that self-exposure is as effective as clinician-accompanied exposure for social phobia. Thus, it appears that clinician assistance during exposure treatment of social phobia might be necessary for optimal treatment outcome. Certainly, our clinical experience supports the contention that most people with social phobia need therapist assistance, at least initially.

The results of these studies, all of which included large samples of patients with clearly diagnosed social phobia, indicated that standard behavioral treatment consisting of exposure, SST, or both led to significant improvement of social phobia symptoms. Furthermore, follow-up data showed that treatment gains were maintained for at least 6 months, with a small amount of data indicating maintenance for as long as 2½ years. Below we describe studies in which a cognitive component was included.

Cognitive–Behavioral Treatment

Heimberg et al. (1990) compared a Cognitive–Behavioral Group Therapy (CBGT) consisting of cognitive restructuring, self-guided in vivo exposure homework, and cognitive restructuring homework with a placebo group consisting of didactic lecture–demonstration–discussion regarding the nature of social phobia. Treatment consisted of 12 two-hour weekly sessions. Although both groups showed significant within-group change, there were no differences between CBGT and the placebo group on most variables at posttreatment. However, at 6-month follow-up, both groups were significantly improved over pretreatment, and the CBGT group was significantly more improved than the placebo control group on most measures. It is clear that CBGT produced improvement in this socially phobic group, although not more improvement than the control group until the 6-month follow-up. Improvement continued in the CBGT group even after treatment had been terminated. Failure to find differences between CBGT and controls at posttreatment might have been due to the fact that the control group contained a number of active treatment components (albeit nonspecific). Thus, a longer period of time was required for differences to emerge.

In a second study, Heimberg, Salzman, Holt, and Blendell (1993) published 5-year follow-up data on a subset of the patients reported in the earlier study. Of the 49 patients originally treated with either CBGT or educational support, 19 were assessed at the follow-up. Both groups maintained their treatment gains, but those treated with CBGT were judged by clinicians to have less severe symptomatology and less interference in daily activities. In addition, the CBGT group had significantly better scores on the Social Avoidance and Distress Scale and the Fear Questionnaire. On a behavioral test, there were no group differences in self-ratings of anxiety, performance quality, or any measures derived from a thought-listing task. Independent raters did judge the CBGT group as significantly less anxious and more skilled during the behavioral task. This study is impressive in terms of the length of its follow-up period. However, only 38% of those initially treated returned for the follow-up, and the data indicated that those who did return were less severely impaired at pretreatment and more invested in their particular intervention (i.e., rated it as more credible and effective for their fears). Thus, conclusions regarding this positive outcome are limited by the particular characteristics of the follow-up sample (i.e., those who returned for follow-up were more likely to be those subjects who thought the treatment was credible). On the basis of these studies CBGT appears to be an efficacious intervention. Below, we discuss studies in which behavioral and cognitive–behavioral treatments have been compared.

Behavioral and Cognitive–Behavioral Comparisons

In an early study, Butler, Cullington, Munby, Amies, and Gelder (1984) compared the effectiveness of exposure with anxiety management (EXP/AM), exposure with an attention-placebo treatment called *associative therapy* (EXP/AT), and a wait-list control using 45 patients with social phobia (none with comorbid APD). AM consisted of relaxation, distraction, and rational restructuring. AT consisted of history taking and allowing thoughts and memories to come freely to the mind. In vivo hierarchial exposure sessions occurred between therapy sessions. Treatment consisted of seven 1-hour individual AM or AT sessions. In addition, two booster sessions were given between posttreatment and the 6-month follow-up. At posttreatment, both exposure groups were significantly more improved than the control group on all but one measure. However, there was no difference between the two exposure groups. In addition, at 6-month follow-up, both exposure groups maintained their treatment gains. Furthermore, the EXP/AM group had scores that were significantly lower than the EXP/AT group on half of the outcome measures. Interestingly, even though the EXP/AM group was more improved than the EXP/AT group at follow-up, both groups continued to improve over the follow-up period (although two booster sessions were used).

Emmelkamp, Mersch, Vissia, and van der Helm (1985) compared in vivo exposure (EXP) to two different cognitive strategies, rational emotive therapy (RET) and self-instructional training (SIT), in 34 individuals diagnosed with social phobia. Treatment consisted of six group sessions conducted by trained therapists in addition to homework assignments. For the EXP group, exposure consisted of in vivo social situations for 120 minutes' duration, but extinction (habituation) was not a criterion for session termination. The SIT treatment consisted of practicing preparing, confronting, coping, and reinforcing self-statements for use during imaginal presentations of problematic social situations (i.e., imagining a scene, assessing anxiety level, becoming aware of negative thoughts, and replacing them with adaptive self-statements). RET consisted of having patients analyze their feelings in terms of activating events, beliefs about the event, and the emotional or behavioral consequences of the beliefs, emphasizing disputing "discomfort and ego anxiety." Although all groups improved from pre- to posttreatment across various domains, there was little difference among the treatments at posttreatment or at 1-month follow-up, suggesting little advantage to adding RET or SIT to EXP. The study is a prime example of the failure to obtain consistent findings across various measurement categories. Also, many of the findings reported reflected within-group improvements as opposed to between-group differences, indicating that all of the treatments were efficacious and that differences among them were minor. Again, it is noteworthy that these behaviorally treated patients (regardless of specific strategy used) continued to improve once the active treatment had been terminated.

In the first of several studies comparing the combination of SST with cognitive treatments for social phobia, Stravynski, Marks, and Yule (1982) compared SST with and without cognitive restructuring in 22 patients with social phobia comorbid for APD. Using twelve 90-minute individual sessions, 11 subjects received SST consisting of instructions, modeling, role-rehearsal, feedback, self-monitoring, and homework. Eleven subjects also received cognitive restructuring consisting of using past situations as material to analyze activating events, irrational beliefs, emotional consequences, disputation of beliefs, and plans for new actions. Some patients were treated in small groups and some were treated individually. Assignment to the different treatment formats was not random. Overall, there were no between-group differences at posttreatment or at 6-month follow-up. However, an analysis of treated versus untreated behavioral targets revealed that as treatment was introduced, frequency of performance and associated anxiety improved for treated but not for untreated target behaviors. The authors concluded that SST was an effective treatment for social phobia but cognitive restructuring did not enhance its effects. Although improvement was maintained at the 6-month follow-up, there was no generalization to in vivo intimate relationships. The authors hypothesized that those patients with social phobia and APD might need intimacy training as well as SST, although no specific training guidance for the former was offered.

Because patients with social phobia differ in the extent to which they experience somatic and cognitive symptoms, Mersch, Emmelkamp, Bogels, and van der Helm (1989) matched patients on the basis of *reactor style* (cognitive or behavioral) with mode of intervention. The rationale was that a cognitive reactor would respond better to a cognitive intervention and vice versa. Among the 74 socially phobic patients, 39 were classified as cognitive or behavioral reactors (the remainder could not be classified). All patients were treated with group SST plus homework or group RET in eight weekly 2½ hour sessions. Although significant within-group changes occurred, there were no between-group differences. Thus, matching reactor types with mode of treatment did not appear to facilitate a more positive outcome. Even when reactor classification was ignored, a significant difference between SST and RET was found on only one measure. Thus, the two treatments appeared about equally efficacious.

In a follow-up study of patients treated in the Mersch et al. (1989) study, Mersch, Emmelkamp, and Lips (1991) reported results for 57 patients after treatment terminated. However, 25 of the 57 patients received additional treatment at some point during the follow-up period. Therefore, follow-up results were reported only for those without additional treatment ($n = 32$). Treatment gains were maintained, and there were no significant differences between SST and RET. Improvement and relapse rates indicated that 12 (38%) of the 32 patients showed additional improvement during the follow-up period, whereas 9 (28%) relapsed. The other 11 patients (32%) did not show any clinical change during the follow-up period. Those who sought additional treatment during follow-up were judged at pretreatment to be significantly more anxious and to have poorer social skills compared with patients who did not seek further treatment. Thus, those who relapsed seemed to have been those who did not have the skill necessary for initiating and maintaining social relationships. This also provides additional evidence that for many socially phobic people some form of social skills training needs to be included in treatment.

Mattick and his colleagues (Mattick & Peters, 1988; Mattick, Peters, & Clark, 1989) conducted two large and well controlled studies of social phobia and cognitive–behavioral treatment. The 1989 study was conducted first (although it was published subsequent to the study published in 1988) using 43 patients with social phobia; 67% generalized and 33% specific subtypes. This study compared three active treatments: graduated exposure, cognitive restructuring (a combination of systematic rational restructuring and RET), and a combination of graduated exposure and cognitive restructuring. Graduated exposure consisted of hierarchical, gradual exposure for a period of 2 hours. In addition, there were self-directed assignments. Therapists modeled, instructed, and encouraged patients, and homework consisted of monitoring exposure situations, anxiety levels, and anxiety-related thoughts. Cognitive restructuring consisted of identifying problematic thoughts and analyzing and reevaluating situations. Homework consisted of recording situations, anxiety level, and rational reappraisal. Active treatments also were compared with a wait-list control. This study was the first in which a cognitive intervention without some element of exposure was used. Patients were randomly assigned, and treatment was conducted over 6 weeks in 120-minute sessions and administered as in the Mattick and Peters (1988) study (see below) except that the cognitive restructuring group was discouraged from entering phobic situations. Instead, homework assignments consisted of analyzing past or hypothetical phobic situations. The study included a 3-month follow-up.

The results indicated that the treatment groups changed significantly from pre- to posttreatment on most variables, and differences between treatment groups and wait-list controls were significant for all but one outcome measure. On the Behavioral Approach Task (BAT), there were overall pre- to posttreatment improvements for all the treatment groups, with no subsequent posttreatment to follow-up improvement. At follow-up, the combined group was judged to be superior to both the exposure and cognitive restructuring alone groups. Also, between posttreatment and follow-up, the cognitive restructuring group improved significantly more than the exposure group on three variables (FQ Target Phobia Avoidance Rating and Self-Rating of Severity and the IRB), although both groups showed continued improvement. Overall, the treatments appeared to be about equally effective. One limitation of this study is that the cell frequencies were rather small, raising questions about the power available in the design for the statistical analysis that was conducted.

Mattick and Peters (1988) reported the results of a second study in which the wait-list control condition from the Mattick et al. (1989) study (published in 1989 but conducted before the 1988 study) along with more than 40 new cases were offered treatment. Patients were randomly assigned to one of two treatments: graduated exposure with or without cognitive restructuring (as described above). Treatment was conducted in group format for 2 hours per week over a 6-week period. At posttreatment, the combined group was superior to EXP on a BAT. The combined group also was superior to EXP on a target phobia avoidance rating, although there were no significant group differences on self-report measures. Of EXP patients, 48% still reported definite avoidance at the 3-month follow-up, whereas only 14% of the combined group did so, a difference that was significant. Of the combined group, 52% were able to complete 100% of BAT items, whereas only 17% of EXP patients were able to do so (a difference that also was significant). In addition the combined group was superior to EXP alone on composite measures of improvement and endstate functioning. Finally, at 3-month follow-up, 24% of the combined group requested additional treatment, whereas 47% of the EXP group made such a request. Contrary to other studies, the overall results here favor the combined group. However, these results need to be interpreted cautiously because of a host of data-analytic questions, which are beyond the scope of this chapter (see Turner et al., 1995).

Mersch (1995) reported on the outcome of 34 socially phobic patients treated with either exposure in vivo or an integrated treatment consisting of RET, social skills training, and exposure in vivo. Each treatment consisted of 14 weekly sessions, encompassing 16 hours of treatment time. Both active treatments were also compared with a waiting list control group. Contrary to the expectations of the authors of this study, the integrated treatment was no better than exposure in vivo alone on any of the measures, although both groups were significantly superior to the wait-list control. Patients in both groups maintained their treatment gains at follow-up. One problem with interpreting the outcome of these data is the abbreviated number of treatment sessions given to SST and RET. The former consisted of only 2 sessions and the latter only 4 sessions. In both cases, the amount of time devoted to these interventions was most likely too short for positive outcomes to emerge.

Most recently, Scholing and Emmelkamp (1996) reported 18-month follow-up data for a group of 59 patients treated with in vivo exposure alone, cognitive therapy followed by in vivo exposure, or a cognitive–behavioral treatment in which both procedures were integrated at the start. Half of the patients were treated in a group format and half in an individual format. At follow-up, those receiving in vivo exposure via a group format fared best, followed by the in vivo exposure alone, and then the integrated treatment. There is a problem in interpreting the results of this study, however. Group sizes were extremely small for the type of analyses performed, no doubt resulting in very low power. Nevertheless, the results once again attest to the central role of exposure in the treatment of social phobia.

In a study designed to "dismantle" the effective ingredients of CBGT, Hope, Heimberg, and Bruch (1995) reported significant treatment outcome differences between exposure only and CGBT. The exposure-only treatment produced superior results. Similarly, using a design to assess the separate effects of exposure and cognitive therapy, Scholing and Emmelkamp (1993a, 1993b) failed to find significant differences across treatment groups at posttreatment or 3-month follow-up. In addition, no differences emerged between individual or group treatment formats.

Finally, Newman, Hofmann, Trabert, Roth, and Taylor (1994) examined changes in cognitions as a result of "pure" behavioral treatment. The intervention included exposure to anxiety-producing situations and didactic training in communication skills and speech-making skills. After 16 hours of treatment, the treated group was improved significantly on most outcome measures when compared with the wait-list control group. In addition, the behaviorally treated group showed significant decreases on cognitive measures even though the program specifically avoided any cognitive intervention. The results of this study were similar to those of others that have attempted similar comparisons (Mattick et al., 1989; Mersch et al., 1989), and suggest that when exposure is the treatment, the pattern of change obtained includes a reduction in maladaptive cognitions.

Substantive Reviews and Meta-Analytic Studies

In addition to individual studies, there are several overall summaries, including formal meta-analytic studies, and we now turn to a discussion of these. Edelman and Chambless (1995) reported that across 8 studies comparing cognitive restructuring with exposure alone, only 1 found an additive effect for the cognitive component. Also Turner et al. (1995) reviewed 13 outcome studies involving approximately 650 patients and concluded that there was no evidence of differential efficacy between behavioral and cognitive–behavioral treatments. Furthermore, they concluded that exposure appeared to be the common ingredient in all of the efficacious treatments.

Further evidence that few differences exist among the treatments and that exposure is the most effective ingredient can be found in the results of meta-analytic studies. First, Taylor (1996), using 49 treatment outcome trials (published and unpublished) with four different interventions, reported that effect sizes for all treatments were superior to those of wait-list controls, but the four active interventions (exposure, cognitive–behavior therapy [CBT], CBT plus exposure, and SST) did not differ significantly among themselves. Furthermore, from posttreatment to follow-up, treated patients showed continued improvement in the absence of further intervention. Finally, exposure and CBT plus exposure had equivalent effect sizes (i.e., there was no statistically significant difference). Although there was a small non-significant difference between these two interventions at posttreatment, even this small difference disappeared at 3-month follow-up.

In a second study, Feske and Chambless (1995) reported a meta-analysis of CBT (combined cognitive strategies and exposure) compared with exposure alone and found that exposure alone was superior to CBT or controls, whereas CBT was not significantly different from controls. In conclusion, the results of both substantive reviews and meta-analytic studies indicate there is little significant difference among available treatment variations, and when there is, the weight of the evidence supports the superiority of exposure. Thus, the findings from meta-analytic studies support our earlier conclusion that the addition of cognitive strategies to exposure-based treatments does not improve treatment efficacy on any type of outcome measure, including measures of cognitions.

It appears that it is time for researchers to shift their attention from minuscule treatment variations to other issues if treatment outcome is to be improved. Chief among the candidates for study are issues of procedural variations. That is, the evidence is abundantly clear that exposure is the critical feature of treatment. Procedural factors such as length and frequency of treatment sessions or exposure to critical elements of the fear (core fear) may provide the answers to further enhance treatment outcome. Similarly, focus on patient characteristics and associated pathology likely will further define the boundaries of current treatments and provide insight into further treatment refinements to address these complications.

Social Phobia Subtype and Treatment Outcome

Despite the substantial data indicating that the subtypes differ on severity, prevalence, associated psychopathology, and developmental factors, few studies have examined differential treatment outcome for social phobia subtypes. In the first reported study, Brown, Heimberg, and Juster (1995) found that those with social phobia improved equally with CBGT regardless of subtype, but the specific subtype was significantly less impaired than the generalized at posttreatment. To understand who improved and who did not in the Turner, Beidel, and Jacob (1994) study, we examined the specific versus generalized subtype (see chapter 1). Although both groups improved significantly over treatment, a comparison on endstate status indicated that all (100%) of those with the specific subtype treated with exposure achieved high or moderate endstate status, compared with only 33% of those with the generalized subtype ($p < .001$).

In addition, examination of the habituation patterns of specific and generalized subtypes revealed several important findings (Turner, Beidel, Long, & Greenhouse, 1992). First, the pattern of reactivity within the flooding session was the same for both subtypes. That is, both groups experienced equivalent subjective distress during the flooding session (see Figure 4). Second, both groups manifested an identical pattern of habituation across the 12 flooding sessions (Figure 4). Thus, both specific and generalized subtypes habituated to the exposure stimuli and did so at about the same rate. These identical patterns suggest that both groups should have had the same clinical response to flooding. However, this clearly was not the case.

Because those in the generalized subtype group did not improve to the same extent as those in the specific group, the data were examined more closely to elucidate factors that might have limited improvement in the generalized subtype. This analysis revealed clearly that the generalized subtype had a more severe and complex symptomatic pattern than the specific, with a higher frequency of comorbidity with other Axis I and II conditions. Also, although data from extant studies are mixed, it appears that the generalized subtype is characterized by deficient social skills (see discussion in chapter 1). In view of the skill deficits, we devised a treatment strategy incorporating exposure and SST, which is designed to improve outcome for the generalized subtype above what is achieved with exposure alone. This treatment is called Social Effectiveness Therapy (SET; Turner, Beidel, & Cooley, 1994).

The efficacy of SET was examined in 13 *DSM-III-R* patients diagnosed with the generalized subtype (Turner, Beidel, Cooley, Woody, & Messer, 1994). Of the 13 patients, 9 had an Axis II disorder (4 had both OCPD and APD). Significant pre- to posttreatment improvement on most of the outcome variables was noted. Those not reaching significance were in the expected direction. On the Social Phobia Endstate Functioning Index (SPEFI), 84% achieved at least a moderate improvement rating at posttreatment. This compares with 33% of the generalized subtype in the Turner, Beidel, and Jacob (1994) study. Therefore,

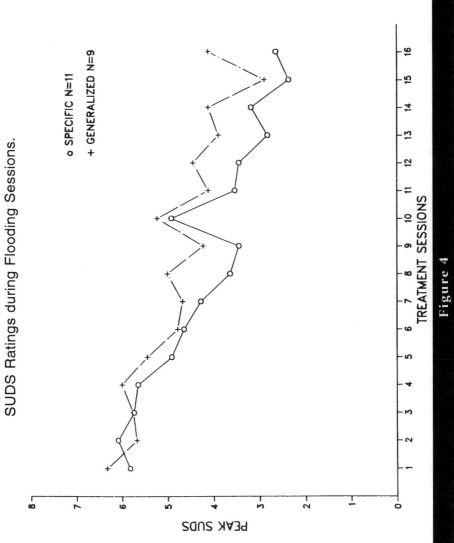

SUDS Ratings during Flooding Sessions.

o SPECIFIC N=11

+ GENERALIZED N=9

Figure 4

Note: Reprinted from Turner, Beidel, Long, & Greenhouse (1992) with permission.

this treatment strategy appeared to result in improved outcome in the generalized subtype.

SET is designed not only to reduce social anxiety but also to improve interpersonal skill and social functioning. Patients participated in two role-play encounters designed to depict traditional social interactions. Based on the judgment of an independent rater, there was significant improvement from pre- to posttreatment on ratings of social effectiveness and anxiety. Given the severity of the sample (including the presence of OCPD and APD) and the relatively short duration of treatment, these results are indeed impressive. Furthermore, treatment gains were maintained over a 2-year follow-up period (Turner et al., 1995). Further conclusions regarding the efficacy of SET must await the results of a controlled trial.

Other Variables Associated With Outcome in Social Phobia Treatment

Although the results of extant studies are impressive, little effort has been directed toward elucidating important clinical features that might predict who will or will not respond well to treatment. We alluded to the issue of subtype response above, but other obvious factors include degree of symptom severity and the presence of concurrent Axis I and II conditions. Similarly, little attention has been directed toward examining the characteristics of those who refuse treatment and those who drop out of treatment. To address this issue, Turner, Beidel, Wolff, Spaulding, and Jacob (1996) reexamined data from the Turner, Beidel, and Jacob (1994) study.

With respect to treatment refusers, 15.5% of those eligible for the study refused to enter. Examination of demographic and clinical characteristics of the refusers revealed that there were no significant differences between refusers and acceptors on gender, age, marital status, educational attainment, or age of onset. Additionally, there were no differences in percentage of subjects with a comorbid diagnosis or distribution of social phobia subtype. There were no significant differences between the refusers and acceptors on self-report, independent evaluator ratings, or behavioral assessment data, either. Interestingly, however, the refusers were rated as slightly less severe by the diagnostic interviewer than the acceptors on a rating of social phobia severity.

When examining the drop-out rate, it was found that 12.7% of those who entered treatment dropped out. This rate is considerably lower than the 23.4% reported by Juster, Heimberg, and Engelberg (1995), but similar to the average of 14% gleaned from other published studies.[1] It appears, then, that the drop-out rate for behavioral treatment studies of social phobia is rather small. There were no significant differences between drop-outs and completers on demographic variables or clinical features (percentage of patients with a comorbid diagnosis, distribution of social phobia subtype, and rating of severity), or on self-report, independent evaluator, or behavioral assessment.

The presence of an Axis I or II condition did not affect the manner in which patients responded to the flooding treatment. Thus, these data indicate that the presence of a comorbid diagnosis did not affect the patient's reactivity during the flooding session, nor did it affect the habituation process. When judgments pertaining to treatment outcome were based on the presence of a comorbid condition, however, there were significant differences on a number of measures. In each case, those with a comorbid condition were less improved than those without. Thus, although both groups improved significantly, overall level of functioning differed at posttreatment for the two groups.

Outcome differences between the specific and the generalized social phobia subtypes particularly were illuminating. The process data indicated that the imaginal flooding intervention produced equal increases in subjective distress during treatment sessions and both groups showed equivalent rates of habituation across sessions. In addition, the treatment outcome data were consistent with the process data. When con-

---

[1] Butler, G., Cullington, A., Munby, M., Amies, P., & Gelder, M. (1984); Emmelkamp, P. M. G., Mersch, P. P., Vissia, E., & Van Der Helm, M. (1985); Falloon, I. R. H., Lloyd, G. G., & Harpin, R. E. (1981); Fava, S. G., & Canestrari, R. (1989); Hope, D. A., Heimberg, R. G., & Bruch, M. A. (1995); Jerremalm, A., Jansson, L., & Ost, L. (1986); Lucock, M. P., & Salkovskis, P. M. (1988); Mattick, R. P., & Peters, L. (1988); Mersch, P. P. A. (1995); Mersch, P. P. A., Emmelkamp, P. M. G., & Lips, C. (1991); Newman, M. G., Hofmann, S. G., Trabert, W., Roth, W. T., & Taylor, C. B. (1994); Scholing, A., & Emmelkamp, P. M. G. (1993a, 1993b); Turner, S. M., Beidel, D. C., Cooley, M. R., Woody, S. R., & Messer, S. C. (1994); Turner, S. M., Beidel, D. C., & Jacob, R. G. (1994); Wlazlo, Z., Schroeder-Hartwig, K., Hand, I., Kaiser, G., & Munchau, N. (1990).

trolling for pretreatment differences, posttreatment scores were not different, with the exception of the SPAI difference score and the FQ Social Phobia subscale (both of which reflected the more severe clinical picture of the generalized subtype). Also, on a composite measure of overall improvement, there was no significant difference between the percentage of those with the generalized and those with the specific subtype who achieved moderate or significant improvement. Thus, the treatment produced equivalent degrees of improvement for both subtypes of social phobia.

However, actual posttreatment scores for the two groups indicated that there was still a substantial difference in the clinical status of these patients even after this intensive behavioral program. Across all categories of outcome data (self-report, behavioral, and independent evaluator ratings), at posttreatment patients with the generalized subtype had a significantly more severe clinical picture than patients with the specific, despite having made equivalent gains during treatment. Similarly, the statistically significant difference in subtype percentages achieving high endstate status indicated that those with the generalized subtype were not functioning at a level as high as their specific counterparts. These data suggested that although flooding produced equivalent amounts of change within both subtypes over treatment, it was not enough for most of the patients with the generalized subtype to reach the same endstate functioning level as their specific subtype counterparts (i.e., a level similar to but not the same as controls who had no disorder).

These data indicated that when comorbid conditions are present, patients with social phobia still respond positively to behavioral (flooding) treatment, but their general clinical status is not as improved as that of those patients without comorbid conditions at posttreatment. Similarly, the patients with specific and generalized subtype improved equally over treatment, but the overall functioning status of the patients with the generalized subtype was less than the functioning status of those with the specific subtype at posttreatment. The results of the Turner, Beidel, Cooley, Woody, and Messer (1994) study suggested that when social skills training is added to exposure treatment, patients with the generalized subtype achieved a clinical status similar to that of patients with the specific subtype (treated with exposure alone) at posttreatment. However, this will need to be substantiated in a study in which the different treatments are compared directly.

Summary of Outcome Findings

Based on the available literature from individual controlled outcome studies, substantive reviews, and meta-analytic studies, there are a number of behavioral and cognitive–behavioral treatments that have some degree of utility in the treatment of social phobia. With respect to the behavioral treatments, all of the interventions used to date (various methods of exposure, SST, SET) have some degree of efficacy after relatively short courses of treatment. Overall, it is clear that behavioral treatment is superior to placebo and that differences between treatment variations (i.e., cognitive–behavioral vs. behavioral) are minor when each embodies some form of exposure. Exposure was a component in virtually all of the behavioral or cognitive–behavioral treatments (one condition in the Mattick et al., 1989, and one in the Scholing and Emmelkamp, 1996, study did not contain exposure). This suggests that exposure is an essential ingredient in current treatments for social phobia. This is illustrated further by the results of meta-analytic studies as well as substantive reviews, and when the evidence is combined, it is clear that exposure is the critical element in current treatment. However, to date, there is no clear consensus about which form of exposure is best. In addition, SST alone results in significant improvement of patients with social phobia as well and, when combined with exposure, appears to be particularly efficacious for treatment of the generalized subtype. There is little evidence that the addition of cognitive strategies enhances the efficacy of behavioral treatment (exposure or social skills training). On the other hand, there were few data to suggest that they detract from the efficacy of exposure or social skills training. Given the current findings, it appears that any of the strategies used in current outcome studies is a reasonable choice for clinicians as long as they include an effectively administered exposure component. Furthermore, the treatments are short term, usually lasting about 3 months.

An important and reasonably consistent finding across most studies is that treatment gains are not only maintained but additional improvement often can be seen at follow-up in the absence of continued treatment. This suggests that patients learned skills during treatment that facilitated additional improvement over time, impressive findings given the relatively brief treatment periods. Most studies have follow-up of at least 6 months, but there are some data for 2-year follow-up and a smaller amount at 5-year follow-up.

Despite the generally encouraging findings, there is some indication that many patients are in need of additional treatment following the typical regimens that have been used. This information comes from several sources. First, there is some indication that booster sessions were needed during follow-up in some cases (e.g., Butler et al., 1984; Mattick & Peters, 1988; Mattick et al., 1989; Mersch et al., 1989, 1991). Second, Mersch et al. (1991) indicated that 9 patients had relapsed at 14-month follow-up. Interestingly, those in need of additional treatment were described as being deficient in social skills. Third, it was our impression from the patients treated in the Turner, Beidel, and Jacob (1994) study that additional treatment would have been helpful in a number of cases, even though the treatment period was longer in this study than in many others. Thus, it is clear that we need to determine further what are the improvement-limiting factors in these treatments. Is it related to characteristics of patients, the treatments, or both? Finally, our clinical experience is that some patients can benefit from longer treatment periods, and many can benefit from such self-improvement groups such as Toastmasters or Toastmistress. Clinicians should make decisions as to who might benefit from longer programs or extra interventions on an individual basis.

TREATMENT IMPLEMENTATION

Whether intentionally, unintentionally, or because a positive, trusting relationship has yet to fully develop, patients with social phobia sometimes initially minimize the extent of their fears in terms of intensity or pervasiveness or both. For example, some patients initially enter treatment indicating that they have concerns only in public speaking situations. However, as we discussed in chapter 5, a detailed assessment often reveals a much more pervasive fear pattern. In many instances, their virtual "cocoon" has become so comfortable that patients do not recognize their extensive social isolation. In other cases there seems to be intense investment in seeing their disorder as very circumscribed. Numerous issues of clinical management are presented in chapter 6, and the reader is referred there for this critical information. To reiterate briefly, the clinician needs to be aware of the role of various clinical issues in the intervention process. In the remainder of this chapter, we will provide an overview of how the major behavioral and cognitive–behavioral treatments are implemented and examine several important clinical parameters. Because exposure is the most critical element of effective treatments, we will begin our discussion here.

Exposure

Exposure involves the patient confronting the feared situation or stimuli. It is the key ingredient in the reduction of anxiety and fear in social phobia and virtually all anxiety disorders. Exposure per se is not a treatment because there are different methods that are based on different behavioral models (cf. Barlow, 1988). Exposure is a generic term used to describe a group of treatments based on different theoretical models of fear reduction. Habituation is the most frequently invoked mechanism of fear reduction to account for change produced by exposure strategies, although there are cognitive interpretations of the process as well. We will limit our discussion here to the nature of exposure treatment, methods of exposure typically used in social phobia treatment, and procedural variables associated with treatment implementation.

When exposure treatment is used, the expectation is that over time the patient will habituate (i.e., cease to become emotionally aroused) to stimuli that previously elicited an emotional reaction. Habituation usually is determined by changes in physiological measures such as pulse rate or blood pressure or, alternatively, subjective feelings of distress such as self-ratings on a rating scale (see chapter 5 in this volume).

At times both types of indices are used. As we have stated throughout this volume, emotional distress is elicited when a patient with social phobia is placed in a social performance situation in which arousal (either physical, subjective, or both) tends to be elicited. If the individual remains in the distressing situation for a sufficient period of time, arousal will decrease (see Figure 5). This decrement is usually referred to as *within-session habituation* (because it occurs during the course of an exposure session). Repeated contact between an individual and the feared stimulus over a number of days hastens the habituation process, and, with sufficient pairings, the stimulus loses its ability to elicit the fear response. When this happens, there eventually is little arousal elicited upon exposure to the feared situation and between-session habituation has occurred (see Figure 6). Some patients report that they have tried this intervention "on their own" and it was unsuccessful. The difference is that when patients attempt this type of exposure alone, the

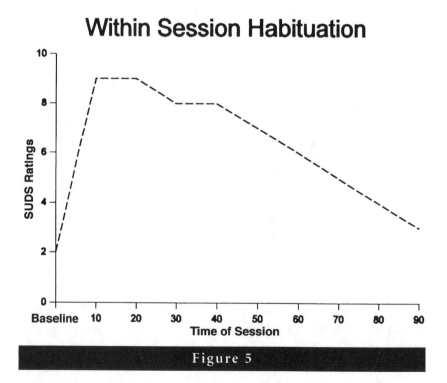

Figure 5

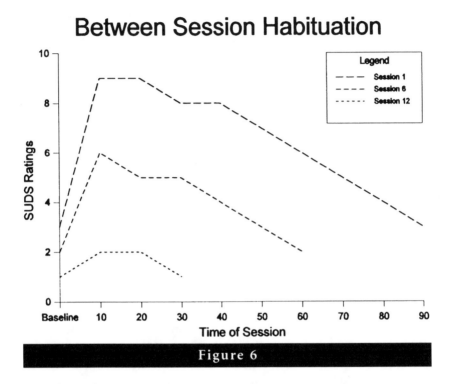

Figure 6

distress they experience is so severe that they cannot continue to maintain contact with the feared stimulus (i.e., long enough for habituation to occur). Rather, they escape or avoid anxiety-producing situations. Escape or avoidance prior to habituation can function to increase or sustain the intensity of the fear response. In contrast, by maintaining contact through exposure treatment, within-session and between-session habituation occurs, and thus the fear response dissipates.

Imaginal Exposure

Imaginal exposure involves presenting the patient with feared situations or stimuli using the process of imagery. The construction of imaginal scenes is required for this form of exposure. The stimulus cues making up the scene are critical to the success of the intervention. In constructing imaginal scenes for social phobia treatment, it is important that the scene captures what we refer to as the *core fear*. By core fear, we mean those critical features that serve to instigate and maintain the anxiety and fear. Although patients with social phobia are described as fearing scrutiny and negative evaluation by others, the problem is more complicated than this implies, and the specific parameters associated with the fear will differ considerably for individual patients. For example, one patient sought treatment for public speaking fears in our clinic. This fear had been present since about midadolescence following an experience in which he was making a presentation in his class and did not do very well. Since that time, during attempts at public presentations he experienced a host of somatic symptoms whenever he spoke before an audience. These included blushing, rapid heart beat, shaking, and stuttering. Because the patient was afraid that others would see these reactions, his anxiety always increased whenever one of these symptoms was perceived, setting off a vicious cycle of spiraling fear. Analysis of this case revealed that the primary concern was that others would be able to see the physiological responses and wonder how anyone could be that anxious. In essence, this patient would be evaluated in a less than positive light by others. The core fear in this case was that others would see and evaluate this reaction in a negative light, and the composition of the audience did not appear to matter. Thus, the scene for this patient would need to include a scenario where others in fact clearly recognized these exaggerated physical symptoms and made a negative evaluation (i.e., the patient must experience the negative consequence during exposure).

On the other hand, consider the case of Mr. X, the head of computer operations for a Fortune 500 company who also reported a severe public speaking phobia. Mr. X did not have a degree in computer science but had become head of the department because of his leadership and organizational skills. Mr. X could give talks (with some difficulty) to groups of people if the audience did not contain computer experts. Size of the audience was of little relevance. Rather, the critical feature was the composition of the audience. In this case, Mr. X harbored considerable doubts about his abilities to head a computer department. He was concerned that his peers would detect his inadequacies, discover how uninformed he really was, and learn that he was not capable of heading the department. In this case, the core fear was the patient's doubts about his own abilities and his peers' evaluation of his intellect and work performance. Thus, a scene incorporating the core fear in this case would include all of the presumed weakness being revealed in front of his peers and the feared negative evaluations in fact being made. From these case scenarios, it can be seen easily that although both patients had speaking fears, and indeed they feared negative evaluation, the parameters associated with the fear were quite different. Effective exposure for these two cases would require exposure to somewhat different cues. It has been our experience that the core fear concept is difficult to grasp by the novice therapist and those not trained in behavior therapy. Also, failure to understand this concept, in our opinion, frequently is related to failure to obtain positive results with exposure treatment. Both of these cases serve to illustrate the importance of addressing what the patient fears will happen (i.e., the catastrophic fears).

Another important element in scene construction is the inclusion of all of the relevant variables of importance (Lang et al., 1968). This means that the scene needs to allow the patient to experience those unique physiological and cognitive symptom patterns associated with their fear. An imaginal scene must capture the essence of each patient's fear and the associated parameters if habituation is to be achieved. Failure to do so could result in incomplete habituation, which has been shown to result in return of fear (Craske & Rachman, 1987). An example of an imaginal exposure scene used in treatment is presented in Table 13. As background clinical information, this patient was a 28 year old male who had received a law degree from a prestigious law school. However, he had been unable to practice as a trial attorney because of his extreme fear when arguing before a judge and jury. When doing so, he experienced heart palpitations, profuse sweating, and blushing. He feared that he would mispronounce words or be unable to speak and that others would criticize his performance. The core of his fear was that he really was an imposter (i.e., not qualified to fill this role) and that others would detect that he was not intelligent

Table 13

Sample Imaginal Flooding Scene for an Adult With Social Phobia

You are arguing a case before a judge and jury. This is an important case, and the senior partners from your firm are here in attendance. The case has received substantial attention from the media, and many reporters are in attendance as well. You are worried about the appearance you will make and whether these people will see you as incompetent and unfit to be an attorney. What if you make a fool of yourself? Your heart is beating rapidly, your palms are sweating, and you feel flushed. You begin to stumble over your words. You can see several members of the jury are yawning. The judge and prosecuting attorney are wondering how you ever passed the bar exam, let alone graduated from such a prestigious law school. The senior partners are shaking their heads in dismay about the mistake they made in hiring you. The media is smirking at your incompetence—you cannot even make a simple argument in your area of expertise.

enough or competent enough to be a trial attorney at a major law firm.

The core fear in this scene was the patient's fear that everyone, but particularly other attorneys whom he respected, would discover his perceived incompetence. Thus, it was not simply performing in a court room that was the primary concern, but rather the judgments of those assumed to be peers and authority figures and the subsequent catastrophic consequence (i.e., these individuals would discover his incompetence). Therefore, this was the core fear included in the imaginal exposure treatment. In addition, physiological cues were included because they represented an important element of the fear complex (i.e., the patient feared that his physical symptoms would be apparent to others). Furthermore, these symptoms, through associative conditioning, had acquired the ability to elicit fear in their own right.

Implementing Imaginal Exposure

Exposure procedures require that the patient stay in contact with the stimulus long enough for habituation to occur. In the case of imaginal exposure, this means that the patient is required to imagine the scene on a prolonged basis. If the session is terminated prematurely, sensitization may occur and there may be an increase, instead of a decrease, in anxiety. On the basis of the available literature, sessions should last for 90 minutes at the minimum. Preferably, the session should conclude when the patient's distress level has been reduced by 50% of the within-session reactivity over baseline (usually judged by using the patients self-rating of anxiety). Figure 7 illustrates a typical response during an early flooding session. Ending the session at 60 minutes would have been counterproductive and could have increased sensitization to the stimulus. Ending the session at 90 minutes would be acceptable (50%

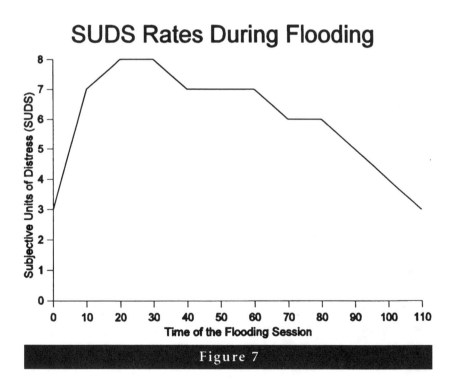

Figure 7

reduction in subjective units of distress, or SUDS, level was reached); however, extending the sessions to 110 minutes would be preferable (SUDS level returned to baseline). Therefore, at 90 or 110 minutes within-session habituation was achieved (by two different definitions). Across sessions, the time required for habituation typically decreases, therefore session length decreases as well. Session length tends to be longer early in treatment and shorter as treatment progresses.

Setting

Imaginal exposure should be carried out in a quiet setting with low lighting. Such a setting is ideal because the intrusion of noise can be distracting and interfere with the patient's ability to concentrate on the imagery. We conduct this treatment in a sound-attenuated room. In the absence of such space, one might choose an internally situated room far away from the possibility of outside noise. In any event, the quietest possible setting should be sought for imaginal exposure sessions.

Spacing of Sessions

Generally, the literature on exposure treatment, although not specifically for social phobia, suggests that sessions occurring within close time proximity (massed sessions) are preferable to those that are spaced further apart. In our treatment program, we use once-per-week sessions for individual flooding, and once-per-week SST sessions (for a total of two sessions per week). Most patients, in our experience, find it difficult to attend treatment sessions more than twice per week. However, one alternative is to use several days of massed treatment (e.g., 10 days), as we do with obsessive–compulsive disorder. Treatment is then reduced in intensity on the basis of the patient's clinical status. Typically, although treatment time is extensive during the early stages of the intervention, overall positive response is achieved more quickly, and total treatment time does not differ in the end. This highly intensive strategy also is useful when there is need to obtain quick relief (e.g., when the patient comes for treatment because of an imminent task that must be completed).

Emergence of New Material During Exposure (Imaginal or In Vivo)

Participation in exposure sessions often will prompt the revelation of new material that is part of the core fear. This material in many cases had not been recognized by the patient prior to the intervention. In many instances, this material consists of additional situations, individuals, or activities that create social distress. Emergence of new material occurs frequently during early exposure sessions. When it does, the new material should be incorporated into the subsequent exposure sessions.

Anxiety Level

The goal of flooding is to make certain that contact with the fear-producing stimuli takes place. The patient's role is to participate fully in the session by imagining the scene (or to participate maximally in the exposure task in vivo; see the section on in vivo exposure below). Thus, although some degree of anxiety is expected, it is not the patient's responsibility to generate distress. It is crucial that patients understand their role in the exposure session. Otherwise, the patient's focus likely will be on increasing and maintaining a high level of arousal, rather than on focusing on the fear cues.

Attention and Distraction

Patients often want to know if they should "do anything" during the exposure sessions, such as trying to relax or using coping statements to assist in fear reduction. Distraction during exposure sessions has been found to interfere with habituation in patients with obsessive–compulsive disorder (e.g., Grayson, Foa, & Steketee, 1986), and this probably is the case for social phobia as well. Therefore, no method of distraction is recommended.

Relaxation After the Exposure Session

A short debriefing session conducted after the exposure intervention should allow the clinician to determine whether the patient is suffering from any residual distress. Clinicians treating patients with posttraumatic stress disorder (PTSD) often provide relaxation instructions to patients to decrease their anxiety after the exposure session. However, this is inconsistent with the habituation model that underlies intensive exposure treatment. Exposure (whatever its mode of presentation) continues until a significant reduction in anxiety is achieved. Therefore, the patient should not be significantly distressed at the end of the therapy session, and thus there should be no need for relaxation training. If the patient does not show a decrease in emotional distress over time, the session might be too short, the core fear may not have been incorporated into the scene, or the diagnosis might be inaccurate or incomplete.

Problems in Implementing Imaginal Exposure

The issue of the inability to use imagery was discussed above. Another potential problem in using imaginal exposure is that some patients engage in cognitive maneuvers to avoid the image. This should not be surprising because patients have spent much of their lives attempting to avoid the stimuli that they now are asked to confront, and the thought of doing so elicits at least some anxiety and fear. To avoid the feared stimuli, they may imagine themselves coping well with the situation, imagining that other people cannot perceive their distress or that the performance is going well rather than poorly. They also may attempt to alter the scene to focus on certain elements that are less anxiety producing. For example, if the patient imagining the scene in Table 13 were using coping behaviors, he might imagine performing flawlessly before the jury and enjoying the presentation, rather than falling apart. Although coping responses can serve to reduce anxiety temporarily, they interfere with the habituation process (Craske, Rapee, & Barlow, 1992). During exposure, and particularly during flooding, there should be an initial increase in distress, followed by a decline over time (habituation). If there are no signs of arousal or distress during the exposure session, the patient should be asked to describe the scene aloud exactly as imagined. If coping behaviors are being used (e.g., the patient imagines doing very well), this strategy often reveals them. Asking the patient to describe the scene aloud also provides a check to ensure that the person is able to imagine the scene. If coping behaviors are being used, patients need to be reminded to devote full attention to the material presented. If the scene is constructed correctly, anxiety should be elicited as a result of the presentation of the core fear.

As noted earlier, the identification of the core fear is the crucial element for the success of the intervention. The scene itself is really just a vehicle to convey the important core fear cues. For example, those with public speaking anxiety may not fear speaking before just any group. Rather, the critical elements often relate to specific aspects of the situation, such as the size and composition of the audience, the type of material to be presented, and specific aspects of the client's behavior. The core fear also includes the meaning of these situations, particularly what patients fear may happen in the situation (e.g., something that will be embarrassing or humiliating) and that others will think badly of them as a result. Therefore, a person with a public speaking fear may be fearful of making a mistake and may fear that others will attribute this fear to the patient's lack of intelligence (incompetence). Others fear that individuals will conclude that the patient is undeserving of a position he or she holds. Still other patients fear that individuals will judge the patient to be of a lower social status than the audience. The core fear is unique for each individual, thus a unique scene must be constructed for each patient.

An often asked question is whether the therapist should present one scene or several different scenes. Even if the patient reports feeling anxious in different situations, such as speaking in public, eating in public, engaging in everyday conversations, and being assertive, the core fear usually cuts across all of these situations. If the clinician has done a proper behavioral analysis and identified the core fear cues, there typically is no need to construct multiple imaginal scenes. Conversely, scenes can be administered in hierarchical fashion, and the clinician might choose this approach when there is concern about patient oversensitivity (see discussion of those with APD, below).

In Vivo Exposure

Exposure conducted *in vivo* means that the individual is exposed to the feared situation or stimuli in real life. In vivo exposure can be carried out in an intensive fashion, or it can be implemented gradually (i.e., through a hierarchy). In vivo exposure is conducted in the same manner as imaginal exposure, and the issue of identifying and addressing the core fears are paramount here as well. In addition, all of the other issues discussed in relation to imaginal exposure pertain to in vivo exposure. The unique challenge in using in vivo exposure is to be able to create the real-life stimuli necessary for the treatment. In settings where trainees and other colleagues are available, the problem is lessened to some degree but not eliminated totally. This is because some of the feared consequences simply cannot be replicated. Thus, the requirements for constructing in vivo exposure opportunities presents the therapist with a considerable challenge. As experience with treating patients with social phobia accumulates, clinicians will be able increasingly to draw on that expertise to generate exposure opportunities. One alternative to creating analogue exposure opportunities is to have patients carry out their own exposure without therapist assistance. This might be possible in some cases, assuming that the specific nature of the individual's fear is understood by the patient and therapist. However, as we have indicated throughout this volume, we have found that *self*-exposure sessions for patients with social phobia are very difficult to accomplish. This conclusion is supported by the work of Al-Kubaisy et al. (1992) described earlier. It has been our clinical experience that in most instances the patient's fear prevents him or her from being able to stay in the situation for an extended period of time. After all, if that were possible, the patient might not have sought therapy in the first place. If the therapist is not able to accompany the patient during the in vivo exposure, an alternative strategy is to use imaginal exposure initially and then follow up with in vivo once the fear has been moderately reduced. Also, in some cases, significant others might be used as surrogate therapists.

Selecting Imaginal or In Vivo Exposure

There is no specific rule regarding the selection of an imaginal or in vivo exposure approach for patients with social phobia, and both have been used successfully. The overall goal of the intervention is to adequately capture and expose the patient to the entire fear complex (i.e., those parameters that contribute to the fear response). In our experience, some amount of imaginal exposure is desirable for most patients with social phobia, but particularly for those with the generalized subtype. In some cases, the intervention may require a combination of both imaginal and in vivo procedures. In these cases the treatment begins with imaginal sessions, and, following success through imagery, the same material is covered as much as possible in vivo. Practical considerations as well as clinical parameters sometimes dictate which approach should be used.

One practical consideration is whether or not a patient can use imagery. Although most patients can do this successfully, occasionally difficulty with imagery will present a problem. If the ability to instigate imagery proves to be difficult, imagery training often helps. However, for those who cannot benefit from this training, in vivo exposure will be necessary. As we have mentioned before, it has been our clinical experience that many who have difficulty with imaginal procedures are those with concomitant OCPD or significant OCPD symptoms. Because of their rigid patterns of thought and behavior, these individuals often have great difficulty imagining a particular scene. They often are so concerned with scene details and spend such an inordinate amount of time making sure that they have all the details "correct" that they are unable to imagine the entire scene and participate fully in the procedure. For example, one patient who was successfully treated with in vivo exposure in our clinic had difficulty focusing on the imaginal scene content because he could not decide whether the table where he was supposed to imagine sitting was square or round. Ambivalence over this detail prevented him from focusing on the most relevant aspects of the imaginal scene (i.e., the specific fear cues). This is but one example, and this problem can be manifested in many different ways. Other examples include preoccupation with ensuring that the exact image is imagined or resistance to the notion that an imagery strategy can be useful. Any of these factors can interfere with effective imaginal exposure. Therefore, if these tendencies cannot be overcome by instruction or imagery training, an in vivo strategy may be necessary.

Another issue that might dictate the use of a particular strategy is whether or not the feared situations can be accessed in real life, and whether the appropriate people necessary to replicate the feared situation, or situations, are available. For example, some patients primarily are concerned about interactions with authority figures. In other instances, in vivo exposure may require the use of students, hospital volunteers, or other clinic personnel to serve as audience members for speeches or social interactions. In some cases, when it is not possible to have such individuals available at the clinic for an in vivo strategy, patients might be able to carry out the exposure sessions alone or with the assistance of a significant other or friend. However, for other patients, these alternatives may not be feasible, and then an imaginal procedure might be the better choice.

It is clear that constructing in vivo exposure situations requires creativity on the part of the therapist. Some patients may be able to quickly generate appropriate assignments. Others will require suggestions or firm direction from the clinician. Likewise, some patients may be able to successfully carry out in vivo exposure sessions on their own (i.e., set up presentations at work in order to practice speaking in front of a group). For others, the clinician may have to accompany the patient to the site of the exposure assignment, at least until the patient is comfortable carrying out the procedure alone. Simulated interactions (role-plays) in the clinician's office may allow for the replication of some situations not available in natural settings. Finally, for those core fears that are not readily available in the course of typical social interactions, some exposure sessions may be replicated in the clinician's office. If such is not possible (as might be the case for many clinicians engaged in private practice settings), an imaginal strategy may be the only alternative.

Use of Homework

Some type of homework assignment typically is used with exposure treatment regardless of the particular strategy chosen. Thus, when imaginal exposure is used, it is typical to give the patient small in vivo assignments to carry out in the natural environment. Although these are not necessarily given in a strict hierarchical fashion, an effort is made to choose those tasks that have a high likelihood of being completed successfully. Homework is just as important for in vivo exposure if the primary strategy is for the treatment to be carried out in the office under therapist direction. Homework is important in aiding the transfer effects from the clinic to the natural environment, and also can provide important information on the effects being obtained from treatment.

Social Skills Training

As noted earlier, there is some evidence that patients with social phobia, particularly the generalized subtype, manifest social skill deficiencies. Furthermore, treatment outcome studies using SST individually (Stravynski, Marks, & Yule, 1982) as well as in combination with other strategies, have produced favorable outcome results. We now turn to a discussion of how to implement SST.

The goal of SST is to help patients acquire those skills necessary for successful social discourse. In addition, as we discussed earlier in this chapter, those with social phobia appear to manifest some rather specific skill deficiencies that also need to be addressed. Furthermore, our SST component includes attention to the skill and art of making speeches because patients with social phobia show substantial deficits in their ability to compose effective presentations. Content areas used in our SST program are presented in Table 14; also see section on SET in this chapter.

SST programs normally make use of basic teaching strategies and include instruction, modeling, behavior rehearsal, corrective feedback,

Table 14
Content Areas for Social Skills Training

Initiating Conversations	Assertiveness Skills (General)
Maintaining Conversations	Assertiveness Skills (Authority Figures)
Attending and Remembering Information	Constructing the Body of a Speech
	Effectively Beginning a Speech
Establishing Friendships	Effectively Ending a Speech
Maintaining Friendships	Informal Presentations
Heterosocial Interactions	

and positive reinforcement. Although these skills can be taught individually, we feel that SST is optimal in a group setting. The training sequence is identical regardless of the format selected. Instruction provides the context for learning the task. When providing instruction, the therapist specifies all of the verbal and nonverbal parameters necessary to correctly perform the behavior that is to be learned.

Modeling then provides an opportunity to see the behavior performed correctly. The therapist first explains what should be observed and then demonstrates the skill. After completing the demonstration, the therapist reiterates the important aspects of the behavior or asks the patient to do so.

Behavior rehearsal (using role-play exercises) is the most crucial component of the skills training program because it provides the opportunity to practice the skill in a controlled environment. As a general guideline, group members should have at least two practice opportunities per instructional component (this can be modified as time permits to address the needs of individual group members). The therapist addresses problems in performance through further instruction, modeling, and rehearsal. Group treatment sessions are an optimal forum for practicing the scenes with a range of interpersonal partners (e.g., male, female, older, younger), thereby further increasing opportunities for rehearsal and generalization of skills. The response of the role-play partner can be held constant or systematically varied to illustrate specific points.

Corrective feedback is used to guide behavior in the desired direction and should be given constructively. Further modeling may be necessary to ensure that patients discriminate between desirable and less desirable performances. Feedback is given by the therapist and elicited from other participants, particularly the role-play partner. After corrective feedback, the patient practices the skill again.

Positive reinforcement is important for acquiring the new skill as well as for facilitating the training process. Some patients are anxious in any type of performance setting. Thus, even the activities that are part of the group and that are designed to ultimately reduce anxiety may be anxiety producing. Thus, SST is likely to produce some anxiety in the patients, particularly during the initial sessions. Therefore, providing positive reinforcement encourages patients to continue participation in the training group.

Implementing Social Skills Training

The clinician must first decide which social skills are in need of improvement. Consideration should be given to improvement in nonverbal skills such as eye contact, body posture, and vocal tone, in addition to verbal content skills such as greetings or assertiveness. Usually, nonverbal skills are taught in conjunction with verbal content. For example, patients are encouraged to make eye contact when they are greeting someone. The following is an example of how these procedures are used to teach patients how to introduce themselves to a stranger.

Instruction. First, the therapist provides didactic information about introductions to a stranger. This includes descriptions of settings where such introductions are appropriate (and perhaps even required), discussion regarding the proper timing of such introductions, and examples of how introductions might be accomplished. The didactic presentation should be brief (no longer than 3 minutes) and provides the background for the skill's acquisition.

Modeling. Next, the therapist models the skill to be acquired. In this case, the therapist would set the appropriate scene and then actually introduce him- or herself to a stranger. One of the group members plays the second role. The therapist acts out the introduction, using all appropriate social skills. After the introduction is completed, the therapist reiterates the crucial information. For example:

> The setting was the cafeteria in the building where I work. I knew this individual worked in an office on the same floor, but we had never met. This person smiled at me and did not seem preoccupied, so I felt that he was interested in a small conversation. I said, "Hello, we seem to work on the same floor, but we haven't been introduced. My name is Mary Jones." Then he told me his name. Then I said, "It's nice to meet you. I guess we will be seeing a lot of each other."

Behavior Rehearsal. Behavior rehearsal allows each group member to practice the skill. Initially, if there is enough time, the therapist should first practice with each patient. This will ensure that the response of the interpersonal partner is consistent. In addition, it will allow the focus of attention to remain on the patient practicing the skill. However, following one or two brief trials for each person with the therapist, group members should continue the rehearsals with each other. In this way, each group member practices with different interpersonal partners (this provides the opportunity for interaction with different people and increases the likelihood of generalization). Instructions similar to the following should be used:

> Now it is your turn to rehearse the skill. Remember to make a small comment in order to start the conversation and then introduce yourself. This is practice, so feel free to use your imagination to fill in the details of the situation. For example, you could give yourself a different occupation if you like.

After rehearsal, corrective feedback and positive reinforcement is provided. As much rehearsal as needed is provided for each group member. Each patient should have several opportunities to practice the skill and also should have the opportunity to play the role of the interpersonal partner.

Constructive Feedback. Feedback should be directed not only at the specific content being taught but at any other aspect of social performance that limits its effectiveness. Therefore, poor eye contact, inaudible voice volume, or inappropriate additional verbal content should be noted and corrected.

Positive Reinforcement. Patients should be reinforced whenever they rehearse a skill. Positive reinforcement should focus on those aspects completed correctly and any improvements. At the very least the therapist should reinforce the patient for attempting the interaction.

Once a specific skill has been acquired, the therapist proceeds to the next skill and repeats the training module. Skills training is cumulative; that is, each new skill builds upon those that were previously acquired. All sessions include concentrated practice with the particular skill introduced in that session.

Social Skills Training Scenes

For behavioral rehearsal to take place, a series of scenarios are developed to address each skill that is to be learned. These scenes are used for the role-playing exercise, which is the vehicle through which behavior rehearsal takes place (just as imaginal scenes are the vehicle through which exposure takes place). Examples of several role-play scenes are presented in Table 15.

Table 15

Sample Role Play Scenes for Social Skills Training

Social Skill	Role-Playing Scene
Initiating a Conversation	You are in the company cafeteria and there are no empty tables, so you have to sit at a table where there is one other person. You walk over to the table and say:
Heterosocial Interactions	You are on jury duty. You introduce yourself to the person sitting next to you, who tells you that he or she works in an office nearby. You, on the other hand, very rarely get to this part of town. At the lunch break, this person turns to you and says, "I know a great place for lunch. The food is good and reasonably priced. Would you like to join me?" You respond:
Assertiveness	You have been planning a weekend getaway for several weeks. Your boss tells you that you will have to work on Saturday. You will lose your deposit if you cancel the trip. Your boss says "I'm leaving now. You will have to work tomorrow to finish this. It is due on Monday." You respond:

Problems in Implementing Social Skills Training

One potential problem in SST is that patients are not familiar with behavior rehearsal (role-playing) and initially may not understand the format. However, a demonstration or two should clarify the purpose of the training. A second difficulty is that patients sometimes observe the therapist modeling the scene, then will imitate the therapist verbatim. However, the goal is to encourage patients to individualize their responses so that the words and actions feel comfortable to them.

A third potential problem is the patient's comfort level during the interaction. Behavior rehearsal requires interaction with others even if all aspects of a situation are not detailed clearly. For example, although a particular setting (e.g., you are at the mall and run into an old friend) might be described, the interaction itself evolves as a result of the on-going role-play. For many patients, their rigid cognitive styles do not allow them to interact freely in an unstructured interaction. Therefore, they may hesitate to participate in the behavior rehearsals by, for example, asking numerous questions prior to starting the interaction, such as What kind of mall is it? How well do I know this old friend? or What do we have in common? Often, these questions are avoidance tactics and sometimes reflect the rather rigid personality style frequently seen in those with social phobia. These types of delay tactics are managed by indicating that all of these details are not necessary and by encouraging the patient to simply begin the interaction.

Although there are some skill deficits that seem to define broadly the behavior of patients with social phobia, participants in any group will have varying levels of skill. Some will require more instruction and practice than others. In those cases, those who show more skill may be used to assist in the role plays.

No optimal size for social skills groups has been identified, but it is our practice to limit group size to 3 to 5 patients. Even though the size typically is rather small, group members may have varying cultural backgrounds, educational or intellectual levels, and occupations (e.g., unemployed, student, part- or full-time employment). Thus, the context of the skills training (e.g., the role-play scenes) can be modified to reflect more accurately personally realistic situations (e.g., work vs.

school). Also, goals should be individualized, depending on the patient background (i.e., difficulty in certain types of social encounters).

Homework

Homework assignments are an integral part of behavioral treatment and are used both with SST and exposure. The issues to be discussed here pertain to all cases except where the patient is carrying out exposure him- or herself. The homework assignment should be reasonable, should allow the patient the opportunity to practice the behavior of interest (skill or exposure), and should have a high likelihood of being completed successfully. Initially, therapists usually have to help patients generate homework, but later, many patients are able to take on much of this task themselves. We sometimes provide patients with a homework form in order to clearly detail the assignment and assist in compliance. In Table 16 we list sample homework assignments for some of the skills listed in Table 14.

Table 16

Sample Homework Assignments for Social Skills Training Program

Topic	Homework Assignment
Initiating Conversation	Initiate a conversation with a familiar person and a stranger.
Maintaining Conversation	Initiate a conversation with a familiar person and a stranger. During both conversations, ask at least one open-ended question.
Establishing Friendships	Identify three potential activities that you would enjoy. Attend at least two and initiate a conversation in each.
Maintaining Friendships	Twice this week, invite someone to join you in an activity.
Assertiveness	Identify a situation in which you need to be assertive. Act on it this week.

HOMEWORK ASSIGNMENT #4

Name: Date:

Identify three potential activities or situations to which you could invite a person to join you:

1.   (easy)

2.   (moderate)

3.   (difficult)

Attend two of these activities and do the following:

1. Initiate a conversation with a familiar person. To maintain the conversation, ask at least two open-ended questions relating to the same topic.

Date completed: Person's name:

Questions asked/Topic discussed:

2. Initiate a conversation with a stranger. To maintain the conversation, ask at least two open-ended questions relating to the same topic.

Date completed: Person's name:

Questions asked/Topic discussed:

3. Invite someone to join you in an activity.

Date completed: Person's name:

Activity asked person to join you in:

Person's response:

Figure 8

Initially, some patients may be reluctant to complete homework assignments, claiming that they did not have time or did not understand the assignment. In the majority of cases, this is avoidance behavior. The noncompletion must be addressed by determining whether the task is too difficult or whether the problem is reluctance due to fear. If necessary, the homework assignment may have to be altered to facilitate completion.

Social Effectiveness Therapy[2]

Social Effectiveness Therapy (SET) is a multicomponent behavioral treatment program specifically designed to decrease social anxiety, improve interpersonal skill, improve social performance (i.e., public speaking skill), and increase patient participation in social activities. With respect to interpersonal skill, it targets general social functioning as well as some unique problem areas typical of social phobia. SET incorporates a strategy to help people with social phobia recognize the inhibitory cocoon that they have constructed and in which they live. The program incorporates the most consistently effective treatment approach to social phobia (exposure) with an SST component geared specifically to the needs of the patient with social phobia. SET consists of several components: education, SST, homework assignments, flexibility exercises, exposure, and programmed practice.

SET includes both individual and group treatment. Group sessions provide patients the opportunity to practice new skills in a relatively safe setting using a variety of interpersonal partners. Thus, in addition to teaching specific skills, the group serves as a social setting, allowing some degree of in vivo exposure (performance) in social situations. However, individual sessions are deemed essential for the success of treatment. The individual sessions are used to elicit the patient's specific social fear pattern, thereby allowing the program to be tailored to the individual's specific needs. Group and individual sessions run concurrently. Patients come to the clinic twice per week, once for group sessions and once for individual exposure sessions, for 3 months. During the fourth month, there is a once per week individual session. Sessions are 90 minutes in duration. The major components of SET are detailed briefly below and are described more completely in Turner, Beidel, and

---

[2] The Social Effectiveness Therapy Treatment Manual (Turner, Beidel, & Cooley, 1994) is available from Multi-Health Systems, Inc., 65 Overlea Boulevard, Suite 210, Toronto, Ontario M4H 1P1 Canada (800) 456-3003.

Cooley (1994). The program is designed to be administered over a 4-month period of time, but can be adjusted easily to meet the needs of individual patients or groups of patients. Thus, we will describe the length of treatment as we typically use it, but the length of time for a specific treatment phase is adjustable.

Education

This phase is used to educate patients about the nature of social fears and anxiety and includes a discussion of potential etiological factors. The patient is thoroughly acquainted with the treatment program and is informed of what is expected of the patient. This can be done individually or in group. When groups are used, this session allows patients to become familiar with each other prior to specific intervention. In fact, the new acquaintances in this session might be viewed as the first in a series of steps designed to alter what typically is a rigid and inhibited social living style.

Social Skills Training

SST is implemented as previously described and consists of three phases: social environment awareness, interactional skills enhancement, and presentation skills enhancement. *Social environment awareness* teaches the nuances of when, where, and why one should start and terminate interpersonal interactions. *Interpersonal skills enhancement* addresses the mechanics (verbal and nonverbal) of how to conduct a successful social encounter, targeting unique areas for the patient with social phobia, such as specific listening exercises and topic transition mastery. The third phase of SST, *presentation skill enhancement,* teaches the mechanics of public speaking, with respect to speech construction and delivery. The goal is to assist the patient in producing well organized, interesting presentations that will assist in creating an overall positive impression.

Exposure

The second major component of SET is the provision of exposure to the anxiety-producing stimuli. The imaginal as well as in vivo exposure components used in this program are implemented as previously described in this chapter. Imaginal exposure is conducted in 12 sessions during the first 12 weeks of the 16-week treatment program (12 individualized treatment sessions held once per week). Individual sessions are used so that exposure can be directed at the patient's specific fears. In addition, some fears, such as those related to catastrophic results of a failed social interaction, can best be addressed imaginally.

Programmed Practice (In Vivo Exposure)

The last 4 weeks of the 16-week individualized sessions consist of weekly planning of in vivo homework exposure assignments. The therapist and patient meet to develop specific in vivo exposure assignments that the patient will carry out between weekly sessions. The expectation for the scope of social activities will be expanded during these sessions, consistent with the patient's newly acquired social skills and decreased anxiety in these settings. These sessions are used to provide assistance to those who might be reluctant to try out their newly acquired skills, to reinforce independent planning of social encounters, and to stimulate and assist those who need encouragement to plan social activities on their own. However, the emphasis during these sessions is on the patient's assuming control of the therapy. Several exposure assignments are developed each week, and sessions are 90 minutes in length.

Cognitive Restructuring

As we have noted throughout this book, adults, and perhaps adolescents, with social phobia worry about how they will be perceived by others. In some instances, this worry may be just an uncomfortable feeling of dread. In other instances, patients report specific cognitions in association with specific situations or tasks. In most cases, these are negative thoughts, such as "Why bother? I will just make a fool of myself," or "I'll say something stupid and be so embarrassed." Although careful assessment indicates that these thoughts can be eliminated through the use of traditional exposure strategies, many psychologists have chosen to address these and other negative cognitions directly through the use of cognitive restructuring procedures. Below is a description of the cognitive restructuring procedures used by Heimberg and his colleagues in CBGT for social phobia.

The rationale presented to patients is that events do not cause anxiety; it is the thoughts about those events that cause one to be anxious. Therefore, changing thoughts can change emotions (however, there is no actual empirical support for this rationale—at least none that does not also include an element of exposure). Cognitive restructuring is used in the context of exposure simulations. Thus, it occurs in conjunction with exposure to the feared stimulus. Cognitive restructuring is taught early in the CBGT program to facilitate acquisition of these skills so that they become part of the exposure simulations and homework assignments. Heimberg (1991) lists five goals to be achieved through the initial training in cognitive restructuring: (a) reconceptualizing thoughts as hypotheses rather than facts, (b) becoming aware of maladaptive thinking, (c) acquiring skills for identifying cognitive distortions, (d) becoming aware of the connection between maladaptive thoughts and anxiety, and (e) acquiring skills for challenging and changing negative thoughts. These skills are acquired through modeling and homework assignments.

Initially, the therapist models negative cognitions that he or she might have had in a distressful situation (e.g., when giving a presentation). Then, each of these negative thoughts are examined carefully using the following questions: (a) How would an objective observer view the situation? (b) What is the evidence that the view of the patient with social phobia is the only way to view the situation? and (c) What are alternative views? For example, a negative thought might be, "I'll forget what I want to say." To dispute this thought, the person might say, "In the past, I never forgot what I was going to say, even though I was very nervous. Even if it does not come out perfectly, the important thing is that the audience understands. If they don't understand, they will ask me a question and I can clarify what I wanted to say." After the therapist models disputing a number of negative thoughts, patients are given some initial practice in recognizing their own negative thoughts and disputing them. The patients are given a homework assignment to record all socially distressful situations over the next week and the negative thoughts that accompany these situations.

At the next session, homework is reviewed and the patient is given a list of potential cognitive distortions. Several such lists are available (Burns, 1980; Heimberg, 1991; Persons, 1989). The list in Table 17 is from Heimberg (1991). All of these cognitive distortions are discussed with the patient to ensure understanding and relevance to social phobia.

Next, patients participate in a series of exercises designed to teach them how to dispute the negative thoughts that they have learned to identify. Patients are given a problematic situation, are then asked to generate potential negative thoughts, and then are directed to dispute the negative cognitions (by asking questions such as "Is that for certain? What evidence exists for that conclusion?"). The final step is to generate more rational responses (thoughts) to replace the negative cognitions. Again, the homework assignment follows the content of the group session and requires the patient to monitor and record their (a) negative thoughts in stressful situations, (b) questions used to dispute the negative thoughts, and (c) substituted rational responses.

Table 17
Common Cognitive Distortions

All or Nothing Thinking
Overgeneralizing
Mental Filtering
Disqualifying the Positive
Jumping to Conclusions
Magnifying or Minimizing
Catastrophizing
Emotional Reasoning
Making "Should" Statements
Mislabeling
Personalizing

The ultimate goal of cognitive restructuring is for the patient to acquire a set of cognitive skills that can be applied in distressful social situations. Thus, the final step in cognitive restructuring is for the patient to use these skills whenever he or she feels anxious in social settings. In CBGT, the patient is given numerous group exposure opportunities (called exposure simulations) to practice cognitive restructuring. Designing exposure simulations is similar to designing any type of in vivo exposure session and can cover the entire range of situations that elicit distress. Heimberg (1991) noted that, unlike an in vivo exposure session, CBGT exposure simulations can be molded to the exact needs of the individual patient because other group members can serve as the interpersonal partners during the simulation. Exposure simulations are 10 minutes in length, and SUDS levels are assessed at 1-minute intervals.

Implementing Cognitive Restructuring

Prior to actually implementing cognitive restructuring, the patient first must learn the rudiments of the procedure. Therefore, in an early treatment session, the clinician first introduces the rationale for this procedure and provides examples of common negative thoughts associated with social situations. Following this, the therapist must teach patients to question the veracity of his or her negative thoughts and to generate alternative explanations. Finally, the clinician assigns homework tasks to help the patient begin to recognize negative thoughts and generate alternatives on his or her own.

At the next session, the therapist introduces the various types of negative distortions that may be found in the negative thought patterns of those with social phobia. Then, the clinician teaches patients all the steps in cognitive restructuring: identify negative distortions, dispute the negative thoughts, and generate rational alternatives. Again, homework is assigned for continued practice of these skills.

At all other sessions and for homework, the patient applies cognitive restructuring procedures when in distressful situations. These situations may consist of exposure situations or actual in vivo exposure settings. In CBGT, for example, there are at least three exposure simulations per patient per session (Heimberg, 1991).

Problems in Implementing Cognitive Restructuring

According to Heimberg (1991), there are several problems that may occur when implementing cognitive restructuring. First, patients might deny the presence of negative cognitions despite high distress when in social settings, instead focusing on their feelings. Questions such as "What did you think might happen in the situation?" may be useful in eliciting the presence of negative cognitions. Second, some patients may not recognize that their thoughts are distorted or irrational. This may seem inconsistent with a diagnosis of social phobia inasmuch as the diagnostic criteria require that the patient recognizes that his or her fear is irrational. However, if it is possible that the patient recognizes the fear, but not necessarily the thoughts, as irrational, it is recommended that the clinician not try to force the patient to recognize the irrationality of the thoughts. Rather, the patient is encouraged to just stop focusing on the thoughts (Persons, 1989). Also, similar to Ellis' rational emotive therapy (Ellis, 1962), patients may be encouraged to perform a behavioral experiment in order to determine whether their predictions actually occur.

A third problem addressed by Heimberg (1991) relates to those patients who do not grasp the core of CBGT (i.e., the cognitive restructuring component). If after repeated attempts the patient still does not understand CBGT's goal or procedures (e.g., thought identification, substitution of positive thoughts for negative ones), clinicians can diminish emphasis on cognitive restructuring and increase attention to the exposure component. A second alternative is to attempt to reduce the complexity of CBGT. For example, rather than a complete cognitive restructuring analysis, patients may be taught a series of simple self-statements to use in the distressful situations.

Other implementation problems include the need to keep the patient on track during the treatment sessions. Heimberg (1991) noted that the exposure simulation is the vehicle through which cognitive restructuring occurs. Thus, therapists must not allow patients to delay the simulations by overly detailed explanations of past anxious experiences or detailed and comprehensive lists of all possible automatic thoughts.

Case Study[3]

Thus far, this chapter has focused on reviewing the available literature and discussing the basics of treatment implementation. Next, we present a case example that illustrates how the various procedures were used in the treatment of an adult with generalized social phobia.

Initial Evaluation

The patient was a 39-year-old, married, African American, female physician who described a long-standing history of becoming "really nervous" in large crowds, especially if the people were unfamiliar. Although unable to recollect the specific onset, she remembered being extremely shy in elementary and junior high school. At social functions, she typically would "hide out" in the bathroom, feigning illness in order to avoid social interactions. She reported no close friends or confidants, was unwilling to get involved with people unless certain of being liked, and did not date until after college. She occasionally would consume alcohol prior to, and frequently during, social events to cope with her discomfort. When in stressful situations, she stuttered. For example, saying her name during introductions, whether to professionals or patients, was particularly difficult. Consequently, she avoided hospitals (where she would have to speak to other professionals), speaking on the telephone, and introducing herself to others, often being perceived as brusque and somewhat rude.

Assessment

A primary diagnosis of social phobia, generalized subtype, was made with the aid of the *Anxiety Disorders Interview Schedule-Revised* (ADIS-R; DiNardo et al., 1985). Also, she met diagnostic criteria for avoidant personality disorder by history and as assessed by the *Structured Clinical Interview for DSM-III-R Personality Disorder* (SCID-II; Spitzer & Williams, 1986). She complained of depressed mood but did not meet criteria for an affective disorder. Prior to treatment at our clinic, she

---

[3]Reprinted from *Journal of Anxiety Disorders, 10,* Fink, C. M., Turner, S. M., & Beidel, D. C., Culturally Relevant Factors in the Behavioral Treatment of Social Phobia: A Case Study. Copyright (1996), with kind permission from Elsevier Science Ltd, The Boulevard, Langford Lane, Kidlington OX51GB, UK.

had received individual therapy and marital therapy in other settings. Although improvements were noted in her marital relationship as a result of marital therapy, no improvement was evidenced in her social–evaluative concerns. She was taking Zoloft (75 mg. per day) initially, but a withdrawal regimen was begun approximately halfway through behavioral treatment, and she was medication-free at treatment termination.

Self-report, clinician-completed, and behavioral measures were used at pre- and posttreatment. These are presented in Table 18. As depicted, the pretreatment assessment scores were consistent with a diagnosis of social phobia. General anxiety and depression were within normal range of functioning.

Public speaking skill and social skills were assessed through an impromptu speech task and a role-play test. She was only able to speak for $3\frac{1}{2}$ (out of 10) minutes, and independent evaluators rated her effectiveness during the social interactions as either a 2 or 3 (on a 0 to 5 point scale), depending upon the gender of the role-play partner. Her SUDS rating of distress was 9 (on a 0 to 10 point scale) during the

Table 18

Scores on Self-Report Instruments and Clinical-Rating Scales

Instrument	Pretreatment	Posttreatment	Follow-up
SPAI Difference Score	113	52	55
Brief Social Phobia Rating Scale			
Fear total score	21	2	–
Avoidance score	19	2	–
Physiological	7	0	–
Total score	47	4	–
Hamilton Depression Scale	5	0	–
Hamilton Anxiety Scale	15	0	–
Social Phobia Endstate Functioning			
Index	0	4	–

Note. Dashes indicate these variables were not assessed at follow-up.

speech and 5 during the role-play interactions, indicating substantial to very significant distress.

Treatment Goals

A. Reduce anxiety and increase skill in social interactions.
B. Increase social interactions in professional and personal settings.
C. Eliminate avoidance of hospital settings.

Treatment Implementation

Goal A. Reduce anxiety and increase skill in social interactions. Because the patient had the generalized subtype of social phobia, treatment consisted of Social Effectiveness Therapy (Turner, Beidel, & Cooley, 1994). She participated in 12 group SST sessions and 12 individualized imaginal exposure sessions, conducted concurrently with the SST. The SST program has been described earlier in this chapter. Careful review of all behavioral material indicated that the core fear was a fear that others would view her as incompetent and, in particular, not worthy of being a physician. This fear was most pronounced when the evaluators were older White, male physicians. The individualized exposure scene is depicted in Table 19. As indicated, the core fear, that others, particularly older, White males, would discover that she was incompetent, was an integral part of the scene, as were the physical symptoms of distress actually experienced by the patient during actual encounters.

Goal B. Increase social interactions in professional and personal settings. This was accomplished through the use of in vivo homework assignments that were initiated after the patient had participated in several imaginal flooding sessions and there was initial evidence of between-session habituation. Homework assignments included the following:

1. Initiating conversations with coworkers.
2. Inviting a White coworker to lunch.
3. Inviting a White neighbor to go out to dinner.
4. While attending a professional meeting, inviting a White physician to lunch.

Table 19
Imaginal Exposure Scene

It is daily rounds at the VA. Today's even more stressful than usual because the chairman, a White, older male, is participating on rounds. The other residents, interns, and medical students are showing off, quoting from the *New England Journal of Medicine* and talking all at once. The whole while, you are thinking to yourself "I should say something." You really want to be at your best. The chairman looks around the group and says, "Before we start, why don't we go around the circle and say who we are." You immediately think, "What if the words don't come out?" You quickly glance around and realize that you are in the middle of the circle. You are the only Black person on the team. . . . You can't say your name! You feel hot and begin to sweat. Everyone is looking at you with smug "I knew it" expressions. You really screwed up. Everyone is thinking that the only reason you are in medical school is because you are a Black female. The department had a certain quota that needed to be filled. Your mouth becomes dry and you feel nauseous. . . You feel absolutely stupid—everyone knows that the only reason you got this far is because you are Black. You see the chairman lean to the person next to him and hear him say, "This is what happens when we let a Black girl into the program." Everyone continues to stare at you. You feel incredibly inferior. You know that the only reason you are still in the program is because you are Black. You do not deserve to be a physician, and everybody knows it.

5. Inviting her employer, a White, middle-aged, male physician, to lunch.

Goal C. Eliminate avoidance of hospital settings. Everyday for a 10-day period, the patient was to enter a local hospital (which had been the location of many distressful encounters in the past and which she currently avoided entering) and remain there until she experienced a 50% reduction in her distress upon initial entry into the setting (initially this was therapist accompanied). Again, it is important to note that this program was not instituted until the data from the individual exposure sessions showed some degree of between-session habituation.

Treatment Outcome

As depicted in Table 18, there was a marked decrease in social anxiety and associated distress. This was evident across self-report measures, and the Social Phobia Endstate Functioning Index (a composite measure based on the social functioning of individuals without social phobia) indicated that the patient was functioning at a level comparable to those who did not have social phobia. In addition, she was able to complete the 10-minute impromptu speech task with a SUDS rating of 3 (on a 0 to 10 point scale). Her interactions during the role-play test were rated as 5 (on a 0 to 5 point scale; 5 = most effective), and her SUDS rating was either 4 or 2, depending on the gender of the interactional partner. At 4-month follow-up, her SPAI scores were still low. She reported that 1 month after the termination of treatment, she moved to a nearby city and commenced specialty residency training, further indicating that hospitals were no longer problematic for her.

This case study illustrates the use of a multicomponent behavioral strategy to treat severe and generalized social phobia in an adult patient. There are several aspects of this case that deserve mention. First, although this woman had achieved a substantial occupational objective, becoming a physician, she still was severely impaired by her social fears. Second, in this particular case, the core fear was her fear of others seeing her as incompetent. There were culturally sensitive aspects to her fear (specifically, that White males who were in authoritative positions would view her as incompetent). Therefore, the exposure situation had to include these elements. As noted in Fink et al. (1996), it is unlikely that the patient would have been able to maintain her long-term treatment gains had not this core fear been extinguished successfully. Additionally, homework assignments played a particularly important role in addressing this fear. Assignments were developed conjointly by the therapist and patient and required some creativity in order to ensure that the assignments would allow the patient to address elements of the core fear. Also, homework assignments were lagged (i.e., were given only after in session exposure no longer resulted in distress) so that there was a high likelihood of successful completion. Finally, this was a very intensive program and required substantial commitment from the patient to participate in both the twice per week clinic sessions and the additional homework assignments. However, most of the assignments could be completed during the course of normal working hours or on the weekends, thus the time commitment was not overwhelming.

CONCLUSION

Research involving the treatment of social phobia has progressed rapidly over the past 15 years, and there now is a sufficient body of literature to draw some conclusions regarding the efficacy and durability of current behavioral and cognitive–behavioral treatments. In fact, the findings regarding overall efficacy and the key element in these treatments are remarkably consistent. Three different strategies (substantive reviews, meta-analyses, and dismantling studies) all indicate that the key ingredient in these interventions is exposure. The efficacy of exposure is so robust that it appears to result in a positive outcome regardless of which variation is used. The most crucial characteristic appears to be that the patient has contact with the distress-producing event for a positive outcome to occur.

One area that has not been examined fully is that of the differential treatment response of social phobia subtypes. When Turner et al. (1996) reanalyzed data from the Turner, Beidel, and Jacob (1994) study, all of those patients with specific social phobia had achieved moderate to high endstate functioning. On the other hand, only 33% of those with the generalized subtype had reached this level. This led Turner et al. (1996) to conclude that for patients with circumscribed social fears (i.e., the specific subtype), exposure alone appears to be sufficient to achieve a positive outcome. However, for those with the generalized subtype (who constitute the majority of those seen in clinics), additional interventions appear to be necessary. This is supported by the preliminary data from the study conducted by Turner, Beidel, Cooley, Woody, and Messer (1994), which suggests that exposure plus the addition of a structured social skills program delivered in a group setting improves outcome for generalized social phobia. Skill deficits appear to be prevalent in the generalized subtype because of its earlier onset and long history of social inhibition and withdrawal and possibly because of the overlap in diagnostic criteria with APD. Because of this overlap, and the fact that APD and social phobia can be diagnosed concurrently, many people with generalized social phobia also suffer from APD.

We have endeavored in this chapter to present the practical side of conducting the major behavioral and cognitive–behavioral interventions used to treat social phobia, highlighting what we believe to be critical parameters and the common pitfalls faced by clinicians during implementation. As noted, developing and conducting the specific exposure sessions often is very straightforward. At other times, considerable resourcefulness is required in order to develop an appropriate exposure venue. Finally, in addition to consideration of the generalized–specific dimension, other factors such as the presence of comorbid Axis I and II disorders may affect treatment outcome or influence the manner in which treatment is conducted. The few data that exist suggest that individuals with comorbid Axis I or II disorders do benefit from behavioral and cognitive–behavioral treatment but that additional attention to the comorbid conditions likely will be necessary. For example, when severe depression is present, this disorder may need to be addressed prior to attempting to treat the social phobia. In other cases, such as when GAD is present, the order in which these disorders are treated may not be a critical issue. Consideration of each disorder's effect on functional impairment or the patient's general emotional status may be useful in making this type of determination. Clinicians need to remember that some patients will be in need of continued exposure opportunities even after formal intervention has terminated. As noted, the Toastmasters programs, Dale Carnegie classes, or becoming a reader at church often can serve as continued opportunities to further enhance or maintain treatment gains.

Behavioral and Cognitive–Behavioral Treatment of Social Phobia in Children and Adolescents

Well, my friends told me that when they used to ask my opinion about something, I would always say, "I don't care" or "I don't know." Now when they ask me, I give them my opinion. They said they like me much better now because I say what I think.

A 10-year-old girl who was asked how she thought she had changed following a 12-week behavioral treatment program for childhood social phobia.

As we have discussed several times throughout this volume, there are few treatment studies that have used a carefully diagnosed sample of children with social phobia. However, there are numerous studies that have reported the treatment of children described as shy, socially isolated, or socially withdrawn. To provide a historical perspective, we will review a few illustrative controlled studies involving nondiagnosed shy, socially isolated, or socially withdrawn children. Then, we will present the few studies using carefully diagnosed socially phobic children. After these reviews, we will describe strategies for the effective implementation of behavioral and cognitive–behavioral treatments. Although we will discuss different behavioral approaches separately, these strategies typically are combined in clinical treatment settings.

EMPIRICAL OUTCOME STUDIES OF SOCIALLY WITHDRAWN AND ISOLATED CHILDREN

Empirical studies reporting the outcome for the treatment of social isolation in children primarily involve the use of behavioral or cognitive–behavioral interventions, and most have involved exposure in one form or another. Below we review the various strategies and then provide a critique of the available literature.

From a social learning perspective, impairment in social functioning may result from a lack of effective social skills, from performance inhibition due to anxiety, or from both (Arkowitz, 1981). Most behavioral clinicians assume that socially isolated children have social skill deficits, which in turn lead to withdrawn behavior, restricted peer interaction, and impairment in interpersonal relationships (cf. Rubin, LeMare, & Lollis, 1990; Vernberg, Abwender, Ewell, & Beery, 1992). One method of addressing these deficiencies is to implement social skills training (SST) programs, which are designed to teach those skills necessary for effective interpersonal discourse. Typically, these programs provide children with instruction in specific behaviors, for example, smiling, eye contact, initiations, conversational skills; modeling of effective social behaviors; opportunities to practice the behaviors; and verbal feedback regarding the appropriate response. The intent is to teach the necessary skills and give children the opportunity to put them to use. In most cases, SST has proved effective in increasing social interactions in children with mild to moderate levels of social withdrawal (Sheridan, Kratochwill, & Elliott, 1990; Whitehill, Hersen, & Bellack, 1980) as well as in shy adolescents (Christoff, Scott, Kelley, Baer, & Kelly, 1985). Among the few existing comparative treatment trials, Jupp and Griffiths (1990) reported that both a traditional discussion psychotherapy group and a psychodramatic role-play group (actually an SST group) successfully improved social interactions in shy adolescents, but only the SST group had a concomitant change in self-concept. Schneider and Byrne (1987) documented a similar outcome with socially withdrawn children. It is important to note that it is unclear how many of the socially isolated children included in these samples might have met criteria for social phobia. Thus, it is difficult to apply these findings directly to the treatment of children with social phobia, although they are quite provocative. Furthermore, if some of these children met criteria for social phobia, SST alone would not be expected to produce an optimal treatment outcome because a crucial component of any successful intervention (prolonged exposure to the feared situation) had not been addressed adequately. However, SST could be an integral component of an overall treatment program.

Most SST strategies have had limited success in increasing peer acceptance (e.g., Berler et al., 1982; Whitehill et al., 1980). Without direct attention to the social fear, even children armed with newly acquired skills will be inhibited and will not use them in peer settings. Firmly established patterns of peer neglect by sociable peers may not allow for the demonstration of new abilities, and thus such opportunities usually have to be planned as part of the intervention (Finch & Hops, 1982; Paine et al., 1982). One alternative is for the therapist (or the parent) to arrange for social experiences by (a) arranging contingencies to promote social interaction and (b) providing immediate reinforcement when social interactions occur. In school settings, using operant strategies and tangible reinforcers (points or prizes) increased interactions in socially isolated children to a level comparable to that of their more sociable peers (Bergsgaard & Larsson, 1984; Guevermont, MacMillan, Shawchuck, & Hansen, 1989). Additionally, several studies of socially isolated children have found that SST plus peer-involvement experiences are effective (e.g. Bierman & Furman, 1984; Finch & Hops, 1982; Paine et al., 1982). In other cases, the use of peer-pairing (peer-mediated) procedures without concomitant social skills training have been investigated. A sociable peer may serve as a role model, provide positive reinforcement, decrease anxiety, increase confidence, and enhance generalization. Peer-pairing procedures (without SST) increased positive social interaction and peer acceptance in socially withdrawn preschoolers (Furman, Rahe, & Hartrup, 1979) and peer-neglected first-

and second-grade students (Morris, Messer, & Gross, 1995). However, because these young children were not diagnosed with social phobia, it is unclear how these samples relate to children with social phobia. For example, if skill deficits are a part of the clinical presentation, it is unlikely that peer pairing alone (without SST) will be effective because there will not be any opportunity for children to acquire social skills. Thus, although the arrangement of socialization experiences probably is an important component of a comprehensive intervention for children with social phobia, factors such as skill acquisition and fear reduction also must be addressed.

To reiterate, behavioral treatment in the form of operant strategies, SST, and peer pairing appear to be successful in increasing young children's social interactions. However, the heterogeneous nature of these samples precludes drawing direct conclusions for those with childhood social phobia. In addition, sample sizes were very small and subject selection was based primarily on a behaviorally observed deficiency rather than on the presence of a specific emotional disorder. Additionally, most samples were recruited through the school system, creating a potential bias because those who are most severely withdrawn (or socially phobic) may not attend school. Finally, outcome was based on behavioral observation, sociometric procedures, or teacher ratings. Therefore, changes in emotional state were inferred through changes in social behavior rather than via clinical ratings and interviews. Nevertheless, this body of research provides guidance in the development of strategies for treating children with social phobia. And as we shall see, early studies of childhood social phobia suggest that the findings from these studies were indeed applicable to social phobia.

EMPIRICAL OUTCOME STUDIES OF CHILDREN WITH SOCIAL PHOBIA

There have been two cognitive–behavioral studies that have included children with social phobia in their treatment sample (Barrett, Dadds, Rapee, & Ryan, 1996; Kendall, 1994). These studies used cognitive–behavioral procedures (CBT) to alleviate children's fears. Kendall's

(1994) program, called *the Coping Cat program*, combines several procedures to treat anxiety disorders in children. Initially, relaxation training is used to decrease the general level of arousal. Next, children are trained in cognitive restructuring to change negative cognitions into positive thoughts. Finally, during exposure to anxiety-producing situations, children are taught to use coping skills. Therapists accompany children into situations that normally create distress and encourage the children to practice relaxation training and cognitive restructuring while in the situation. Compared with a wait list control group, those children who were treated with the Coping Cat program had significantly lower scores on child measures of general anxiety and greater ability to cope with fearful situations. Parents' ratings of anxiety and depression and social competence also changed significantly as a result of the intervention, but teacher ratings did not differentiate the two groups. Finally, although behavioral observation of the children did not reveal differences across the groups on individual behavioral variables, a total behavioral observational score did differentiate the groups, suggesting that overall, children receiving the active treatment were less anxious and distressed. It should be noted that parents' participation in therapy was variable, and the degree of parental involvement (on the basis of therapist ratings) was modestly related to treatment outcome. Finally, long-term follow-up (3.35 years later) indicated that children maintained their treatment gains (Kendall & Southam-Gerow, 1996).

In addition to demonstrating the efficacy of CBT using the Australian version of the Coping Cat program, Barrett et al. (1996; the Coping Koala Program) demonstrated that parental behaviors may affect treatment outcome. This study compared the Coping Koala program (which contains all elements of the Coping Cat program) for children with either separation anxiety disorder, overanxious disorder, or social phobia with a combination of Coping Koala and family anxiety management (FAM). FAM included three components: discipline training (rewarding courageous behavior and extinguishing excessive anxiety), anxiety management of parental distress, and communication and problem-solving skills designed to help parents work together to solve problems and help the children maintain their gains. The addition of

FAM enhanced treatment outcome on some, but not all, clinician and self-report measures. At posttreatment and at 12-month follow-up, significantly more of those treated with the combined intervention no longer met diagnostic criteria. It is important to note that two of the three FAM components were directed at the parent's problems rather than those of the child. Thus, the usefulness of a parent training component, specifically directed at the child's anxiety disorder, remains to be studied.

As noted, both of these programs included children with social phobia in the treatment samples. For example, 27% of the children in the Barrett et al. (1996) program were diagnosed as having social phobia. However, the results were not analyzed separately by specific diagnosis. Therefore, it is unclear whether these interventions were specifically effective for children with social phobia. In contrast, Albano, Marten, Holt, Heimberg, and Barlow (1995) and Albano, DiBartolo, Heimberg, and Barlow (1995) described a cognitive–behavioral group treatment program specifically for adolescents with social phobia (CBGT-A). According to the authors, this treatment combines procedures used successfully to treat adult social phobia (Heimberg, Salzman, Holt, & Blendall, 1993) with the skills development approach for adolescents proposed by Christoff et al. (1985). There are two overall components to CBGT-A, psychoeducation and skill building and behavioral exposure. Each component is 8 weeks in length. During the psychoeducational and skill building phase, children participate in SST, problem solving training, assertiveness training, and cognitive restructuring. During the second phase, simulated within-session and in vivo exposure sessions are introduced. In conjunction with the therapist, each child develops an individual fear hierarchy. Using the hierarchy, children enact items within session, with other children in the group as the interpersonal partners. These exposure simulations are 10 minutes in length, and afterwards the therapist and group members discuss the just-completed interactions, including both positive and negative aspects. For details on the administration of CBGT-A, see Albano, Marten, et al. (1995) and Albano, DiBartolo, et al. (1995). The results of the pilot group (with 5 adolescents) indicated that 3 months after the completion of treatment, social phobia had decreased to subclinical levels for 4 out of 5 adolescents. At 1-year follow-up, 4 adolescents were free of any disorder, whereas the fifth still had some vestiges of social phobia but at only a subclinical level. The mean number of negative cognitions during a behavioral assessment decreased, although heightened physiological arousal remained unchanged. Data from a controlled trial examining the effectiveness of this program to an educational control group are forthcoming.

During the past 3 years, we constructed an intervention program directed at preadolescent children (ages 8 through 12). Our program, called *Social Effectiveness Therapy for Children* (SET-C; Beidel, Turner, & Morris, 1996a), was developed as a result of our studies of the psychopathology and treatment of adult social phobia. As is the case with CBGT-A, SET-C is based on the SET program that we have used successfully with adults who have social phobia. The specifics of implementing SET-C components (exposure and SST) are presented below. Preliminary results ($n = 16$) for the SET-C program were positive. After 12 weeks of treatment, children showed a significant decrease on the Social Phobia and Anxiety Inventory for Children. In addition, parents reported a significant decrease on the Child Behavior Checklist Internalizing Scale. The behavioral assessment included participation in 5 role-play scenes and a read-aloud task. Ratings by an independent observer, blind to time of assessment, indicated a significant improvement in interactional skill and read-aloud skill, and a significant decrease in observed anxiety. Furthermore, at posttreatment, children's self-ratings of anxiety indicated a significant decrease from pretreatment. Currently, a study comparing SET-C with a credible control group is underway.

To date, there only are 4 reports of behavioral treatment for children or adolescents with social phobia. Two (Barrett et al., 1996; Kendall, 1994) included children with social phobia as part of a mixed sample of anxiety disorders. Although containing a larger number of participants, the studies did not examine the effectiveness of the interventions separately for children with social phobia. Two more recent trials (Albano, Marten, et al., 1995; Beidel et al., 1996) were based on smaller samples but included only children with social phobia. However, the efficacy of these latter two interventions have not yet been compared with control groups, although studies are underway. All programs used some form of exposure. One important difference among these studies is that the Coping Cat and Coping Koala programs do not include SST as part of the intervention, whereas CBGT-A and SET-C address social skill deficits directly. In light of the recent data suggesting that children with social phobia have substantial social skill deficits, a systematic skills training strategy would appear to be an important treatment component. Also, the form of exposure in CBGT and SET-C is more intense than the Coping Cat and Coping Koala treatments, and the exposure in SET-C is more intense than that used in CBGT-A. Whether the intensity of exposure is related to the achievement of positive outcome remains an empirical question.

Developmental considerations also may play a role in the specific procedures selected to be part of the intervention. For example, the CBT (Coping Cat and Coping Koala programs) and CBGT-A programs included a cognitive restructuring component. This presumes that children with social phobia have negative cognitions and that they are responsible for the social anxiety and fear. Furthermore, cognitive therapists assume that patients with social phobia have negative cognitions when in socially distressful situations, and it is the negative cognitions that are the basis of the fear. However, one of the cardinal features of this disorder, as reported by the patients themselves, is an inability to think when they are anxious. Adults with social phobia frequently characterize their experience as one in which they are flooded with many thoughts such that they are unable to think clearly and focus at all. Children under the age of 12 rarely are able to describe having specific thoughts when in the fear-producing situation. Thus, it is not entirely clear whether the "negative thoughts" reported by those with social phobia actually occur during social situations or perhaps only on retrospective reflection about the experience.

An additional consideration for children is that they have not yet reached Piaget's stage of formal operations in which consideration of the future is possible. Thus, younger children may not have the catastrophic thinking style typical of adults with this disorder. Although to date developmental studies have not addressed this issue, a similar argument has been raised regarding the absence of negative cognitions in children and adolescents with panic disorder (Nelles & Barlow, 1988). Despite the various hypotheses about why there may be an absence of negative cognitions in individuals with social phobia, our investigations of psychopathology in young children do not reveal the presence of specific negative cognitions when children actually are engaged in socially distressful situations. Similarly, we have been unable to detect them in our clinical interviews. Furthermore, our research with adult patients indicated that negative cognitions decrease when patients are treated with traditional behavior therapy. Specific attention to the cognitive component was not necessary to reduce negative cognitions because of these factors. Our program for 8- to 12-year-old children does not include a cognitive component.

TREATMENT IMPLEMENTATION

In chapter 8, we discussed considerable evidence suggesting that exposure is the critical element in the treatment of social phobia in adults. Our review of the literature on the treatment of socially isolated children (and more recently, children with social phobia) suggests that exposure strategies are critical to the effective treatment of maladaptive social anxiety in children as well. Also, SST (which includes some exposure elements) has been used widely to address social isolative behavior in children. On the basis of the review of the literature in the area, it appears that a combination of exposure and SST is likely to be most effective in addressing these problems. Two pilot studies with children diagnosed with social phobia support this conclusion. The evidence presented here also suggests that cognitive restructuring may be efficacious as well. We now turn to a description of how these treatment strategies are implemented.

Exposure

As with adults, the most critical part of exposure treatment is an understanding of all the fear parameters, and in particular, the identification of the core fear. Although adults often can provide enough information for clear identification, such is frequently not the case for children and adolescents. Young children or adolescents may admit to being shy but not be able to further clarify the nature of their fears. Adolescents also often refuse to further clarify their fears, even when they appear to understand them, because they have not come in to treatment willingly and are reluctant to talk to a therapist. Therefore, when treating children and adolescents, there are many instances in which information about the fear's components must be collected from secondary sources, such as parents, teachers, self-report data, behavioral assessments, or self-monitoring data and clinical conjecture, rather than from direct interview. Such data can be collected using several different methods.

The *Anxiety Disorders Interview Schedule-Parent Version* (ADIS-P) and *Anxiety Disorders Interview Schedule for Children-Child Version* (ADIS-C; Silverman & Albano, 1995) sections on school and social phobia contain lists of potential social situations (see Table 20). Each of these situations can be rated for extent of anxiety and avoidance. Although parents may not always be able to provide exact ratings of distress, they often easily identify a broad range of situations. This identification can be of great assistance in efforts to develop exposure situations by providing information on the types of situations in which the child experiences distress. Similarly, administration of the Social Phobia and Anxiety Inventory for Children (SPAI-C; parent or child versions; Beidel et al., 1995) also can help identify potentially distressful situations. Additionally, daily diary ratings (see chapter 5) can provide a wealth of information about socially distressful situations the children typically encounter. Any or all of these methods may be useful in determining the parameter's of the child's fear.

Once the specific parameters are determined, the clinician should decide how to structure the exposure treatment. Although the same method of exposure used to treat adults (see chapter 8) can be used in treating children and adolescents, there are a number of factors that need to be considered carefully. Three important decisions regarding how to implement exposure treatment with children include (a) inten-

Table 20

Situations Listed in the Anxiety Disorders Interview Schedule for Children

Answering questions in class	Eating in front of others
Giving a report or reading aloud in front of the class	Eating in the school cafeteria
	Answering or talking on the telephone
Asking the teacher a question or for help	Meetings such as girl/boy scouts or team meetings
Taking tests	Ordering food in a restaurant
Writing on the blackboard	Musical or athletic performances
Working or playing with a group of kids	Inviting a friend to get together
	Speaking to adults (e.g., store clerk)
Gym class	Attending dances or activity nights
Walking in the hallways/hanging out by your locker	Having your picture taken
	Parties
Starting a conversation	Dating
Joining in on a conversation	
Using school or public bathroom	

From *Anxiety Disorders Interview Schedule for Children.* Copyright ©1995 by Graywind Publications. Reproduced by permission of publisher, The Psychological Corporation. All rights reserved.

sity of exposure, (b) mode of exposure, and (c) extent of therapist involvement in the session. Although these factors are important when treating adults, they particularly are important for children. In each of the ensuing sections, these variables will be discussed in turn.

Intensity of Exposure

One of the first decisions the therapist must make is whether to use a high- or low-intensity exposure strategy. As noted in chapter 8, exposure can be graduated or intensive. Intensive exposure requires substantial cooperation on the part of the child to enter and remain in the social situation for the appropriate period of time (see section on intensive exposure below). In addition, the rationale often is difficult for young children to understand, at times resulting in crying or tantrumming behaviors. Thus, because of their reluctance or apprehension concerning treatment, a graduated approach often is considered preferable for young children. A graduated approach also helps control the parent's anxiety level, thus avoiding some of the pitfalls of the "protection trap" described by Silverman and Kurtines (1996), where the parent adopts the posture of protecting the child from experiencing distress (see chapter 6 in this volume). Similarly, children under 12 may have difficulty using imagery. Thus, in vivo strategies primarily are used with young children.

Graduated Exposure for Children

The purpose of graduated in vivo exposure is to provide systematic, gradual, and repeated contact with the feared situation. Graduated exposure allows small amounts of the feared stimuli to be presented one step at a time (i.e., hierarchically), and repeated pairings across a number of sessions, using progressively more fearful stimuli, is necessary for the treatment to be effective. Attainment of the highest step on the hierarchy with minimal distress is the goal of the graduated exposure process.

Hierarchy Construction

Deciding to use a graduated approach necessitates the construction of a fear hierarchy. As with adults, the child's assistance in constructing the hierarchy is helpful. When explaining this concept to children, it is often helpful to describe the hierarchy as a ladder. For very young children, drawing a picture of a ladder will help the presentation of the concept. Children (and their parents) should be told that the first part of treatment will consist of building a ladder representing their fears. Those situations that are less fearful will be the bottom rungs of the ladder, whereas those that are more fearful will be the highest rungs of the ladder. Situations or activities are constructed on the basis of the assessment material that outlined the range of the fears rated for the associated degree of distress and from the child's input when this is possible.

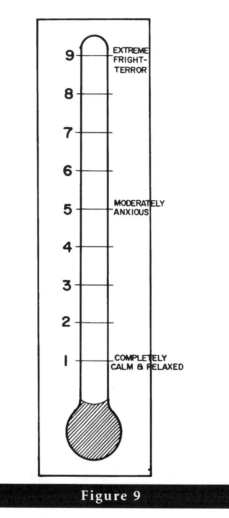

Figure 9

Fear Thermometer

There are many ways to construct the hierarchy, but one common way is to use index cards. Each situation can be written on an individual index card. Ratings of the situation described on each index card are usually made using a Subjective Units of Distress Scale (SUDS). Then, the cards can be ordered to represent the degree of distress elicited. For children, rating scales of 8 or 9 points are most common. Again, the caveat with respect to rating scales noted in chapter 5 is important here. A fear thermometer (such as the one depicted in Figure 9) or pictures depicting various numerical ratings of distress will assist young children in ordering the hierarchy.

When working with young children, it is recommended that the clinician and the child develop and order the hierarchy together. Then, it can be reviewed with the parent for accuracy and completeness. Typical hierarchies usually range between 10 and 20 steps (index cards). Because this is a graduated approach, the hierarchy should include situations representing all steps on the SUDS scale. Therefore, if the review indicates that there are "gaps" in the ladder (i.e., there are situations rated as a 3 and some are rated as a 6 but none that is rated as 4 or 5), additional items should be constructed. This might be accomplished by varying the scene content of items already in the hierarchy. For example, the item "reading in front of one child" might be rated as a 3, whereas "reading in front of an adult" might be rated as a 6. Therefore, items representing 4 or 5 might be "reading in front of 2 children" and "reading in front of the babysitter (a teenage girl)," respectively. An important key to the success of the intervention is that the therapist should not try to impose any type of order on the hierarchy. That is, it is not necessary that the order of the items "make sense" to the therapist. It only needs to make sense in terms of representing increasing levels of distress for the child. In other words, maladaptive fear by nature is irrational. Hence, the sequence might not be logical. A hierarchy used for the treatment of a 10-year-old girl with social phobia is presented in Table 21.

Implementation of Graduated Exposure

Once the hierarchy is constructed, one or two items are addressed each week. The items may be assigned to be completed in session or as homework assignments, depending upon their nature. In some cases, an item may be completed in the session as well as for homework. Prior to presenting an item, the child's baseline level of distress is assessed (using either physiological or subjective ratings). As each item is presented, the therapist asks the child to rate current distress using a SUDS scale. Because this is a graduated approach, distress should be low (i.e.,

Table 21

Sample Hierarchy for the Treatment of Social Phobia

Fear	SUDS rating
Answering a question in class when you know the answer	1
Eating at a fast food restaurant	2
Reading aloud in front of 1 person, knowing and practicing the material ahead of time	2
Reading unfamiliar material aloud, in front of one person	3
Writing on the blackboard	3
Saying hello to a person your age—someone you know but not well	4
Taking a spelling test on the blackboard	4
Ordering food in a fast-food restaurant	4
Making mistakes—tripping in front of someone	5
Saying hello to an adult that you know	5
Reading aloud in front of a group	6
Being around a group of "popular" peers but not required to talk to them	7
Giving a report in class	7
Talking to an adult and disclosing information about self	8
Requesting information from clerks in stores or from the principal	8
Introducing self to a "popular" peer	9
Joining in with a group of peers (walking to class, playing a game)	9

1 or 2 units on the SUDS scale above the child's baseline distress level). Thus, if the child's baseline distress is rated as a "1," exposure to the fearful item should not be rated higher than a "3." The item should continue to be presented until the distress rating decreases to baseline. At the completion of the session, the items (or some variation) should be prescribed as a homework assignment to be completed several times during the ensuing week. For example, children who have difficulty greeting strangers may be required to answer the telephone at home

for the next week. Alternatively, under their parents' guidance, they might go to the mall and ask questions of unfamiliar store clerks.

As depicted in Table 21, some of the items occur during school, and therefore it would be unlikely that the therapist would be present during the exposure session. If the items themselves are to be assigned solely as homework (i.e., completed outside of the therapy session), the parent and child should be instructed carefully about how to conduct the session and how long the session should last (at least 90 minutes or until distress returns to baseline).

In the case of items such as greeting someone, the child would not necessarily continue to greet the same person for an extended period of time. However, the child should continue to greet different individuals until the distress dissipates. Thus, the child should be taken to a park or a playground where there are numerous other individuals available to participate in the exposure session.

The following are the steps for implementating graduated exposure:

1. The therapist, in conjunction with the child and the parent, using all of the available assessment data, develops a hierarchy of anxiety-producing situations.
2. One or two items per session are presented (or assigned as homework). Children should be reassured that items further up the ladder will not be presented until the bottom rungs are successfully completed. The items should elicit only minimal distress and the child should continue to engage in the situation until that distress has dissipated.
3. Items addressed in the session should be assigned for further practice as homework assignments.
4. If the items are to be completed outside of the therapy session, the therapist needs to provide clear instructions concerning implementation to the parent and child, including the time frame.

Problems in Implementing Graduated Exposure

As noted, the anxiety-producing situations should be ranked from least to most anxiety-producing. If the presentation of an item from the hierarchy list results in a moderate to high level of distress, it usually indicates that (a) the initial placement of the item in the hierarchy was incorrect, or (b) the item represents too large a step on the ladder from the previous item (i.e., there are rungs missing on the ladder). In the case of the former, the item should be withdrawn and placed further up the hierarchy. In the case of the latter, the item should be broken down into smaller steps. As discussed above, additional items, to fill in the gaps, should be constructed.

The most important potential complication associated with graduated exposure is deriving the hierarchy for a young child. The child may have only a limited understanding of the fear, and parents also may have only limited insight into the exact nature of the child's distress. Thus, parents may recognize the child's anxiety but not have the depth of understanding necessary to provide all of the fear cues needed to construct a hierarchy. Often, extremely stressful situations (e.g., SUDS ratings at the top of the hierarchy) are easily identified, as are nonstressful settings. It is the middle items that are the most difficult to identify. Experienced clinicians often are able to suggest items that fill in the middle of a hierarchy. Also, an empirical approach can be used to test the various steps to determine whether they are relevant, although this will add to the length of treatment time. Should items for a hierarchy not be identified, a graduated approach may not be feasible, and a more intensive alternative might need to be considered (see imaginal exposure section).

A final consideration with graduated exposure sessions is the necessity for parental involvement in the program. In the majority of cases, children do not carry out assignments on their own very well. An exception might be when assignments are carried out in the school setting. In such cases, only minimal parental involvement is required (such as praise when the child completes the task). However, other assignments, such as having a friend over to play, inviting a friend to a movie, or eating in a fast food restaurant, require the parent to play an active role in facilitating successful completion of the assignment. Thus, an important key to the success of graduated exposure with children is parental willingness and ability to assist in carrying out tasks as assigned. In many cases, this will require only that the parent understand the rationale for the assignments and be willing to help the child complete it, including scheduling the appropriate amount of time. In other cases, it may require transporting the child or spending their money. There are a number of factors that may inhibit active parental participation. For example, parents may not have the physical or economic resources, may be unwilling, or may be impaired by their own social fears such that they are unable to help their children engage in the exposure assignments. In these cases, there are a few alternatives that might be considered. For parents without physical or economic resources (e.g., they do not own a car), or for those who have severe social fears themselves, constructing all assignments to be conducted at the school is one alternative. In such cases, it may be possible to enlist a guidance counselor or favorite teacher to assist the child in carrying out the assignments. A second, and perhaps better, alternative for those parents who have social fears themselves is to help them enter treatment. Finally, for those parents who are just "too busy" to help their child, the clinician may remind the parent that improperly administered treatment programs are not effective and that they may need to reconsider whether they judge the child's problem to be severe enough to warrant treatment at this time.

Intensive Exposure (Flooding)

The theoretical basis for flooding has been discussed in chapter 8 in this volume. However, to reiterate briefly, flooding is based on a habituation paradigm and a substantial amount of laboratory data that has shown that repeated exposure to an anxiety-producing situation without the opportunity for escape will result in decreasing anxiety (see chapter 8). However, most individuals become so overwhelmed by their anxiety that they cannot "wait it out." Rather, they escape or avoid the distressful situation. The goal of intensive exposure (flooding) is to place the children in the fearful situation and help them stay there until the anxiety dissipates.

For older children or adolescents (e.g., age 12 or older) flooding may be the treatment of choice for the same reason that it frequently is for adults (see chapter 8). Also, it may be used if an appropriate hierarchy cannot be constructed, or if there is no suitable adult to oversee a gradual exposure program. Rather than a hierarchy, exposure, using an intensive (flooding) paradigm, means that the child immediately faces the most distressful situation (i.e., the top rung of the ladder). Such situations usually involve performing in front of others, for example, reading, speaking, or writing in front of a group of people. There are subtle differences among these behaviors, and it should not be assumed that just any performance situation will do. Careful assessment is needed to identify the core fear. One of the children treated in our clinic had no difficulty speaking in front of large groups if she had a prepared text. However, she became quite distressed if she had to extemporaneously speak to a group or interact casually with a small group of children. Her concern was that others would think she was not intelligent, and if she could not prepare in advance, her fears were magnified. It should be pointed out here that this child had an intense need for perfection as she interpreted it. Thus, presenting the material in the exact way was very important to her and to the core fear needed for proper exposure.

Implementing Intensive Exposure (Flooding) Sessions

Constructing the appropriate stimuli for intensive exposure therapy also can be problematic and often requires considerable ingenuity on the part of the therapist. However, because reading in front of others is a common performance activity for children and adolescents, and a common fear for those with social phobia, this often can be used for intensive exposure. It is recommended that a series of children's books be kept on hand, representing various reading levels. This provides ready access to read-aloud material. An alternative is to instruct children to bring in their own school texts; however, children's apprehensions are such that often they "forget" their book. Having the books on hand does not allow the child the opportunity to escape from participating in the exposure activity.

In the intensive flooding paradigm, in which performance is the critical factor, a child would be given a book and be required to read in front of several audience members (volunteers or undergraduate students) and to keep reading until the anxiety dissipates. Other exposure activities could include writing spelling words on the board or taking a math test at the blackboard while others observe the performance. At times, the critical factor might revolve around whether the audience was made up of peers or adults, or perhaps authority figures. Also, children who are afraid to join groups of other children could be taken to a beach, playground, or park and be required to interact with other children who are there.

Whatever the situation might be, the clinician should assess SUDS levels (distress ratings) at least every 10 minutes. If possible, keeping a written record of the distress ratings will help determine patterns of within- and between-sessions habituation. The therapist must be prepared to deal with significant levels of distress often elicited by this high-intensity procedure and encourage the child to engage in the exposure setting despite his or her distress. Sometimes providing a small reward at completion of the session is very helpful. The child (assisted by the therapist) continues to engage in the feared activity for an extended period of time (usually 90 minutes) or ideally until arousal dissipates (within-session habituation; see chapter 8).

Flooding is not a one-session treatment. Children must be exposed to the same distressful situation repeatedly until the situation no longer elicits distress (between-session habituation; see chapter 8). On average, between 10 and 12 flooding sessions are needed to achieve between-session habituation when treating social phobia. Figure 10 depicts within-session and between-session habituation during an in vivo task for a 10-year-old girl with a severe fear of reading in front of others. Figure 11 depicts within-session and between-session habituation during an imaginal task for a 16-year-old boy. For the sake of readability, habituation curves illustrating only several of the sessions are shown.

Many of the problems in implementing intensive in vivo exposure are the same as for intensive imaginal exposure (to be discussed below). Thus, the discussion of problems in implementation will be addressed following the presentation of the procedure referred to as *imaginal flooding*.

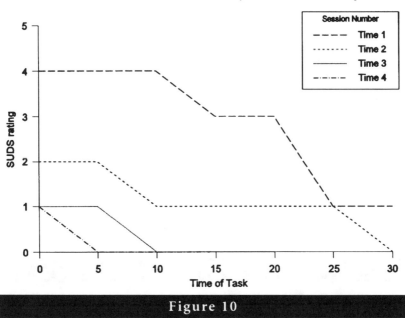

Figure 10

Imaginal Versus In Vivo Exposure

To return to the issues the clinician must consider when implementing exposure with children (intensity, mode, therapist accompaniment), another overall consideration is whether the stimuli should be presented imaginally or in vivo (real life). Both the graduated and intensive exposure procedures discussed above used in vivo exposure. Although in vivo exposure may seem preferable, it sometimes is difficult to arrange the in vivo situations, particularly when not in university or specialty clinic settings. In such cases, imaginal presentation of the distressful situation may be necessary. As we noted earlier in this chapter, we do not recommend the use of imaginal procedures for children under age 10. However, for older children and adolescents, the use of imaginal procedures may be effective and cost-efficient. Furthermore, they allow for exposure to fears that cannot be replicated in vivo.

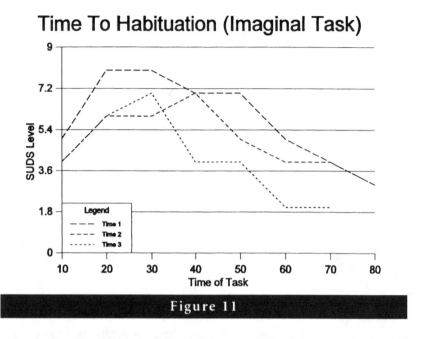

Time To Habituation (Imaginal Task)

Legend
- — — Time 1
- – – – Time 2
- ······· Time 3

Y-axis: SUDS Level (0, 1.8, 3.6, 5.4, 7.2, 9)
X-axis: Time of Task (10, 20, 30, 40, 50, 60, 70, 80)

Figure 11

Imaginal Flooding

As we noted in chapter 8, the key to conducting imaginal exposure is the construction of the imaginal scene. To reiterate briefly, it is crucial that the patient be exposed to the core fear. Those with social phobia are not afraid of people per se, but rather they fear that they might do something humiliating or embarrassing in front of others and that the other people will think critically of them. Therefore, the imaginal scene must capture this element. Table 22 presents two imaginal scenes used in actual treatment cases. The first (Scene 1) is for a 14-year-old boy with a severe fear of reading in front of the class, and the second (Scene 2) is for a 16-year-old boy with generalized social phobia.

There are several points that should be made about these scenes. First, they include the core fear and depict the child's specific concern. Second, there is no option for the patient to cope with the distress or to "handle" the situation. Because this is a strict habituation paradigm, it is important to make sure that the child is exposed to what he or

Table 22
Sample Imaginal Flooding Scenes

Scene 1

You are in your English class at school. There are about 25 students in the class. Your class has been studying Shakespeare, and everyone in the class has been taking turns reading aloud. You are really worried about this. You are scared that you might make a fool out of yourself. Your heart is racing, your hands are trembling, you are sweating, and your face feels hot and red. What will you do if the teacher calls on you to read? Everyone will see how nervous you are. Even if they don't, you are likely to mispronounce one of the words and everyone might laugh. No one else has made a mistake.

The teacher looks at you and says, "Barry, please read the next part aloud." Everyone turns to look at you. They can see how red your face is and how your hands are trembling. You open your mouth to speak but nothing comes out. You try again and you mispronounce the first word. The guys are all snickering and the girls are smiling. You keep reading but you keep mispronouncing even the easiest words. Even the teacher is trying hard not to laugh at you. The other kids are whispering "He doesn't read correctly." The teacher is thinking "I thought he was smarter than that." Your face is bright red. You feel embarrassed and humiliated.

Scene 2

You are at your locker at school. There are many kids around, but you still feel very lonely. No one talks to you, and you have not been able to talk to anyone either. You think that they are looking at you funny, although you cannot be sure. You feel really nervous. You are sweaty and your heart is beating fast. They are probably thinking that there is something wrong with you, that they should stay away from you. You just want them to talk to you, to treat you like they treat everyone else.

Very close to you are two of your classmates. They are talking about soccer, something you know a lot about. They have not been rude to you in the past, and so you decide that maybe you should talk to them. You inch over toward them

Table continues

Table 22 (*Continued*)

and they do not move away. You think to yourself "Maybe it will be okay. Maybe they will let me talk to them." You are really nervous. Your heart is pounding and you can barely get the words out. You are talking so softly you can hardly hear what you are saying. You say something about soccer. They both stop talking and just look at you for a second. They don't really respond to you. They don't ask you anything else, and then they just go back to talking to each other. Once again, you have failed. What's wrong with you that you cannot even say a couple of sentences without getting so nervous that people turn away? You are just a total failure.

she fears. If the child is allowed to "cope," in essence, the child is being allowed to escape or minimize the distress. This is inconsistent with the habituation model that underlies this paradigm. Third, the specific content of the scene is less relevant than the fact that the specific fear is presented. Thus, in the first scene in which the adolescent mispronounces words and embarrasses himself in front of others, the scene used a classroom. However, it just as easily could have been a scene where the child was reading in front of a church congregation or speaking at a party. The particular scene background is less important than exposure to the specific feared consequences (i.e., the core fear). The procedures for implementing imaginal exposure have been presented in chapter 8, and the reader is referred there for details.

Problems in Implementing Intensive Imaginal or In Vivo Exposure

One potential problem using exposure is the failure of the child, adolescent, or perhaps even the parent to understand the rationale for the treatment. Most adults will understand that in order to conquer fear, one must face the anxiety-producing situation. However, because children and adolescents initially may be distressed by the procedure, it is important that the rationale be explained carefully and completely. Pictorial illustrations of within-session habituation and between-session habituation often are helpful in explaining the concepts and goals of intensive exposure. Furthermore, we recommend keeping track of the SUDS levels assessed during the treatment sessions and graphing them as illustrated in Figures 10 and 11. These graphs often are useful to share with children and parents to track the effectiveness of the program and demonstrate progress. Compliance often can be increased when children and parents see that intensive exposure is having an effect.

Even if they understand the rationale, some children may not have the motivation to participate in this procedure. Children and adolescents usually are brought in to a clinic because an adult feels that they have a problem. Thus, they usually are more reluctant and fearful about what treatment will entail. When children are hesitant or noncompliant about participation in treatment, we have found that allowing them some control over the exposure situations engenders their trust and makes them more compliant. Thus, similar to the advice given by March and Mulle (1993) for treatment of children and adolescents with OCD, we advise setting up an agreement (contract) with children. The agreement is that once exposure situations are identified, the child can choose which exposure task will occur first, and as long as there is continued progress toward the ultimate goal, the decisions to move to a second task are made jointly by the therapist and the child. With this agreement, children often willingly attempt the first task, and once they are involved in the process, issues of control typically are no longer a problem.

When using imaginal exposure, another potential problem is difficulty imaging the scene. As we have noted before, we do not recommend imaginal exposure for children under age 10. However, even older children and adolescents may have difficulty with the requirements of this procedure. Some children do not have well-developed cognitive capabilities and thus are not able to imagine the scene. In such cases, simple training in imagery procedures may enhance their abilities. This can be accomplished by having the child practice imagining situations, places, or things that are familiar. For example, children can practice imagining their bedroom by naming all of its contents and describing them in detail. Similarly, a favorite place or activity can be used. After some practice, a child's imagery capability often improves. However, in some cases, the child's complaint of not being able to imagine the scene is not due to an inability to image but is a way of avoiding the distress associated with a scene. If this happens, the first step is to repeat the rationale for exposure. If this does not eliminate the problem, asking the child to verbalize aloud what he or she is imagining is often effective. Another alternative is to arrange for parents to provide positive reinforcement as a reward for participating. If each of these strategies is unsuccessful, an in vivo strategy should be considered.

Finally, as noted in chapter 8, children, like adults, may try to minimize distress by attempting to cope during the imaginal procedure. For example, in the second scene in Table 22, an adolescent who is attempting to cope may change the scene content such that the classmates smile and respond rather than ignore the conversational attempt. Actually, this coping behavior is more common in adults than in children or adolescents, but the older the child or adolescent is, the more likely such a problem will arise. Remediation of this problem is discussed in chapter 8.

Therapist Accompanied Versus Therapist Directed Exposure

A final consideration in the implementation of exposure therapy is whether the therapist should accompany the child during in vivo exposure. Our advice is that if at all possible, at least the first several sessions should be therapist accompanied. There are several reasons behind this recommendation. First, initial sessions often can reveal additional information about the parameters of the disorder. Second, therapist accompaniment may facilitate compliance. Third, one study that addressed this issue found that clinician-accompanied sessions were more effective than self-exposure for adults with social phobia (Al-Kubaisy et al., 1992). We do recognize that in many settings, therapists may not always be able to leave the clinic to conduct the exposure session. If clinician accompaniment is not an option, and the in vivo situation cannot be replicated within the clinic setting, it may be possible to use the parents or some other significant person to conduct the exposure session. However, parents or others need to be given specific instructions and make a commitment to conduct the exposure session for at least 90 minutes. Furthermore, a practice session in the clinic should be conducted in order to ensure that the parent or significant person can conduct the session appropriately.

Social Skills Training

As we noted earlier, SST embodies some elements of exposure treatment. This is because SST usually occurs in groups (although individual treatment is possible), thus providing a naturalistic exposure session. However, SST is not formal exposure treatment and cannot take its place. Also, SST is more than just exposure to a group. The goal of SST is to teach children specific skills and give them an opportunity to practice these skills in a controlled setting. As noted in chapter 2, children with social phobia exhibit specific skill deficits in areas including conversational skills and positive and negative assertion. Table 23 presents content areas that we have found lacking in children with social phobia. In addition, clinicians have noted nonverbal deficits such as poor eye contact, low voice volume, and inappropriate vocal tone. This list is not exhaustive but represents difficulties typically encountered.

Elements of Social Skills Training

The primary objective of SST is skills building, not fear reduction. Typically, one behavior (whether verbal or nonverbal) is targeted at each

---

Table 23

Content Areas Included in Social Skills Training

Greetings and Introductions	Establishing and Maintaining Friendships
Initiating Conversations	Giving and Receiving Compliments
Maintaining Conversations	Assertiveness With Peers
Listening Skills	Assertiveness With Adults
Skills for Joining Groups	Telephone Skills

---

session, but the entire treatment process is cumulative. Nonverbal content skills such as eye contact and voice volume are taught consistently and integrated with the teaching of the content areas. All skills are taught using traditional procedures for SST: instruction, modeling, behavioral rehearsal, feedback, and positive reinforcement. *Instruction* means that the therapist presents the skill to be learned and a rationale for why learning it is important. For example, if the skill is "giving a compliment," children are told that giving compliments is a way to make friends. They are asked to give examples of compliments so that their understanding of the concept can be assessed. Then, the therapist *models* appropriate and inappropriate ways to give compliments. Particularly with younger children, we think that it is very important to use exaggerated modeling to make the distinctions clear. For example, when modeling how to give a compliment, therapists could use an extremely aversive vocal tone, no eye contact, and perhaps a low voice volume in order to demonstrate the wrong way to give a compliment. This should be followed by modeling the appropriate way. Children should be questioned regarding differences between the right or wrong way.

The core of SST, *behavioral rehearsal*, is how the majority of the session time should be spent. Children should be given extensive opportunities to practice the skills. This is usually accomplished by setting up a context in which the behavior can be rehearsed. Although sometimes called role-playing, it is important to remember that the child is not encouraged to play a role. The scene is merely a vehicle through which rehearsal occurs, and the child uses the scene context to practice the skill. The child is instructed to treat the situation as if it were a real social encounter. To continue with the example of giving a compliment, the child may be asked to imagine the following:

> You are sitting in math class. The boy next to you has been studying really hard to improve his grades. The class gets back the most recent test, and he turns to you and says "I finally got an A!"

The child is to respond to this situation with an appropriate compliment. Because skill acquisition will not occur with a single trial, the child should be provided with several practice opportunities with the same scene and with many additional opportunities using other scenes.

After each role-play, the child should be given *corrective feedback* and *positive reinforcement*. Recalling that this is a performance situation and performing in public is feared by children with social phobia, it is important to praise the child for any attempt to engage in the rehearsal. However, it also is important to point out areas in need of further improvement. Thus, the clinician may respond to the child's attempt as follows:

> Chris, you did very well when you said "Congratulations, you worked really hard and you deserve an A." I want you to do it again, and this time, I want you to look at me and smile when you say, "Congratulations."

Implementing Social Skills Training

SST can be conducted individually or in small group settings. In the individual setting, the therapist serves as the interpersonal partner in the behavioral rehearsal. Because the therapist then is required to play two roles simultaneously (interpersonal partner and observer of the child's performance), we prefer a group setting whenever possible. This allows one of the other group members to serve as the interpersonal partner, thereby allowing the therapist to concentrate fully on observing the child's performance. In addition, the group setting allows the child the opportunity to practice with a number of different children who are representative of the child's peers.

An initial step in conducting SST is taking an inventory of the child's social skill deficits. There are no self-report measures widely available to do this, thus, the clinician must rely on behavioral observation, parental report, the child's report of behavior in various social settings, and clinical observations. The content areas listed in Table 23 represent those deficits most commonly encountered in children and adolescents with social phobia, so clinicians might use this list to assist in an initial inventory.

Once the list of social skills deficits has been constructed, the next

step is to construct appropriate scenes to be used in the behavior rehearsal. Some "standard" scenes should be constructed in advance of
the session, but the training will be most effective if the child can supply
some situations from daily interactions. Thus, there should be a battery
of scenes available in case the child does not volunteer any situations,
but scenes drawn from the child's daily experiences and that tap specific
difficulties experienced by the child are most useful.

Ideally, the skill should be presented as described above. If an individual format is used, one or two skills should be presented at each
session, depending upon the child's ability to understand and acquire
the particular behaviors. In a group setting, only one content skill per
session should be used, thereby allowing each child sufficient practice
opportunities. Rehearsal should continue with the same scene until each
child has mastered all components. Then, as noted above, another scene
(requiring each child to practice the same skill) is used.

As we noted with exposure sessions, it is important that the child
continue to practice the skill between therapy sessions. Therefore, the
therapist must design appropriate homework assignments. This homework should provide the opportunity for continued practice but should
not take long to complete (so that the task does not become aversive
or a point of contention between parent and child). In addition, these
homework assignments serve as generalization experiences, allowing the
child to practice the skill outside of the therapist's office and in a variety
of natural settings. For example, continuing with the skill of giving
compliments, the child might be required to give two compliments per
day. Children should be given a homework form so that they (and the
therapist) can monitor completion of the assignments. The assignment
should include specific instructions regarding what the child is to do
and how to do it. Examples of homework assignments for each of the
skills listed in Table 23 are presented in Table 24. Clinicians are cautioned that these are "generic" assignments. The assignments will be
more effective if they are tailored to the particular child.

Problems in Implementing Social Skills Training

We noted that children often may be reluctant to rehearse the behavior
in front of others, particularly in a group setting. We have found that

with preadolescent children, small tokens such as stickers often enhance children's motivation to participate. Similarly, for both preadolescent and adolescent children, coupons for fast food or movie passes are substantive motivators. Often, if requested, fast food restaurants will supply free coupons for french fries (or a similar item), know-

Table 24	
Generic Homework Assignments for Social Skills Training	
Skill	*Homework*
Greetings and Introductions	Smile and say hello to two people you know everyday; introduce yourself to three new people
Initiating Conversations	Greet a friend and ask a question (each day)
Maintaining Conversations	Greet a friend and ask two questions about the same topic (each day)
Listening	Talk to someone in your class. Ask them a question. When you get home, write down the answer
Joining Groups	Ask someone to join you in an activity.
Establishing and Maintaining Friendships	Telephone a friend each night. Talk for 10 minutes.
Giving and Receiving Compliments	Give two compliments each day.
Being Assertive With Peers	If possible, be assertive with a peer. If no situation arises, ask two friends to sleep over at your house.
Being Assertive With Adults	If possible, be assertive with your parents. If no situation arises, talk to as many adults as possible.
Using the Telephone	Make three telephone calls per day. For example, call pet stores and ask if they sell parakeets.

ing that additional foods will be purchased when the coupon is redeemed. The coupons can be used as a reward for group (or individual) participation.

Another potential problem is patients not completing homework assignments. There may be several different reasons for this. First, it should be determined that the assignment is not too difficult for the child. If it is too difficult, the assignment should be adjusted to make it more likely that the child will be able to accomplish the task successfully. If it is a matter of motivation and not difficulty, just encouraging the child to complete the task may be insufficient. Rather, it may be necessary for the parent to reinforce the child for the completion of the assignment. Reinforcement need not be expensive. Increased privileges such as a later bedtime or a later curfew for adolescents may be all that is necessary to engage the child in the task.

A final potential problem is the behaviors learned in the office or clinic not transferring to other settings. Again, the most effective method to ensure generalization is by repeated practice in other group settings. In certain instances, it may be necessary for the parent and therapist to engineer appropriate activities. For example, parents may have to arrange for another child to visit the house in order for there to be opportunities to play with other children. Similarly, when the assignment calls for the child to talk to as many adults as possible, parents can assist their children by providing many practice opportunities. For example, children could go into fast food restaurants and order a meal. They could go into a convenience store and pay for the gas or buy a quart of milk or go into a post office and buy stamps. Generalization opportunities are only as limited as the therapist's creativity and the parent's cooperation.

In our opinion, SST is an integral part of the treatment of social phobia in children. Based on the clinical presentation data in chapter 2, the etiological data in chapter 4, and the adult data in chapters 1 and 8, there is substantial support for the conclusion that those with social phobia (particularly the generalized subtype) have substantial social skill deficits that require remediation if children are to interact appropriately with others. However, although we believe that SST is an integral treatment component, we do not believe that it is sufficient treatment by itself. Two recent meta-analyses of treatment outcome studies with adults (see chapter 8 in this volume) indicated that exposure generates the largest effect size. In one of these reports (Taylor, 1996), the effect size for SST alone was found to be inferior to treatments that included exposure. Some reasons for this have been discussed previously. For example, social skills do not generalize "automatically" to nonclinic settings. Even when generalization programs are a part of the intervention, only 21% of the programs produce partial or complete generalization (Chandler, Lubeck, & Fowler, 1992). Although we noted that SST may provide a group setting and as a result serve as an exposure situation, it does not include a systematic exposure intervention. Furthermore, as we have stressed several times, exposure therapy must be individualized, exposing the patient to very specific fear cues. Therefore, it is highly unlikely that participating in an SST group always would address each group member's unique fear components. Individualized SST would be even less effective at providing a proper exposure setting. Thus, although SST can be an important aspect of the treatment of social phobia in children and adolescents, treatment is most effective when combined with some form of exposure, as in the case of *Social Effectiveness Therapy for Children* (SET-C; Beidel, Turner, & Morris, 1996a).

Social Effectiveness Therapy for Children[1]

SET-C is a 12-week program during which sessions are conducted twice per week for a total of 24 treatment sessions. Each week the child participates in one group social skills training session and one individual exposure session. SET-C includes an individualized exposure therapy component that is implemented as previously described in this chapter. For each child, exposure opportunities, either in the clinic or in the child's natural environment, are developed. In addition, the chil-

---

[1]The Social Effectiveness Therapy for Children Treatment Manual (Beidel et al., 1995) is available from Deborah C. Beidel, Ph.D., Anxiety Prevention and Treatment Research Center, Medical University of South Carolina, Suite 200, 615 Wesley Drive, Charleston, SC 29407.

dren are given homework assignments geared to the content of the exposure sessions. For example, if a child was fearful of interacting with adults, the child may be given the assignment to go into 12 stores over the next week and ask questions of adults. Obviously, parental cooperation is a crucial aspect of the success of the homework program.

SET-C also includes a group SST component because studies of the behavioral interactions of children with social phobia indicate that compared with their nonanxious peers, these children have poorer social skills and higher levels of observable anxiety (see chapter 2). Thus, the second weekly session is an SST group. In SET-C, the content of the social skills sessions is geared to the specific deficits known to be present in these children (see section on SST in chapter 8 for details of the training procedures and Table 23 for the social skills content areas). Finally, a unique aspect of SET-C is the use of a peer-generalization component. This was considered necessary because prior studies with socially withdrawn or isolated children indicated that often behaviors acquired in the clinic do not generalize to other settings without direct intervention. In addition, this component provides opportunities for social learning through the observation of nonanxious peers. Specifically, as part of our SET-C intervention program, we have recruited a group of nonanxious peers who serve as peer helpers in the program. After each SST group, the children with social phobia and the peer helpers go on an outing that lasts for approximately 90 minutes. These activities occur at various places throughout the city, including parks, roller skating rinks, pizza parlors, bowling alleys, and other popular recreation venues for children. The goal of these outings is to allow the children with social phobia to practice the skill learned in group in a natural setting and to provide an opportunity to interact with children who are not anxious (i.e., the type of child who usually ignores them). The peer helpers (who are the same age as the children in the treatment group) are selected on the basis of their friendly, outgoing nature and their desire to help other children who are "shy." They are given minimal instructions and training, but are simply told to talk to the shy children, include them in the activity, and to help them have fun. Peers do, however, receive instruction in confidentiality issues.

Cognitive Restructuring

Some intervention programs, such as the Coping Cat, Coping Koala, or CBGT-A programs discussed earlier, include a component to teach children how to identify and change negative cognitions that might accompany social phobia. As noted, we have not found evidence of a preponderance of negative cognitions in preadolescent children. However, such cognitions may be more common in more mature patients, such as adolescents. Kendall (1994) conducts cognitive restructuring as follows: First, negative thoughts are identified: for example, "She'll never like me, why should I even bother to say hello?" Then rational alternatives are generated: for example, "She always smiles at me, so she probably doesn't hate me," or "Maybe she's just as nervous as I am," or "It's okay to be nervous, everybody's nervous when they meet for the first time." Children then are given practice through behavioral rehearsal or actual exposure sessions whereby they can practice substituting positive thoughts for negative ones. With repeated practice, negative thoughts cease to occur.

Implementing Cognitive Restructuring

One of the first steps in implementing cognitive restructuring is training the child to recognize automatic negative thoughts. Automatic thoughts are usually considered to be unrecognized by the individual even though they can influence behavior. Making one aware of these unrecognized thoughts is usually accomplished by asking children or adolescents to enter into socially distressful situations and pay attention to what they are thinking in the situation. Children are requested to monitor and record these thoughts for the next treatment session.

Once the negative thoughts are identified, the therapist and the patient together examine these thoughts and conclusions and determine their veracity. The child is then taught to generate alternative, positive thoughts for these situations. Beidel, Neal, and Lederer (1991) reported that children with social phobia spontaneously use positive coping statements to cope with their fears. Thus, children have the ability to generate such statements, and it is a matter of teaching them to generate them on a more consistent basis. After the child becomes proficient in generating positive coping statements, the child is taught to substitute positive for negative thoughts. As with traditional exposure or SST, children are assigned homework opportunities to continue to practice the cognitive restructuring task.

Problems in Implementing Cognitive Restructuring

As noted, one difficulty in implementing cognitive restructuring might be the failure of children or adolescents to report the presence of negative cognitions. This might be because young children have not yet achieved a level of cognitive development that allows for the presence of "future-oriented" cognitions. Furthermore, sometimes children mistake the presence of negative feelings ("I felt very nervous") for negative thoughts ("What if I make a mistake?"). Alternatively, if these thoughts are present but unrecognized or for some reason not reported, there is some indication that children might be trained to become adept at recognizing their presence. One strategy advocated by Kendall (1994) that appears helpful in training children to identify and clarify the nature of these negative thoughts is through the use of cartoons and thought bubbles (see Figure 12). Children are very familiar with cartoons and the use of bubbles to indicate that the character is thinking about something. The exercise entails using a collection of such cartoons illustrating various emotions and asking children to write in the bubble what the character must be thinking. By externalizing the task to the use of cartoon characters and providing a broad range of cartoons (between 15 and 20), we have found that children can become more adept at reporting negative thoughts. As a matter of fact, we have found that when these cartoon bubbles are assigned as homework, children need very little encouragement or reinforcement to complete the homework. The cartoons also can be useful when teaching the substitution of positive coping thoughts for negative ones. In this case, cartoons are altered so that two thought bubbles appear. In the first, the child writes the negative thought. Then in the second, the child constructs a positive coping statement.

We believe that with young children the use of cartoons may be quite beneficial. In addition to possibly teaching children to recognize negative cognitions, the cartoons help to externalize the process. By this

Figure 12

Sample cartoon used to help children clarify the nature of negative thoughts

we mean that by identifying the negative thoughts of cartoon characters, children can practice the procedure separately from focusing on their own distress. Thus, children can become proficient at the technique prior to directing it to their own distressing cognitions.

Relaxation Training

We do not view relaxation training as an intervention suitable for the treatment of social phobia when used alone. There is no empirical evidence (either in adults or children) to suggest that this procedure, by itself, is efficacious in the treatment of this disorder. However, because several CBT programs use relaxation training as part of the treatment protocol, we will discuss it briefly here. Relaxation training is an effective strategy to decrease general distress. In children and adolescents, relaxation sessions are generally shorter than for adults (no more than 15–20 minutes) and they address fewer muscle groups. Below we list some guidelines for the implementation of relaxation training with children and adolescents.

Implementing Relaxation Training

Some children who are noticeably tense and anxious to others often are unable to recognize their physical distress. Learning and using relaxation training effectively requires the recognition that one is tense and anxious and the ability to discriminate when one is anxious or relaxed. Thus, prior to teaching relaxation training, we often engage the children in exercises designed to heighten their awareness of somatic sensations of anxiety. We use the interoceptive conditioning exercises designed by Barlow and colleagues (Barlow, Craske, Cerny, & Klosko, 1989) to illustrate what "bodies can feel like when someone is anxious." Interoceptive exercises include such strategies as running in place for one minute, breathing through a small straw for a minute, and shaking the head from side to side (see Barlow et al., 1989, for details). Children can try the exercise and then discuss with the therapist whether the symptom elicited is similar to what happens to them when they feel anxious.

There are two formalized scripts that have been used to teach relaxation training. The first was a script developed for younger children (Koeppen, 1974). This script addresses the cognitive limitations of young children; that is, most relaxation scripts instruct patients to tense and relax various muscle groups. Koeppen's script, recognizing that young children may have difficulty with this type of command, uses images and descriptions of how to tense and relax muscle groups to make the instructions more salient to the child. For example, rather than saying, "Tense the muscles in your right hand by making a fist," the script by Koeppen instructs the child to "Imagine you have a lemon in your right hand and you want to make lemonade. Squeeze the lemon as hard as you can." Although empirical studies are not available, our clinical impression is that young children (ages 10 and under) respond positively to this script. Ollendick (as cited in Ollendick & Cerny, 1981) modified this script for use with older children and adolescents. Essentially, Ollendick's modification removes the imagery components and returns the script to simple instructions to tense and relax muscle groups. This latter script is probably most useful for children over the age of 10.

The child should assume a comfortable position for the session. Tell children to wear "play clothes" for this session, so they can feel comfortable participating either in the interoceptive or relaxation exercises. Prior to conducting the actual session, demonstrate the tension-reduction exercises with the child to be assured that what he or she will be asked to do is understood. Instruct the child in a low voice, using a faster tempo when telling the child to tense muscles and a slower tempo when giving instructions to relax. The therapist should make a cassette tape of the first relaxation session, instructing the child to practice relaxation everyday at home.

Problems Implementing Relaxation

There really are few problems in implementing relaxation training. Clinicians should explain that relaxation training is a skill, like riding a bicycle, and likewise it will take some time to become proficient. Motivation to practice may be the biggest obstacle to successful implementation. The reinforcement practices discussed above would be useful here as well.

Treatment of Selective Mutism

As we noted in chapter 2, selective mutism may be a severe variant of social phobia. Case descriptions suggest that behavior therapies or combination treatments may be effective, but controlled trials have not been conducted (Albert-Stewart, 1986; Cunningham, Cataldo, Mallion, & Keyes, 1983; Krohn, Weckstein, & Wright, 1992). However, in addition to social phobia, children with selective mutism often exhibit forms of defiant and oppositional behaviors (Black & Uhde, 1995) that complicate the clinical presentation and thus the intervention for this disorder. Furthermore, the onset of the difficulty frequently is associated with emotional distress. Therefore, treatment of this disorder must encompass several considerations.

First, the clinician needs to be assured that the refusal to speak has a social–evaluative component. Because a selectively mute child will not, in all likelihood, express such feelings to the therapist, this information will have to be collected from parents or other caretakers with whom the child will communicate and from a behavioral analysis of the situation. Children often will express to parents that they are scared or nervous in some situations and that that is why they refuse to speak. Once the behavior is determined to have a social–evaluative component, interventions such as exposure or SET-C may be helpful. These should be developed and conducted as described above.

However, an important consideration for children with this condition is the amount of attention (i.e., positive reinforcement) that is given to the negative behavior of not talking by parents and others in the environment. Our clinical experience suggests that selectively mute children receive much positive reinforcement for not talking. They get to sit close to their parents, who then translate their whispers or meaningful looks. We have seen some mothers who actually laugh and smile when the child refuses to answer the interviewer's questions or whispers the answer to the mother. In addition, parents can become quite upset because of their child's defiant behavior and devote substantial attention to trying to force the child to talk, making the difficulty a contest of wills. It is important to understand that even if the attention is negative, it is a form of reinforcement (parents are paying attention to the child) and probably functions to increase the likelihood that the selective mutism will continue. In many cases, it is not only parents who reinforce this negative behavior. For example, in addition to having others respond for her at home, one selectively mute child in our clinic never responded or asked questions in class, relying instead on classmates to do it for her. In essence, a pervasive pattern of reinforcement of the maladaptive behavior existed.

In cases of selective mutism, a careful behavioral analysis perhaps is even more important in order to fully understand the condition. In particular, relevant operant aspects associated with the condition need to be revealed, and a plan for addressing this component will need to be developed. In the treatment of this condition it is almost always necessary to pay attention to patterns of behavior that serve to reinforce its occurrence. This may be accomplished by first making the parents aware of the negative effects of their current behavior. The parents should then be taught to provide reinforcement when the child talks rather than when he or she does not talk or when he or she uses other nonverbal forms of communication. The parent may need to be trained in how to differentially reinforce behavior, and a program designed to foster a pattern of positive interaction may have to be instituted. In some cases, more elaborate contingency management programs might be needed.

There are no published controlled empirical studies of the behavioral treatment of selective mutism. Our approach is twofold. First, we use exposure treatment (or a combination of exposure and SST, as in SET-C) as described previously. Parents are encouraged to involve their children in social activities such as scouts, soccer, or dancing lessons, using the parameters described above. Second, we enlighten the parents (and train them if necessary) about the role of positive reinforcement and other factors in maintaining the behavior and teach the parents how to reinforce appropriate behavior (talking) and extinguish non-appropriate behavior (not talking). Thus, parents are instructed that they must stop communicating for the child and "translating" what the child would like to say. This puts the onus of communication back on the child, where it belongs. Basically, the operant aspects of the behavior are explained to the parent, and the need for effective management of the problem is articulated.

The issue of parental reinforcement for not talking is not one that is trivial for the treatment of children with selective mutism. The ina-

Table 25

Sample Graduated Hierarchy for Treatment of Selective Mutism

1. Whisper aloud to Mom and Dad so that David and Sarah (same-aged peers) can hear.
2. Talk aloud to David
3. Talk aloud to David and Sarah together
4. Talk aloud to Mom and Dad in front of an unfamiliar adult.
5. Say one sentence to an unfamiliar adult.
6. Talk for 2 minutes with an unfamiliar adult (with Mom or Dad in the room).
7. Talk for 2 minutes with an unfamiliar adult (no parents present).
8. Say "hello" to teacher at school—no children present
9. Say "hi" to a classmate
10. Talk to teacher in presence of two children
11. Answer a question in front of the class

bility of the parents to recognize the role their attention plays in maintaining the child's disorder may be specific to the selective mutism or may be merely one aspect of an overall pattern of inadequate parenting skills. In either case, simply pointing out the relationship between the parental attention and the maintenance of selective mutism usually will not be sufficient to alter the behavior. Rather, parents will need direct intervention in order to change their behavior. In these cases, effective intervention should include a parent management program that includes specific attention to the role of reinforcement in the maintenance of behaviors and that addresses training in DRO (differential reinforcement of other behavior) schedules (e.g., teaching the parent to ignore nonverbal or whispered communications and to respond to the child only when audible words are spoken). If the parental behaviors associated with selective mutism are part of a broader pattern of inadequate parenting skills, a general parent training program should be implemented.

In Table 25, we present an exposure hierarchy used to treat selective mutism in a 6-year-old boy. The parents in this case provided positive reinforcement (in the form of special desserts or small toys) for achievement of each step on the hierarchy. The parents (with much difficulty at first) ignored the child's attempt to communicate nonverbally or the child's attempt to force the parent to communicate for him. The program was successful once the parents understood their role. One year follow-up indicated treatment gains were maintained.

Case Study

Throughout this chapter we have described the implementation of procedures for the treatment of social phobia in children. Below we present a case illustrating the assessment and treatment of a 14-year-old boy with social phobia and school refusal.

Initial Clinical Interview

Max is a 14-year-old boy who was accompanied to the clinic by his parents because of school refusal behavior. Both Max and his parents described a long history of social anxiety and social awkwardness. In addition, Max did not have any friends and participated in few activities (other than soccer) with peers his age. Over the past year, his parents had noticed that he had become even more reclusive and concerned about negative evaluation by others. Since the onset of school (2 months previously), he had become increasingly withdrawn. When interviewed, he had not been to school for the past 28 days. He described significant fears in a wide range of social situations, stating that he feared embarrassment and humiliation. In addition to school avoidance, he was afraid to speak or write in front of others, to eat in front of others, or to use public restrooms. In addition, he avoided almost any type of general social interactions, including casual conversations. Max complained of physical symptoms of distress, including heart palpitations, sweating, trembling, and occasional blushing. He had been treated previously at a local mental health clinic with Prozac (20mg.); however, his response had been poor. In addition, he exhibited numerous features of APD, including no friends, extreme sensitivity to criticism, and an unwillingness to interact with anyone unless certain of being liked. The behaviors described at this initial interview were consistent with a diagnosis of severe generalized social phobia and traits consistent with

Table 26

Max's Scores on Self-Report Instruments Assessing Anxiety and Depression

Scale	Scores		
	Pre	Post	Follow-Up
State-Trait Anxiety Inventory			
State	31	–	–
Trait	52	–	–
Fear Survey Schedule for Children	42	–	–
Social Phobia and Anxiety Inventory			
Social Phobia Subscale	168	120	90
Agoraphobia Subscale	27	20	10
Difference Score	141	100	80
Beck Depression Inventory	6	–	–

Note: Dashes indicate no scores recorded

APD. A decision was made to accept Max as a patient at the Anxiety Prevention and Treatment Research Center and to offer a course of behavioral treatment.

Assessment Phase

After the initial interview, Max was administered the *Anxiety Disorders Interview Schedule for Children (ADIS-C)*. This interview was conducted for two reasons: first, to confirm the diagnostic impressions of social phobia and to assess more closely for other anxiety disorders, and second, to begin to collect the behavioral data necessary to construct the behavioral treatment plan. The results of the ADIS-C confirmed the initial diagnostic impressions and revealed that Max had high levels of distress and avoidance across a broad range of social situations (both public performances and general social interactions). In addition to the ADIS-C, he completed several self-report inventories. His scores on these inventories are depicted in Table 26. It should be noted that a decision was made, based on Max's age, to administer the *Social Phobia* and Anxiety Inventory (SPAI) rather than the Social Phobia and Anxiety Inventory for Children (SPAI-C) because the former assesses a broader range of potentially distressful situations with a wider variety of interactional partners.

The scores in Table 26 indicate very severe social phobia as measured by the SPAI. In addition, the STAI-C trait score was high, indicating he had a tendency to become anxious and worried in a range of situations, a concept we referred to in chapter 4 as anxiety proneness. His scores on other measures were in the low to average range, suggesting he did not suffer from a more generalized anxiety disorder.

Max also was instructed in self-monitoring procedures. However, because he was avoiding almost all social encounters, he reported only minimal distress on a daily basis but virtually no social contact. Thus, the important use of self-monitoring in this case was that it confirmed the social isolation. In other words, the ratings of distress were deceptive because he did not have the opportunity to feel distressed. The patient's efforts to minimize distress by avoiding all anxiety-eliciting situations had been successful. Thus, a decision was made to monitor Max's progress in terms of the number of days that he attended school. Finally, a behavioral assessment of Max's social skill was conducted using a similar-aged male confederate and several role-play scenes. The assessment revealed that Max had adequate verbal social skills (that is, he knew what to say in various social situations) but he exhibited poor nonverbal skills (poor eye contact, voice volume, etc.).

Initial Treatment Plan

The initial treatment plan had the following goals:

A. Reduce social anxiety and fears of negative evaluation using intensive imaginal and in vivo flooding.
B. Return Max to school using a graduated in vivo shaping program
C. Monitor improvement in nonverbal social behaviors as social distress is decreased
D. Establish social relationships with same-age peers

Goal A: Reduce social anxiety and fear using intensive flooding procedures. To address the first goal of the treatment program, Max participated in a course of imaginal flooding. The scene was constructed (see Scene 1, Table 22, this chapter) to expose him to his core fear of performing poorly in front of others and having others consider him stupid. This scene was presented to Max over the course of six sessions. Blood pressure, pulse rate, and SUDS levels were monitored. There was evidence of within-session and between-session habituation over the course of the six sessions, as depicted in Figure 11. At that point, a decision was made to replicate the imaginal scene in vivo, and Max participated in six in vivo flooding sessions where he read aloud to a small audience. Again, within-session and between-session habituation was noted, and Max showed substantial between-session habituation (see Figure 11). During this phase, Max also had homework assignments to complete, consisting of attending church with his family, accompanying them to restaurants for meals, and keeping up with his schoolwork by participating in the homebound instruction program arranged for him by his parents.

Goals B and D: Return Max to school using a graduated in vivo program and establish social relationships with same-age peers. After achieving between-session habituation in the clinic, the next step was to return Max to the school setting, using the graduated exposure hierarchy that is depicted below. The SUDS ratings (using a 0–100 point scale) reflected Max's judgment about how anxious he would be in each situation.

Max's Graduated Hierarchy

1. Sit in "community program room" located on the school campus but in a building separate from his classes (SUDS 30).
2. Sit in the library, which was in the same building as the school (SUDS 40)
3. Attend one class and spend the rest of the day in the library (SUDS 50)

4. Attend two classes and spend the rest of the day in the library (SUDS 65)
5. Attend the entire morning session and spend the afternoon in the library (SUDS 80)
6. Attend all classes (SUDS 90)
7. Attend all classes and speak to the teacher (SUDS 95)
8. Attend all classes and interact with two peers in each class (SUDS 100)

Max completed each of these steps sequentially and did not advance to the next step until his SUDS level in the previous task did not exceed 20. The entire hierarchy took 25 days to complete. In addition, he was given homework assignments to continue social activities outside of school and to once again attend his church youth group. These latter assignments served to increase his social relationships (Goal D).

Goal C: Monitor nonverbal social skills. As Max's social anxiety decreased, there was improvement in his nonverbal social skills concomitant with the lessening of his social fears and avoidance. This improvement was noted both in his interactions with the therapist and by his parents, who often had the opportunity to observe Max interact with peers. Therefore, no additional intervention was considered necessary.

Assessment of Improvement

Figure 13 depicts Max's school attendance during the course of treatment and during follow-up. Prozac was discontinued at the end of the active treatment intervention. Although he occasionally still refused to go to school during the immediate posttreatment period, by 6-month follow-up his only absences were for documented illness.

Case Summary

This case illustration depicts the treatment of a 14-year-old with severe social phobia and school refusal behavior. There are several aspects to this intervention that deserve mention. First, Max's parents were very supportive but at the same time very firm. They did not want to reinforce his avoidant behavior and were very clear with him that the expectation was that he would return to school as soon as possible. They complied with all aspects of the treatment plan and provided much encouragement for Max to do the same. Thus, this case illustrates a situation where the parents were a very positive asset to treatment and no intervention in this domain was necessary. Second, although it may be possible in some cases to conduct the graduated and intensive programs concurrently, in Max's case it was felt that his distress was so severe that he would not be able to make progress on the in vivo hierarchy until his fear had been decreased, although not necessarily eliminated. Third, it was necessary to engage the cooperation of the school in several respects: (a) to provide homebound instruction during the time that Max was not in school so that he did not fall behind in his schoolwork, thus creating another source of distress, and (b) to

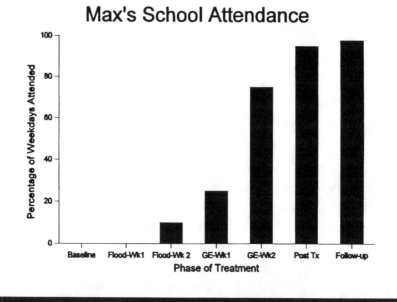

Figure 13

Percentage of Days that Max Attended School on a Weekly Basis. Flood = Imaginal and In Vivo Flooding; GE = Graduated Exposure

allow Max to be on the school grounds when school was in session, even though he was not in his classes. In Max's case, school cooperation was easy to obtain. For others, an in-person conference to discuss the nature of the disorder and how the school may assist in the intervention may be necessary.

It also is important to note that Max was not "cured" at the end of the active intervention program. His posttreatment SPAI difference score had decreased by 40 points (SPAI difference score of 100) but was still in the range of untreated social phobia. Therefore, although much improved, he continued to score in the range of those who would be considered to have social phobia. During follow-up, he continued to receive homework assignments to engage in activities with peers. Thus, he was instructed to rejoin the school soccer team and, in the soccer off-season, join one after-school club. In addition, he became involved in youth activities at his church. At 6-month follow-up, he was attending school regularly, had a small circle of friends, and his difference score on the SPAI had dropped another 20 points, reaching the range on the SPAI where those without social phobia score.

CONCLUSION

In this chapter, we reviewed the available treatment outcome literature in child and adolescent social phobia. This is a relatively small literature because interest in childhood social phobia developed only recently. However, there are several behavioral and cognitive–behavioral treatments that show early promise of being successful in treating this disorder. On the basis of findings from studies addressing social isolation and withdrawn behavior in young children, both SST and exposure strategies seem necessary to overcome social fear and to instigate the development of socially appropriate relationships. All of the behavioral and cognitive–behavioral strategies recently developed for the treatment of social phobia in children and adolescents include some form of exposure, and two combine exposure and SST (i.e., CBGT-A, SET-C). Currently, there are no empirical data to suggest that either of these treatments is more efficacious than another. However, on the basis of the weight of the evidence, studies of socially withdrawn and isolated children, and the results of preliminary findings from CBGT-A and SET-C, some form of skills training in addition to exposure seems appropriate. We noted that a particular problem associated with the treatment of children is that in most cases, the decision to seek treatment for social anxiety was not their own. Indeed, in many cases the child does not want to come to the clinic, and in fact, may not feel that there are any problems at all. In younger children, even when they acknowledge that they have a problem, they may not be able to provide information needed to construct an individualized treatment plan. In such cases, parents, teachers, or significant others become important sources of information needed to establish a diagnosis and to fully characterize the disorder.

We discussed the implementation of each of the psychological treatments that have been developed specifically for the treatment of social phobia in children and adolescents, emphasizing procedural issues as well as significant clinical problems frequently encountered. In particular, we emphasized the necessity for parental involvement in the assessment and treatment process. Also, teachers and significant others often can provide information that will be useful in establishing a diagnosis and helping to identify or clarify critical parameters associated with the condition.

In addition, we reviewed the syndrome of selective mutism and examined similarities and dissimilarities of this condition with social phobia. Clearly, there is significant overlap with social phobia, and we have diagnosed and treated a number of selectively mute children who also met criteria for social phobia. In our experience with these children, factors other than social fear frequently are associated with the manifestation of the non-talking behavior. Primarily, the maladaptive behavior pattern seems to be under the control of operant control. Thus, in addition to social phobia treatment, parent management training, contingency management programs, or both might be needed for the effective treatment of this syndrome.

Finally, we have attempted to present details regarding the implementation of these interventions and some of the common pitfalls. Of course, the hierarchies and flooding scenes presented here cannot be used with other children or adolescents and only represent an example of how they might be constructed. They are presented merely as examples of the type of materials that are used in the interventions. The challenge for the clinician is to construct materials that represent the unique characteristics of each individual child.

Epilogue

Throughout this book, we have attempted to address the broad spectrum of issues related to the disorder known as social phobia—its etiology, clinical syndrome, and treatment. Within this broad spectrum, we wanted to devote particular attention to two issues: developmental considerations and a clinician's-eye view of the challenges of diagnosing and treating this disorder.

In discussing developmental considerations, we addressed the clinical manifestation and treatment of social phobia across the life span, through childhood, adolescence, and adulthood. This examination indicated that although there are many similarities in the manner in which social phobia is manifested, there also are important differences. The core fear of doing something embarrassing or humiliating appears to be consistent across various ages. Even young children report the presence of this type of worry, although they may not report it spontaneously. Avoidance also is common across all ages, although sometimes it can be subtle or be mislabeled as oppositional behavior. The presence of negative cognitions, however, may be a feature that differentiates the presentation of this disorder in adults and children. In the case of preadolescent children, the presence of such cognitions rarely are found. It might be speculated that these cognitions exist in young children, but, because of their immature stage of cognitive development, they do not have the verbal capacity to express their thoughts. However, as we have pointed out, a hallmark of social phobia is the often-expressed complaint that when in social encounters, "my mind goes blank" or "I cannot think of anything to say." This would suggest that when in a distressful situation, those with the disorder are so overwhelmed by emotion that they cannot think at all. Thus, the negative cognitions may represent anticipatory worry or retrospective reflection to explain their heightened arousal. Studies designed to address this issue are necessary to fully understand the cognitive dimension of this disorder in adults and children.

A question commonly encountered by those who provide treatment for anxiety disorders (or any disorder for that matter) is "How did I get this way?" The answer is not simple, even though patients wish to hear otherwise. Social phobia does appear to run in families, although the evidence indicates that it is unclear whether the basis for the familial predisposition is biological, psychological, environmental, or some combination. In our view, it is most likely that some combination of all of these factors are involved in its etiology. Moreover, there may be different pathways. We delineated a number of factors (shyness, behavioral inhibition) that appear to be related to social phobia. At this time, however, it is unclear whether these constructs represent separate predispositional factors or milder forms of the disorder. Studies conducted during the next decade should further illuminate these relationships.

It is evident that we firmly believe intervention will not be successful unless there is a thorough assessment of the patient's clinical condition. This is another area where attention to developmental stage is most important. For example, impromptu speech tasks often are used as part of a behavioral assessment for adults. However, this task is not relevant (i.e., face valid) for most children, whereas reading aloud in front of a group is relevant. On the basis of a consideration of developmental stage, the latter task would be more appropriate for children and represent a more valid assessment strategy.

Not only must the assessment materials and measurement strategies be geared to the age of the patient, the clinician must be aware of patient motivational factors as well. That is, adult patients are more likely to comply with self-monitoring forms and other assessment strategies than are young children because the latter usually do not enter treatment of their own volition. Thus, in this group providing tangible rewards may be necessary to achieve compliance.

Developmental considerations play perhaps their greatest role when it comes to intervention. Not only must the form of the intervention be appropriate for the age of the patient, but additional factors such as comorbid Axis I or II disorders, patient compliance, and the therapist's ability to implement treatment must be considered. For example, Axis II disorders are found commonly in adult patients and present a unique treatment challenge. In contrast, implementing in vivo exposure or homework assignments usually is less difficult with adult patients. Adults usually are able to complete their homework assignments independently. Thus, instructing an adult patient to go out to eat in a restaurant usually requires only the "standard" homework preparation, that is, helping the patient decide on the day and time the assignment will be completed, and which restaurant will be used. However, giving this same assignment to a child or adolescent requires that parents or other adults be available in order to transport and stay with the child. The number of schedules that now must be considered has doubled. Additional difficulties arise if parents themselves have an anxiety disorder. Each developmental stage presents unique challenges for the clinician.

To date, data on treatment maintenance, particularly for the behavioral and cognitive–behavioral treatments for adults, are quite promising. As noted in chapter 7, a substantial number of adult patients who are treated with pharmacological agents appear to relapse when they are switched to placebo or otherwise discontinued from the medication. Thus, although these medications may be useful in the short term, they do not appear to have lasting effects. It is possible, however, that longer term discontinuation schedules or other types of discontinuation strategies (perhaps coupled with cognitive–behavior therapy) may provide more lasting effects.

Short- and long-term follow-up of patients treated with behavioral or cognitive–behavioral therapy indicates that patients maintain, and in some cases, show additional improvement. The most parsimonious explanation for this is that patients continue to apply the skills learned through these interventions and thus enhance their treatment gains. When discharging patients, we always discuss strategies for treatment maintenance. The most obvious recommendation is for patients to continue to place themselves in situations that formerly elicited anxiety. Those with public speaking fears should arrange to continue making presentations in front of groups (such as being a reader at a church), whereas those with more general fears of social interactions should continue to find opportunities (such as adult education classes or community groups) where they can continue to meet and interact with others.

Although no studies have been conducted to determine specifically which factors might enhance treatment maintenance in patients with social phobia, patients treated for OCD often are prescribed interventions designed to reduce general levels of stress (relaxation training, exercise, or assertiveness training), all of which may be helpful in decreasing stress and maintaining treatment gains. Particularly for the substantial number of patients with social phobia who also have generalized anxiety disorder, these interventions might be very helpful.

A second major goal of this volume was an attempt to infuse this book with information sufficient to provide a rich clinical perspective on the disorder. We hope that the patient quotes and descriptions illustrate to the reader the challenges faced by those who suffer from the disorder and those who treat them. To further assist clinicians, we have included actual assessment devices and procedures that we have found useful. In addition, we felt that merely providing a description of how treatments are implemented would be insufficient. Thus, we included examples of exposure hierarchies, imaginal flooding scenes, and homework assignments. Our hope is that these actual patient materials illustrate more clearly how these interventions are developed and implemented.

A common comment by those who provide clinical services is that rarely does treatment proceed as described in journal articles or book chapters. We often have faced similar challenges in our clinical practice. Therefore, we included a discussion of problems and solutions in treatment implementation to illustrate some of the more common problems and how they might be addressed successfully. We hope this presentation illustrates the flexibility of these interventions to address common variations. In 1985, social phobia was called "the neglected anxiety disorder (Liebowitz, Gorman, & Fyer, 1985). As illustrated by the contents of this book, social phobia is neglected no longer. We hope this book will serve to enlighten the field about the nature and manifestation of this disorder and that our experiences will serve to help other clinicians effectively treat the disorder.

References

Achenbach, T. M. (1985). Assessment of anxiety in children. In A. H. Tuma & J. D. Maser (Eds.), *Anxiety and the anxiety disorders* (pp. 703–734). Hillsdale, NJ: Erlbaum.

Akiskal, H. S. (1985). Anxiety: Definition, relationship to depression and proposal for an integrative model. In A. H. Tuma & J. D. Maser (Eds.), *Anxiety and the anxiety disorders* (pp. 787–797). Hillsdale, NJ: Erlbaum.

Albano, A. M. (1995, April). *Psychopathology and treatment of childhood anxiety disorders.* Paper presented at the Anxiety Disorders Association of America Annual Convention, Pittsburgh, PA.

Albano, A. M., DiBartolo, P. M., Heimberg, R. G., & Barlow, D. H. (1995). Children and adolescents: Assessment and treatment. In R. G. Heimberg, M. R. Liebowitz, D. A. Hope, & F. R. Schneier (Eds.), *Social phobia: Diagnosis, assessment and treatment* (pp. 387–425). New York: Guilford Press.

Albano, A. M., Marten, P. A., Holt, C. S., Heimberg, R. G., & Barlow, D. H. (1995). Cognitive–behavioral group treatment for social phobia in adolescents. *Journal of Nervous and Mental Disease, 183,* 649–656.

Albert-Stewart, P. (1986). Positive reinforcement in short-term treatment of an electively mute child: A case study. *Psychological Reports, 58,* 571–576.

Al-Kubaisy, T., Marks, I. M., Logsdail, S., Marks, I. M. P., Lovell, K., Sungur, M., & Araya, R. (1992). Role of exposure homework in phobia reduction: A controlled study. *Behavior Therapy, 23,* 599–621.

American Psychiatric Association. (1980). *Diagnostic and statistical manual of mental disorders* (3rd ed.). Washington, DC: Author.

American Psychiatric Association. (1987). *Diagnostic and statistical manual of mental disorders* (3rd ed., rev.). Washington, DC: Author.

American Psychiatric Association. (1994). *Diagnostic and statistical manual of mental disorders* (4th ed.). Washington, DC: Author.

Amies, P. L., Gelder, M. G., & Shaw, P. M. (1983). Social phobia: A comparative clinical study. *British Journal of Psychiatry, 142,* 174–179.

Anderson, J. C., Williams, S., McGee, R., & Silva, P. A. (1987). DSM-III disorders in preadolescent children. *Archives of General Psychiatry, 44,* 69–76.

Arkowitz, H. (1981). Assessment of social skills. In M. Hersen & A. S. Bellack (Eds.), *Behavioral assessment* (pp. 296–327). New York: Pergamon.

Asendorpf, J. B. (1990). Beyond social withdrawal: Shyness, unsociability, and peer avoidance. *Human Development, 33,* 250–259.

Asendorpf, J. B. (1993). Beyond temperament: A two-factorial coping model of the development of inhibition during childhood. In K. H. Rubin & J. B. Asendorpf (Eds.), *Social withdrawal, inhibition, and shyness in childhood.* Hillsdale, NJ: Erlbaum.

Attili, G. (1989). Social competence versus emotional security: The link between home relationships and behavior problems at school. In B. H. Schneider, G. Attilli, J. Nadel (Eds.), *Social competence in developmental perspective* (pp. 293–311). London: Kluwer.

Bandura, A. (1969). *Principles of behavior modification.* New York: Holt, Rinehart, & Winston.

Barlow, D. H. (1988). *Anxiety and its disorders.* New York: Guilford Press.

Barlow, D. H., Craske, M. G., Cerny, J. A., & Klosko, J. S. (1989). Behavioral treatment of panic disorder. *Behavior Therapy, 20,* 261–282.

Barrett, P. M., Dadds, M. R., Rapee, R. M., & Ryan, S. M. (1996). Family intervention for childhood anxiety: A controlled trial. *Journal of Consulting and Clinical Psychology, 64,* 333–342.

Barrios, B., & O'Dell, S. (1989). Fear and anxieties. In E. J. Mash & R. A. Barkley (Eds.), *Treatment of childhood disorders* (pp. 167–221). New York: Guilford Press.

Becker, W. C. (1971). *Parents are teachers.* Champaign, IL: Research Press.

Beidel, D. C. (1991). Social phobia and overanxious disorder in school-age children. *Journal of the American Academy of Child and Adolescent Psychiatry, 30,* 545–552.

Beidel, D. C., Borden, J. W., Turner, S. M., & Jacob, R. G. (1989). The Social Phobia and Anxiety Inventory: Concurrent valdity with a clinic sample. *Behaviour Research and Therapy, 27,* 573–576.

Beidel, D. C., Christ, M. A. G., & Long, P. J. (1991). Somatic complaints in anxious children. *Journal of Abnormal Child Psychology, 19,* 659–670.

Beidel, D. C., & Morris, T. L. (1995). Social phobia. In J. S. March (Ed.), *Anxiety disorders in children and adolescents* (pp. 181–211). New York: Guilford Press.

Beidel, D. C., Neal, A. M., & Lederer, A. S. (1991). The feasibility and validity of a daily diary for the assessment of anxiety in children. *Behavior Therapy, 22,* 505–517.

Beidel, D. C., & Turner, S. M. (1988). Comorbidity of test anxiety and other anxiety disorders in children. *Journal of Abnormal Child Psychology, 16,* 275–287.

Beidel, D. C., & Turner, S. M. (1992a). Scoring the Social Phobia and Anxiety Inventory: Comments on Herbert et al. (1991). *Journal of Psychopathology and Behavioral Assessment, 14,* 377–379.

Beidel, D. C., & Turner, S. M. (1992b, October). *Are social phobic children the same as social phobic adults?* Paper presented at the Academy of Child and Adolescent Psychiatry Annual Meeting, Washington, DC.

Beidel, D. C., Turner, S. M., & Cooley, M. R. (1993). Assessing reliable and clinically significant change in social phobia: Validity of the Social Phobia and Anxiety Inventory. *Behaviour Research and Therapy, 31,* 331–337.

Beidel, D. C., Turner, S. M., & Dancu, C. V. (1985). Physiological, cognitive and behavioral aspects of social anxiety. *Behaviour Research and Therapy, 23,* 109–117.

Beidel, D. C., Turner, S. M., & Fink, C. M. (1996). The assessment of childhood social phobia: Construct, convergent and discriminative validity of the Social Phobia and Anxiety Inventory for Children (SPAI-C). *Psychological Assessment, 8,* 235–240.

Beidel, D. C., Turner, S. M., Jacob, R. G., & Cooley, M. R. (1989). Assessment of social phobia: Reliability of an impromptu speech task. *Journal of Anxiety Disorders, 3,* 149–158.

Beidel, D. C., Turner, S. M., & Morris, T. L. (1995). A new inventory to assess childhood social anxiety and phobia: The Social Phobia and Anxiety Inventory for Children. *Psychological Assessment, 7,* 73–79.

Beidel, D. C., Turner, S. M., & Hamlin, K. (1997). The Social Phobia and Anxiety Inventory for Children: Further discriminative validity. Manuscript in preparation.

Beidel, D. C., Turner, S. M., & Morris, T. L. (1996). *Social Effectiveness Training for Children: A treatment manual.* Unpublished manuscript, Medical University of Charleston, South Carolina.

Beidel, D. C., Turner, S. M., & Morris, T. M. (1997). *Social skills deficits in children with social phobia.* Manuscript in preparation.

Beidel, D. C., Turner, S. M., Stanley, M. A., & Dancu, C. V. (1989). The Social Phobia and Anxiety Inventory: Concurrent and external validity. *Behavior Therapy, 20,* 417–427.

Beidel, D. C., Turner, M. W., & Trager, K. N. (1994). Test anxiety and childhood anxiety disorders in African American and White school children. *Journal of Anxiety Disorders, 8,* 169–179.

Benca, R., Matuzas, W., & Al-Sadir, J. (1986). Social phobia, MVP, and response to imipramine. *Journal of Clinical Psychopharmacology, 6,* 50–51.

Bergsgaard, M. O., & Larsson, E. V. (1984). Increasing social interaction between an isolate first grader and cross-cultural peers. *Psychology in the Schools, 21,* 244–251.

Berler, E. S., Gross, A. M., & Drabman, R. S. (1982). Social skills training with children: Proceed with caution. *Journal of Applied Behavior Analysis, 15,* 41–53.

Biederman, J. (1991) Sudden death in children treated with a tricyclic antidepressant. *Journal of the American Academy of Child and Adolescent Psychiatry, 30,* 495–498.

Biederman, J., Balessarini, R. J., Wright, V., Knee, D., Harmatz, J. S., & Goldblatt, A. (1989). A double-blind placebo controlled study of desipramine in the treatment of ADD. II. Serum drug levels and cardiovascular findings. *Journal of the American Academy of Child and Adolescent Psychiatry, 28,* 903–911.

Biederman, J., Rosenbaum, J. F., Hirshfeld, D. R., Faraone, S. V., Bolduc, E. A., Gersten, M., Meminger, S. R., Kagan, J., Snidman, N., & Reznick, S. (1990). Psychiatric correlates of behavioral inhibition in young children of parents with and without psychiatric disorders. *Archives of General Psychiatry, 47,* 21–26.

Bierman, K. L., & Furman, W. (1984). The effects of social skills training and peer involvment on the social adjustment of preadolescents. *Child Development, 55,* 151–162.

Birmaher, B., Waterman, S. G., Ryan, N., Cully, M., Balach, L., Ingram, J., &

Brodsky, M. (1994). Fluoxetine for childhood anxiety disorders. *Journal of the American Academy of Child and Adolescent Psychiatry, 33,* 993–999.

Bisserbe, J. C., Lepine, J. P., & GRP Group. (1994). Moclobemide in social phobia: A pilot study. *Clinical Neuropharmacology, 17,* 588–594.

Black, B., & Uhde, T. W. (1992). Elective mutism as a variant of social phobia. *Journal of the American Academy of Child and Adolescent Psychiatry, 31,* 1090–1094.

Black, B., & Uhde, T. W. (1994). Treatment of elective mutism with fluoxetine: A double-blind, placebo-controlled study. *Journal of the American Academy of Child and Adolescent Psychiatry, 33,* 1000–1006.

Black, B., & Uhde, T. (1995). Psychiatric characteristics of children with selective mutism: A pilot study. *Journal of the Americam Academy of Child and Adolescent Psychiatry, 34,* 847–856.

Black, B., Uhde, T. W., & Tancer, M. E. (1992). Fluoxetine for the treatment of social phobia. *Journal of Clinical Psychopharmacology, 12,* 293–295.

Bowen, R. C., Cipywnyk, D., D'Arcy, C., & Keegan, D. (1984). Alcoholism, anxiety disorders, and agoraphobia. *Alcoholism: Clinical and Experimental Research, 8,* 8–50.

Brawman-Mintzer, O., Lydiard, R. B., Emmanuel, N., Payeur, R., Johnson, M., Roberts, J., Jarrell, M. P., & Ballenger, J. C. (1993). Psychiatric comorbidity in patients with generalized anxiety disorder. *American Journal of Psychiatry, 150,* 1216–1218.

Breier, A., Charney, D. S., & Nelson, J. (1984). Seizures induced by abrupt discontinuation of alprazolam. *American Journal of Psychiatry, 141,* 1606.

Bromberg, A. D. (1993). Inhibition and children's experiences of out-of-home care. In K. H. Rubin & J. B. Asendorpf (Eds.), *Social withdrawal, inhibition, and shyness in childhood* (pp. 151–176). Hilldsdale, NJ: Erlbaum.

Brown, E. J., Heimberg, R. G., & Juster, H. R. (1995). Social phobia subtype and avoidant personality disorder: Effect on severity of social phobia, impairment, and outcome of cognitive-behavioral treatment. *Behavior Therapy, 26,* 467–486.

Brown, E. J., Turovsky, J., Heimberg, R. G., Juster, H. R., Brown, T. A., & Barlow, D. H. (1997). Validation of the Social Interaction Anxiety Scale and the Social Phobia Scale across the anxiety disorders. *Psychological Assessment, 9,* 21–27.

Brown, J. B., & Lloyd, H. (1975). A controlled study of children not speaking at school. *Journal of the Association of Workers for Maladjusted Children, 3,* 49–63.

Bruch, M. A. (1989). Familial and developmental antecedents of social phobia: Issues and findings. *Clinical Psychology Review, 9,* 37–47.

Bruch, M. A., Giordano, S., & Pearl, L. (1986). Differences between fearful and self-conscious shy subtypes in background and current adjustment. *Journal of Research in Personality, 20,* 172–186.

Bruch, M. A., & Heimberg, R. G. (1994). Differences in perceptions of parental and personal characteristics between generalized and nongeneralized social phobics. *Journal of Anxiety Disorders, 8,* 155–168.

Bruch, M. A., Heimberg, R. G., Berger, P., & Collins, T. M. (1989). Social phobia and perceptions of early parental and personal characteristics. *Anxiety Research, 2,* 57–63.

Burns, D. D. (1980). *Feeling good: The new mood therapy.* New York: William Morrow & Co., Inc.

Buss, A. H., & Plomin, R. (1984). *Temperament: Early developing personality traits.* Hillsdale, NJ: Erlbaum.

Butler, G., Cullington, A., Munby, M., Amies, P., & Gelder, M. (1984). Exposure and anxiety management in the treatment of social phobia. *Journal of Consulting and Clinical Psychology, 52,* 642–650.

Caspi, A., Elder, G. H., Jr., & Bem, D. J. (1988). Moving away from the world: Life course patterns of shy children. *Developmental Psychology, 24,* 824–831.

Chambers, W. J., Puig-Antich, J., Hirsch, M., Paez, P., Ambrosini, P. J., Tabizi, M. A., & Davies, M. (1985). The assessment of affective disorders in children and adolescents by semistructured interview: Test-retest reliability of the Schedule for Affective Disorders and Schizophrenia in School-Age Children, Present Episode Version. *Archives of General Psychiatry, 42,* 696–702.

Chambless, D. L., Cherney, J., Caputo, G. C., & Rheinstein, B. J. G. (1987). Anxiety disorders and alcoholism: A study with inpatient alcoholics. *Journal of Anxiety Disorders, 1,* 9–40.

Chambless, D. L., Tran, G. Q., & Glass, C. R. (1997). Predictors of response to cognitive-behavioral group therapy for social phobia. *Journal of Anxiety Disorders, 11,* 221–240.

Chandler, L. K., Lubeck, R. C., & Fowler, S. A. (1992). Generalization and maintenance of preschool children's social skills: A critical review and analysis. *Journal of Applied Behavioral Analysis, 25*, 415–428.

Chang, S. C. (1984). [English-language review of Yamashita, I., *Taijin-Kyofu.* Tokyo: Kenehara]. *Transcultural Psychiatry Review 21*, 283–288.

Chapman, T. F., Mannuzza, S., & Fyer, A. J. (1995). Epidemiology and family studies of social phobia. In R. G. Heimberg, M. R. Liebowitz, D. A. Hope, & F. R. Schneier (Eds.), *Social phobia: Diagnosis, assessment, and treatment* (pp. 21–40). New York: Guilford Press.

Cheek, J. M., & Buss, A. H. (1981). Shyness and sociability. *Journal of Personality and Social Psychology, 41*, 330–339.

Christoff, K. A., Scott, W. O. N., Kelley, M. L., Baer, G., & Kelly, J. A. (1985). Social skills and social problem-solving training for shy young adolescents. *Behavior Therapy, 16*, 468–477.

Clark, D. B. (1993, March). *Assessment of social anxiety in adolescents.* Paper presented at the Anxiety Disorders Association of America Annual Convention, Charleston, SC.

Clark, D. B., & Agras, W. S. (1991). The assessment and treatment of performance anxiety in musicians. *American Journal of Psychiatry, 148*, 59–65.

Clark, D. B., Turner, S. M., Beidel, D. C., Donovan, J. E., Kirisci, L., & Jacob, R. G. (1994). Reliability and validity of the Social Phobia and Anxiety Inventory for adolescents. *Psychological Assessment, 6*, 135–140.

Cook, M., & Mineka, S. (1991). Selective associations in the origins of phobic fears and their implications for behavior therapy. In P. Martin (Ed.), *Handbook of behavior therapy and psychological science: An integrative approach* (pp. 413–434). Elmsford, NY: Pergamon Press.

Craske, M. G. (1991). Phobic fear and panic attacks: The same emotional states triggered by different cues? *Clinical Psychology Review, 11*, 599–620.

Craske, M. G., & Rachman, S. J. (1987). Return of fear: Perceived skill and heart rate responsivity. *British Journal of Clinical Psychology, 26*, 187–199.

Craske, M. G., Rapee, R. M., & Barlow, D. H. (1992). Cognitive–behavioral treatment of panic disorder, agoraphobia, and generalized anxiety disorder. In S. M. Turner, K. S. Calhoun, & H. E. Adams (Eds.), *Handbook of clinical behavior therapy* (2nd ed.) (pp. 39–66). New York: Wiley.

Cunningham, C. E., Cataldo, M. F., Mallion, C., & Keyes, J. B. (1983). A review and controlled single case evaluation of behavioral approaches to the management of elective mutism. *Child and Family Behavior Therapy, 5,* 25–49.

Dadds, M. R., Barrett, P. M., Rapee, R. M., & Ryan, A. (1996). Family process and child anxiety and aggression: An observational analysis. *Journal of Abnormal Child Psychology, 24,* 715–734.

Daniels, D., & Plomin, R. (1985). Origins of individual differences in infant shyness. *Developmental Psychology, 21,* 118–121.

Darby, W. B., & Schlenker, B. R. (1986). Children's understanding of social anxiety. *Developmental Psychology, 22,* 633–639.

Davidson, J. (1993, March). *Childhood histories of adult social phobics.* Paper presented at the Anxiety Disorders Association Annual Convention, Charleston, SC.

Davidson, J. R. T., Ford, S. M., Smith, R. D., & Potts, N. L. S. (1991). Long-term treatment of social phobia with clonazepam. *Journal of Clinical Psychiatry, 52,* 16–20.

Davidson, J. R. T., Potts, N. L. S., Richichi, E. A., Ford, S. M., Krishnan, K. R. R., Smith, R. D., & Wilson, W. (1991). The Brief Social Phobia Scale. *Journal of Clinical Psychiatry, 52,* 48–51.

Davidson, J. R. T., Potts, N., Richichi, E., Krishnan, R., Ford, S. M., Smith, R., & Wilson, W. H. (1993). Treatment of social phobia with clonazepam and placebo. *Journal of Clinical Psychopharmacology, 13,* 423–428.

Delgado, P. L., & Gelenberg, A. J. (1996). Antidepressants and antimanic medications. In G. O. Gabbard & S. D. Atkinson (Eds.), *Synopsis of treatments of psychiatric disorders* (2nd ed., pp. 487–503). Washington, DC: American Psychiatric Press.

den Boer, J. A., van Vliet, I. M., & Westenberg, H. G. M. (1994). Recent advances in the psychopharmacology of social phobia. *Progress in Neuro-Psychopharmacology and Biological Psychiatry, 18,* 625–645.

DiNardo, P. A., Barlow, D. H., Cerny, J. A., Vermilya, B. B., Vermilya, J. A., Himaldi, W. G., & Waddell, M. T. (1986). *Anxiety Disorders Interview Schedule-Revised (ADIS-R).* Unpublished manuscript, State University of New York at Albany.

DiNardo, P. A., Brown, T. A., & Barlow, D. H. (1995). *Anxiety Disorders Inteview Schedule for DSM-IV (Lifetime Version).* San Antonio, TX: Psychological Corporation.

DiNardo, P. A., Moras, K., Barlow, D. H., Rapee, R. M., & Brown, T. A. (1993). Reliability of *DSM-III-R* anxiety disorder categories: Using the Anxiety Disorders Interview Schedule-Revised (ADIS-R). *Archives of General Psychiatry, 50,* 251–256.

DiNardo, P. A., O'Brien, G. T., Barlow, D. H., Waddell, M. T., & Blanchard, E. B. (1983). Reliability of *DSM-III* anxiety disorders categories using a new structured interview. *Archives of General Psychiatry, 40,* 1070–1074.

Disilver, S. C., Qamar, A. B., & Del Medico, V. J. (1992). Secondary social phobia in patients with major depression. *Psychiatry Research, 44,* 33–40.

Dummit, E. S., III, Klein, R. G., Tancer, N. K., Asche, B., Martin, J., & Fairbanks, J. A. (1997). Systematic assessment of 50 children with selective mutism. *Journal of the American Academy of Child and Adolescent Psychiatry, 36,* 653–660.

Edelman, R. E., & Chambless, D. L. (1995). Adherence during sessions and homework in cognitive-behavioral group treatment of social phobia. *Behaviour Research and Therapy, 33,* 573–577.

Ellis, A. (1962). *Reason and emotion in psychotherapy.* New York: Lyle Stuart.

Emmelkamp, P. M. G., Mersch, P. P., Vissia, E., & van der Helm, M. (1985). Social phobia: A comparative evaluation of cognitive and behavioral interventions. *Behaviour Research and Therapy, 23,* 365–369.

Endicott, J., & Spitzer, R. L. (1978). A diagnostic interview: The Schedule for Affective Disorders and Schizophrenia. *Archives of General Psychiatry, 35,* 837–844.

Falloon, I. R. H., Lloyd, G. G., & Harpin, R. E. (1981). The treatment of social phobia: Real life rehearsal with nonprofessional therapists. *The Journal of Nervous and Mental Disease, 169,* 180–184.

Feske, U., & Chambless, D. L. (1995). Cognitive–behavioral versus exposure treatment for social phobia: A meta-analysis. *Behavior Therapy, 26,* 695–720.

Finch, M., & Hops, H. (1982). Remediation of social withdrawal in young children: Considerations for the practitioner. *Child and Youth Services, 5,* 29–42.

Fink, C. M., Turner, S. M., & Beidel, D. C. (1996). Culturally relevant factors in the behavioral treatment of social phobia: A case study. *Journal of Anxiety Disorders, 10,* 201–209.

Finnie, V., & Russell, A. (1988). Preschool children's social status and their mothers' behavior and knowledge in the supervisory role. *Developmental Psychology, 24,* 789–801.

Furman, W., Rahe, D. F., & Hartrup, W. W. (1979). Rehabilitation of socially withdrawn preschool children through mixed-age and same-age socialization. *Child Development, 50,* 915–922.

Fyer, A. J., Mannuzza, S., Chapman, T. F., Liebowitz, M. R., & Klein, D. F. (1993). A direct interview family study of social phobia. *Archives of General Psychiatry, 50,* 293–586.

Garcia-Coll, C., Kagan, J., & Reznick, J. S. (1984). Behavioral inhibition in young children. *Child Development, 55,* 1005–1019.

Gelernter, C. S., Uhde, T. W., Cimbolic, P., Arnkoff, D. B., Vittone, B. J., Tancer, M. E., & Bartko, J. J. (1991). Cognitive-behavioral and pharmacological treatments of social phobia: A controlled study. *Archives of General Psychiatry, 48,* 938–945.

Ginsburg, G. S., & Silverman, W. K. (1996). Phobic and anxiety disorders in Hispanic and Caucasian youth. *Journal of Anxiety Disorders, 10,* 517–528.

Golwyn, D. H., & Weinstock, R. C. (1990). Phenelzine treatment of elective mutism: A case report. *Journal of Clinical Psychiatry, 51,* 384–385.

Gorman, J. M., & Gorman, L. F. (1987). Drug treatment of social phobia. *Journal of Affective Disorders, 13,* 183–192.

Gorman, J. M., Liebowitz, M. R., Fyer, A. J., Campeas, R., & Klein, D. F. (1985). Treatment of social phobia with atenolol. *Journal of Clinical Psychopharmacology, 5,* 298–301.

Gossard, D., Dennis, C., & Debush, R. F. (1984). Use of beta-blocking agents to relieve stress of presentation at an international cardiology meeting: Results of a survey. *American Journal of Cardiology, 54,* 240–241.

Grayson, J. B., Foa, E. B., & Steketee, G. (1986). Exposure in vivo of obsessive–compulsives under distracting and attention-focusing conditions: Replication and extension. *Behaviour Research and Therapy, 24,* 475–479.

Grenyer, B. F. S., Williams, G., Swift, W., & Neill, O. (1992). The prevalence of social-evaluative anxiety in opiod users seeking treatment. *International Journal of the Addictions, 27,* 665–673.

Griest, J. H., Kobak, K. A., Jefferson, J. W., Katzelnick, D. J., & Chene, R. L. (1995). In R. G. Heimberg, M. R. Liebowitz, D. A. Hope, & F. R. Schneier (Eds.), *Social phobia: Diagnosis, assessment, and treatment* (pp. 185–201). New York: Guilford Press.

Guevremont, D. C., MacMillan, V. M., Shawchuck, C. R., & Hansen, D. J. (1989). A peer-mediated intervention with clinic-referred socially isolated girls. *Behavior Modification, 13*, 32–50.

Hamilton, M. (1959). The assessment of anxiety states by rating. *British Journal of Medical Psychology, 32*, 50–55.

Hamilton, M. (1960). A rating scale for depression. *Journal of Neurology, Neurosurgery, and Psychiatry, 23*, 56–62.

Hathaway, S. R., & McKinley, J. C. (1940). A multiphasic personality schedule (Minnesota): I. Construction of the schedule. *Journal of Psychology, 10*, 249–254.

Heckelman, L. R., & Schneier, F. R. (1995). Diagnostic issues. In R. G. Heimberg, M. R. Liebowitz, D. A. Hope, & F. R. Schneier (Eds.), *Social phobia; Diagnosis, assessment and treatment* (pp. 3–20). New York: Guilford Press.

Heimberg, R. G. (1991). *Cognitive-behavioral treatment of social phobia in a group setting: A treatment manual* (2nd ed.). Unpublished manuscript, University at Albany-SUNY.

Heimberg, R. G., Dodge, C. S., Hope, D. A., Kennedy, C. R., Zollo, L., & Becker, R. E. (1990). Cognitive behavioral treatment for social phobia: Comparison with a credible placebo control. *Cognitive Therapy and Research, 14*, 1–23.

Heimberg, R. G., Holt, C. S., Schneier, F. R., Spitzer, R. L., & Liebowitz, M. R. (1993). The issue of subtypes in the diagnosis of social phobia. *Journal of Anxiety Disorders, 7*, 249–269.

Heimberg, R. G., Hope, D. A., Dodge, C. S., & Becker, R. E. (1990). *DSM-III-R* subtypes of social phobia: Comparison of generalized social phobics and public speaking phobics. *Journal of Nervous and Mental Disease, 178*, 172–179.

Heimberg, R. G., Hope, D. A., Rapee, R. M., & Bruch, M. A. (1988). The validity of the Social Avoidance and Distress Scale and the Fear of Negative Evaluation Scale with social phobic patients. *Behaviour Research and Therapy, 26*, 407–410.

Heimberg, R. G., Juster, H. R., Brown, E. J., Holle, C., Makris, G. S., Leung, A. W., Schneier, F. R., Gitow, A., & Liebowitz, M. R. (1994, November). *Cognitive-behavioral versus pharmacological treatment of social phobia: Post-treatment and follow-up effects.* Paper presented at the annual meeting of the Association for Advancement of Behavior Therapy, San Diego, CA.

Heimberg, R. G., Mueller, G., Holt, C. S., Hope, D. A., & Liebowitz, M. R. (1992). Assessment of anxiety in social interaction and being observed by others: The Social Interaction Anxiety Scale and the Social Phobia Scale. *Behavior Therapy, 23,* 53–73.

Heimberg, R. G., Salzman, D. G., Holt, C. S., & Blendall, K. A. (1993). Cognitive-behavioral group treatment for social phobia: Effectiveness at five year follow-up. *Cognitive Therapy and Research, 17,* 325–339.

Hembree-Kigin, T. L., & McNeil, C. B. (1995). *Parent-child interaction therapy.* New York: Plenum.

Herbert, J. D., Bellack, A. S., & Hope, D. A. (1991). Concurrent validity of the social phobia and anxiety inventory. *Journal of Psychopathology and Behavioral Assessment, 13,* 357–368.

Herbert, J. D., Hope, D. A., & Bellack, A. S. (1992). Validity of the distinction between generalized social phobia and avoidant personality disorder. *Journal of Abnormal Psychology, 101,* 332–339.

Hersen, M., Bellack, A. S., Himmelhoch, J., & Thase, M. E. (1984). Effects of social skill training, amitriptyline, and psychotherapy in unipolar depressed women. *Behavior Therapy, 15,* 21–40.

Hinde, R. A., & Tamplin, A. (1983). Relations between mother–child interaction and behavior in pre-school children. *British Journal of Developmental Psychology, 1,* 231–257.

Hirshfeld, D. R., Rosenbaum, J. F., Biederman, J., Bolduc, E. A., Faraone, S. V., Snidman, N., Reznick, J. S., & Kagan, J. (1992). Stable behavioral inhibition and its association with anxiety disorder. *Journal of the American Academy of Child and Adolescent Psychiatry, 31,* 103–111.

Hofmann, S. G., Newman, M. G., Becker, E., Taylor, C. B., & Roth, W. T. (1995). Social phobia with and without avoidant personality disorder: Preliminary behavior therapy outcome findings. *Journal of Anxiety Disorders, 9,* 427–438.

Hofmann, S. G., Newman, M. G., Ehlers, A., & Roth, W. T. (1995). Psychological differences between subgroups of social phobics. *Journal of Abnormal Psychology 104,* 224–231.

Holt, C. S., Heimberg, R. G., & Hope, D. A. (1992). Avoidant personality disorder and the generalized subtype of social phobia. *Journal of Abnormal Psychology, 101,* 318–325.

Holt, C. S., Heimberg, R. G., Hope, D. A., & Liebowitz, M. R. (1992). Situational domains of social phobia. *Journal of Anxiety Disorders, 6,* 63–77.

Hope, D. A., Heimberg, R. G., & Bruch, M. A. (1995). Dismantling cognitive-behavioral group therapy for social phobia. *Behaviour Research and Therapy, 33,* 637–650.

Hymel, S., Rubin, K. H., Rowden, L., & LeMare, L. (1990). Children's peer relationships: Longitudinal prediction of internalizing and externalizing problems from middle to late childhood. *Child Development, 61,* 2004–2021.

Ihenaga, K., Kiriike, N., Matasuyama, M., Oishi, S., Kaneko, K., & Yamagami, S. (1996, August). *Phobic and anxiety symptoms in preadolescent and adolescent children.* Paper presented at the World Congress of Psychiatry, Madrid, Spain.

Ishiyama, F. I. (1984). Shyness: Anxious social sensitivity and self-isolating tendency. *Adolescence, 19,* 903–911.

Jacobson, N. S., & Truax, P. (1991). Clinical significance: A statistical approach to defining meaningful change in psychotherapy research. *Journal of Consulting and Clinical Psychology, 59,* 12–19.

Johnson, M. R., Turner, S. M., Beidel, D. C., & Lydiard, R. B. (1995). Personality function and social phobia. In M. D. Stein (Ed.), *Social phobia: Clinical perspectives and research* (pp. 77–117). Washington, DC: American Psychiatric Press.

Jupp, J. J., & Griffiths, M. D. (1990). Self-concept changes in shy, socially isolated adolescents following social skills training emphasising role plays. *Australian Psychologist, 25,* 165–177.

Juster, H. R., Heimberg, R. G., & Engelberg, B. (1995). Self selection and sample selection in a treatment study of social phobia. *Behaviour Research and Therapy, 33,* 321–324.

Kagan, J., Arcus, D., Snidman, N., Feng, W. Y., Hendler, J., & Greene, S. (1994). Reactivity in infants: A cross-national comparison. *Developmental Psychology, 30,* 342–345.

Kagan, J., Reznick, J. S., & Snidman, N. (1987). The physiology and psychology of behavioral inhibition in children. *Child Development, 58,* 1459–1473.

Kashani, J. H., & Orvaschel, H. (1990). A community study of anxiety in children and adolescents. *American Journal of Psychiatry, 147,* 313–318.

Kearney, C. A., & Silverman, W. K. (1990). A preliminary analysis of a functional model of assessment and treatment for school refusal behavior. *Behavior Modification, 14,* 340–366.

Kendall, P. C. (1994). Treating anxiety disorders in children: Results of a randomized clinical trial. *Journal of Consulting and Clinical Psychology, 62,* 100–110.

Kendall, P. C., & Southham-Gerow, M. A. (1996). Long-term follow-up of a cognitive–behavioral therapy for anxiety disordered youth. *Journal of Consulting and Clinical Psychology, 64,* 724–730.

Kendall, P. C., & Warman, M. J. (1996). Anxiety disorders in youth: Diagnostic consistency across *DSM-III-R* and *DSM-IV. Journal of Anxiety Disorders, 10,* 453–463.

Kendler, K. S., Neale, M. C., Kessler, R. C., Heath, A. C., & Eaves, L. J. (1992). The genetic epidemiology of phobias in women: The interrelationship of agoraphobia, social phobia, situational phobia, and simple phobia. *Archives of General Psychiatry, 49,* 273–281.

Kerr, M., Lambert, W. W., & Bem, D. J. (1996). Life course sequelae of childhood shyness in Sweden: Comparison with the United States. *Developmental Psychology, 32,* 1100–1105.

Kessler, R. C., McGonagle, K. A., Zhao, S., Nelson, C. B., Hughes, M., Eshelman, S., Wittchen, H., & Kendler, K. S. (1994). Lifetime and 12-month prevalence of DSM-III-R psychiatric disorders in the United States. *Archives of General Psychiatry, 51,* 8–19.

Klein, D. F. (1964). Delineation of two drug responsive anxiety syndromes. *Psychopharmacologia, 5,* 397–408.

Koeppen, A. S. (1974). Relaxation training for children. *School Guidance and Counseling, 9,* 521–528.

Krohn, D. D., Weckstein, S. M., & Wright, H. L. (1992). A study of the effectiveness of a specific treatment for elective mutism. *Journal of the American Academy of Child and Adolescent Psychiatry, 31,* 711–718.

Kushner, M. G., Sher, K. J., & Beitman, B. D. (1990). The relation between alcohol problems and the anxiety disorders. *American Journal of Psychiatry, 147,* 685–695.

Kutcher, S., Reiter, S., & Gardner, D. (1995). Pharmacotherapy: Approaches and applications. In J. S. March (Ed.), *Anxiety disorders in children and adolescents* (pp. 341–385). New York: Guilford.

Ladd, G. W. (1981). Effectiveness of a social learning method for enhancing children's social interaction and peer acceptance. *Child Development, 52,* 171–178.

Ladd, G. W., & Golter, B. S. (1988). Parents' management of preschoolers' peer relations: Is it related to children's social competence? *Developmental Psychology, 24,* 109–117.

Lader, M. H. (1967). Palmer skin conductance measures in anxiety and phobic states. *Journal of Psychosomatic Research, 11,* 271–281.

LaGreca, A. M., Dandes, S. K., Wick, P., Shaw, K., & Stone, W. L. (1988). Development of the Social Anxiety Scale for Children: Reliability and concurrent validity. *Journal of Clinical Child Psychology, 17,* 84–91.

LaGreca, A. M., & Stone, W. L. (1993). Social Anxiety Scale for Children-Revised: Factor structure and concurrent validity. *Journal of Clinical Child Psychology, 22,* 17–27.

Lang, P. J. (1968). Fear reduction and fear behavior: Problems in treating a construct. In J. M. Shlien (Ed.), *The structure of emotion* (pp. 18–30). Seattle, WA: Hogrefe & Huber.

Last, C. G. (1986). *DSM-III anxiety disorders of childhood and adolescence.* Unpublished manuscript, University of Pittsburgh.

Last, C. G., Hersen, M., Kazdin, A. E., Finkelstein, R., & Strauss, C. C. (1987). Comparison of *DSM-III* separation anxiety disorder and overanxious disorder: Demographic characteristics and patterns of comorbidity. *Journal of the American Academy of Child and Adolescent Psychiatry, 26,* 527–531.

Last, C. G., Hersen, M., Kazdin, A., Finkelstein, R., & Strauss, C. C. (1991). Anxiety disorders in children and their families. *Archives of General Psychiatry, 48,* 928–937.

Last, C. G., Perrin, S., Hersen, M., & Kazdin, A. E. (1992). *DSM-III-R* anxiety disorders in children: Sociodemographic and clinical characteristics. *Jour-*

nal of the American Academy of Child and Adolescent Psychiatry, *31*, 928–934.

Last, C. G., & Strauss, C. C. (1990). School refusal in anxiety disordered children and adolescents. *Journal of the American Academy of Child and Adolescent Psychiatry, 29*, 31–35.

Last, C. G., Strauss, C. C., & Francis, G. (1987). Comorbidity among childhood anxiety disorders. *Journal of Nervous and Mental Disease, 175*, 726–730.

Lepine, J. P., & Lellouch, J. (1995). Classification and epidemiology of social phobia. *European Archives of Psychiatry and Clinical Neuroscience, 244*, 290–296.

Liberman, R. P., King, L. W., DeRisi, W. J., & McCann, M. (1975). *Personal effectivness: Guiding people to assert themselves and improve their social skills.* Champaign, IL: Research Press.

Liebowitz, M. R. (1987). Social phobia. *Modern Problems in Pharmacopsychiatry, 22*, 141–173.

Liebowitz, M. R., Gorman, J., Fyer, A., Campeas, R., Levin, A., Davies, S., & Klein, D. (1985). Psychopharmacological treatment of social phobia. *Psychopharmacology Bulletin, 21*, 610–614.

Liebowitz, M. R., Gorman, J. M., Fyer, A. J., & Klein, D. F. (1985). Social phobia: Review of a neglected anxiety disorder. *Archives of General Psychiatry, 42*, 729–736.

Liebowitz, M. R., & Marshall, R. D. (1995). Pharmacological treatments: Clinical applications. In R. G. Heimberg, M. R. Liebowitz, D. A. Hope, & F. R. Schneier (Eds.), *Social phobia: Diagnosis, assessment, and treatment* (pp. 366–383). New York: Guilford Press.

Liebowitz, M. R., Quitkin, F. M., Stewart, J. W., McGrath, P. J., Harrison, W., Rabkin, J., Tricamo, E., Markowitz, J. S., & Klein, D. F. (1984). Phenelzine vs. imipramine in atypical depression: A preliminary report. *Archives of General Psychiatry, 41*, 669–677.

Liebowitz, M. R., Schneier, R., Campeas, R., Hollander, E., Hatterer, J., Fyer, A., Gorman, J., Papp, L., Davies, S., Gully, R., & Klein, D. F. (1992). Phenelzine vs. atenolol in social phobia. *Archives of General Psychiatry, 49*, 290–300.

Lydiard, R. B., Larria, M. T., Howell, E. F., & Ballenger, J. C. (1988). Alprazolam in social phobia. *Journal of Clinical Psychopharmacology, 49*, 17–19.

MacDonald, K. (1987). Parent–child physical play with rejected, neglected, and popular boys. *Developmental Psychology, 5*, 705–711.

Mancini, C., Van Ameringen, M., Szatmari, P., Fugere, C., & Boyle, M. (1996). A high-risk pilot study of the children of adults with social phobia. *Journal of the American Academy of Child and Adolescent Psychiatry, 35*, 1511–1517.

Mannuzza, S., Fyer, A. J., Klein, D. F., & Endicott, J. (1986). Schedule for Affecitve Disorders and Schizophrenia-Lifetime version (modified for the study of anxiety): Rationale and conceptual development. *Journal of Psychiatric Research, 20*, 317–325.

Mannuzza, S., Fyer, A. J., Liebowitz, M. R., & Klein, D. F. (1990). Delineating the boundaries of social phobia: Its relationship to panic disorder and agoraphobia. *Journal of Anxiety Disorders, 4*, 41–59.

Mannuzza, S., Schneier, F. R., Chapman, T. F., Liebowitz, M. R., Klein, D. F., & Fyer, A. J. (1995). Generalized social phobia: Reliability and validity. *Archives of General Psychiatry, 52*, 230–237.

March, J., & Mulle, K. (1993). *"How I ran OCD off my land": A cognitive–behavioral program for the treatment of obsessive-compulsive disorder in children and adolescents.* Unpublished manuscript, Duke University.

Marks, I. M. (1970). The classification of phobic disorders. *British Journal of Psychiatry, 116*, 377–386.

Marks, I. M. (1985). Behavioral psychotherapy for anxiety disorders. *Psychiatric Clinics of North America, 8*, 25–35.

Marks, I. M., & Gelder, M. G. (1966). Different ages of onset in varieties of phobia. *American Journal of Psychiatry, 123*, 218–221.

Mattick, R. P., & Clarke, J. C. (1989). *Development and validation of measures of social phobia, scrutiny fear and social interaction anxiety.* Unpublished manuscript.

Mattick, R. P., & Peters, L. (1988). Treatment of severe social phobia: Effects of guided exposure with and without cognitive restructuring. *Journal of Consulting and Clinical Psychology, 56*, 251–260.

Mattick, R. P., Peters, L., & Clarke, J. C. (1989). Exposure and cognitive restructing for severe social phobia: A controlled study. *Behavior Therapy, 20*, 3–23.

Mavissakalian, M. R. (1996). Antidepressant medications for panic disorder. In

M. R. Mavissakalian & R. F. Prien (Eds.), *Long-term treatments of anxiety disorders* (pp. 265–284). Washington, DC: American Psychiatric Press.

McGee, R., Feehan, M., Williams, S., Partridge, F., Silva, P. A., & Kelley, J. (1990). DSM-III disorders in a large sample of adolescents. *Journal of the American Academy of Child and Adolescent Psychiatry, 29,* 611–619.

McNeil, D. W., Ries, B. J., Taylor, L. J., Boone, M. L., Carter, L. E., & Lewin, M. R. (1995). Comparison of social phobia subtypes using Stroop tests. *Journal of Anxiety Disorders, 9,* 47–57.

McNeil, D. W., Ries, B. J., & Turk, C. L. (1995). Behavioral assessment: Self-report, physiology, and overt behavior. In R. G. Heimberg, M. R. Liebowitz, D. A. Hope, & F. R. Schneier (Eds.), *Social phobia: Diagnosis, assessment and treatment* (pp. 202–231). New York: Guilford Press.

Mersch, P. P. A. (1995). The treatment of social phobia: The differential effectiveness of exposure in vivo and an integration of exposure in vivo, rational emotive therapy and social skills training. *Behaviour Research and Therapy, 33,* 259–269.

Mersch, P. P. A., Emmelkamp, P. M. G., Bogels, S., & van der Helm, J. (1989). Social phobia: Individual response patterns and the effects of behavioral and cognitive interventions. *Behaviour Research and Therapy, 27,* 421–434.

Mersch, P. P. A., Emmelkamp, P. M. G., & Lips, C. (1991). Social phobia: Individual response patterns and the long-term effects of behavioral and cognitive interventions. A follow-up study. *Behaviour Research and Therapy, 29,* 357–362.

Mersch, P. P. A., Jansen, M. A., & Arntz, A. (1995). Social phobia and personality disorder: Severity of complaint and treatment effectiveness. *Journal of Personality Disorders, 9,* 143–159.

Messer, S. C., & Beidel, D. C. (1994). Psychological correlates of childhood anxiety disorders. *Journal of the American Academy of Child and Adolescent Psychiatry, 33,* 975–983.

Mineka, S. (1987). A primate model of phobic fears. In H. Eysenck & I. Martin (Eds.), *Theoretical foundations of behavior therapy* (pp. 87–111). New York: Plenum Press.

Mineka, S., & Cook, M. (1988). Social learning and the acquisition of snake fear in monkeys. In T. Zentall & G. Galef (Eds.), *Comparative social learning* (pp. 51–73). Hillsdale, NJ: Erlbaum.

Mineka, S., & Zinbarg, R. (1991). Animal models of psychopathology. In C. E. Walker (Ed.), *Clinical psychology: Historical and research foundations* (pp. 51–86). New York: Plenum Press.

Mineka, S., & Zinbarg, R. (1995). Conditioning and ethological models of social phobia. In R. G. Heimberg, M. R. Liebowitz, D. A. Hope, & F. R. Schneier (Eds.), *Social phobia: Diagnosis, assessment, and treatment* (pp. 134–162). New York: Guilford Press.

Morris, T. L., Messer, S. C., & Gross, A. M. (1995). Enhancement of the social interaction and status of neglected children: A peer-pairing approach. *Journal of Clinical Child Psychology, 24,* 11–20.

Mullaney, J. A, & Trippett, C. J. (1979). Alcohol dependence and phobias: Clinicial description and relevance. *British Journal of Psychiatry, 135,* 565–573.

Munjack, D., Baltazar, P., Bohn, P., Cabe, D., & Appleton, A. (1990). Clonazepam in the treatment of social phobia: A pilot study. *Journal of Clinical Psychiatry, 51,* 35–40.

Munjack, D. J., Bruns, J., Baltazar, P. L., Brown, R., Leonard, M., Nagy, R., Koek, R., Crocker, B., & Schafer, S. (1991). A pilot study of buspirone in the treatment of social phobia. *Journal of Anxiety Disorders, 5,* 87–98.

Neftel, K. A., Adler, R. H., Kappell, L., Rossi, M., Dolder, M., Kaser, H. E., Bruggesser, H. H., & Vorkauf, H. (1982). Stage fright in musicians: A model illustrating the effects of beta-blockers. *Psychosomatic Medicine, 44,* 461–469.

Nelles, W. B., & Barlow, D. H. (1988). Do children panic? *Clinical Psychology Review, 8,* 359–372.

Newman, M. G., Hofmann, S. G., Trabert, W., Roth, X., & Taylor, C. B. (1994). Does behavioral treatment of social phobia lead to cognitive changes? *Behavior Therapy, 25,* 503–517.

Noyes, R., Jr., Crowe, R. R., Harrs, E. L., Hamra, B. J., McChesney, C. M., & Chaudhry, D. R. (1986). Relationship between panic disorder and agoraphobia: A family study. *Archives of General Psychiatry, 43,* 227–233.

Ollendick, T. H., & Cerny, J. A. (1981). *Clinical behavior therapy with children.* New York: Plenum Press.

Ontiveros, A., & Fontaine, R. (1990). Social phobia and clonazepam. *Canadian Journal of Psychiatry, 35,* 439–441.

Ost, L. G. (1985). Ways of acquiring phobias and outcome of behavioral treatments. *Behaviour Research and Therapy, 23,* 683–689.

Ost, L. G. (1987). Age of onset in different phobias. *Journal of Abnormal Psychology, 96,* 223–229.

Ost, L. G., & Hughdahl, K. (1981). Acquisition of phobias and anxiety response patterns in clinic patients. *Behaviour Research and Therapy, 16,* 439–447.

Paine, S. C., Hops, H., Walker, H. M., Greenwood, C. R., Fleischman, D. H., & Guild, J. J. (1982). Repeated treatment effects: A study maintaining behavior change in socially withdrawn children. *Behavior Modification, 6,* 171–199.

Parke, R. D., & Bhavnagri, N. P. (1989). Parents as managers of children's peer relationships. In D. Belle (Ed.), *Children's social networks and social supports* (pp. 241–259). New York: Wiley.

Patterson, C. J., Kupersmidt, J. B., & Griesler, P. C. (1990). Children's perceptions of self and of relationships with others as a function of sociometric status. *Child Development, 61,* 1335–1349.

Perrin, S., & Last, C. G. (1993, March). *Comorbidity of social phobia and other anxiety disorders in children.* Paper presented at the Association for Advancement of Behavior Therapy Annual Convention, Charleston, SC.

Persons, J. B. (1989). *Cognitive therapy in practice: A case formulation approach.* New York: Norton.

Pollack, M. H., Otto, M. W., Sabatine, S., Majcher, D., & Rosenbaum, J. (1995, April). *Relationship of childhood anxiety disorders to course of adult panic disorder.* Paper presented at the Anxiety Disorders Association of America Annual Convention, Pittsburgh, PA.

Pollard, C. A., & Henderson, J. G. (1988). Four types of social phobia in a community sample. *Journal of Nervous and Mental Disease, 176,* 440–445.

Potts, N. L. S., & Davidson, J. R. T. (1995). Pharmacological treatments: Literature review. In R. G. Heimberg, M. R. Liebowitz, D. A. Hope, & F. R. Schneier (Eds.), *Social phobia: Diagnosis, assessment and treatment* (pp. 334–365). New York: Guilford Press.

Putallaz, M., & Heflin, A. H. (1990). Parent-child interaction. In S. R. Asher & J. C. Coie (Eds.), *Children's status in the peer group* (pp. 189–216). New York: Cambridge University Press.

Radke-Yarrow, M., & Zahn-Waxler, C. (1986). The role of familial factors in the development of prosocial behavior: Research findings and questions. In D. Olweus, J. Block, & M. Radke-Yarrow (Eds.), *Development of antisocial and prosocial behavior: Research, theories, and issues* (pp. 207–233). Orlando, FL: Academic Press.

Rapee, R. M. (1995). Descriptive psychopathology of social phobia. In R. G. Heimberg, M. R. Liebowitz, D. A. Hope, & F. R. Schneier (Eds.), *Social phobia: Diagnosis, assessment and treatment* (pp. 41–66). New York: Guilford Press.

Rapee, R. M., Brown, T. A., Antony, M. A., & Barlow, D. H. (1992). Response to hyperventilation and inhalation of 5.5% carbon dioxide-enriched air across the *DSM-III-R* anxiety disorders. *Journal of Abnormal Psychology, 101,* 538–552.

Reich, J., & Yates, W. (1988a). Family history of psychiatric disorders in social phobia. *Comprehensive Psychiatry, 29,* 72–75.

Reich, J., & Yates, W. (1988b). A pilot study of treatment of social phobia with alprazolam. *American Journal of Psychiatry, 145,* 590–594.

Reiter, S. R., Pollack, M. H., Rosenbaum, J. F., & Cohen, L. S. (1990). Clonazepam for the treatment of social phobia. *Journal of Clinical Psychiatry, 51,* 470–472.

Renfry, G. S. (1992). Cognitive–behavior therapy and the Native American client. *Behavior Therapy, 23,* 321–340.

Rennenberg, B., Goldstein, A. J., Phillips, D., & Chambless, D. L. (1990). Behavioral group treatment of avoidant personality disorder. *Behavior Therapy,* 363–377.

Reznick, J. S., Kagan, J., Sniderman, N., Gersten, M., Boak, K., & Rosenberg, A. (1986). Inhibited and uninhibited children: A follow-up study. *Child Development, 57,* 660–680.

Robins, L. N., Helzer, J. E., Weissman, M. M., Orvaschel, H., Greenberg, E., Burke, Jr., J. D., & Regier, D. A. (1984). Lifetime prevalance of specific psychiatric disorders at three sites. *Archives of General Psychiatry, 41,* 949–958.

Rosenbaum, J. F., Biederman, J., Bolduc, E. A., Hirshfeld, D. R., Faraone, S. V., & Kagan, J. (1992). Comorbidity of parental anxiety disorders as risk for childhood-onset anxiety in inhibited children. *American Journal of Psychiatry, 149,* 475–481.

Rosenbaum, J. R., Biederman, J., Gersten, M., Hirshfeld, D. R., Meminger, S. R., Herman, J. B., Kagan, J., Reznick, J. R., & Snidman, N. (1988). Behavioral inhibition in children of parents with panic disorder and agoraphobia. *Archives of General Psychiatry, 45,* 463–470.

Rosenbaum, J. F., Biederman, J., Hirshfeld, D. R., Bolduc, E. A., & Chaloff, J. (1991). Behavioral inhibition in children: A possible precursor to panic disorder or social phobia. *Journal of Clinical Psychiatry, 52*(11, suppl.), 5–9.

Rubin, K. H., & Asendorpf, J. B. (1993). Social withdrawal, inhibition, and shyness in childhood: Conceptual and definitional issues. In K. H. Rubin & J. B. Asendorpf (Eds.), *Social withdrawal, inhibition, and shyness in childhod* (pp. 3–17). Hillsdale, NJ: Erlbaum.

Rubin, K. H., LeMare, L. J., & Lollis, S. (1990). Social withdrawal in childhood: Developmental pathways to peer rejection. In S. R. Asher & J. D. Coie (Eds.), *Peer rejection in childhood* (pp. 217–249). Cambridge, England: Cambridge University Press.

Rubin, K. H., & Mills, R. S. L. (1988). The many faces of social isolation in childhood. *Journal of Consulting and Clinical Psychology, 56,* 916–924.

Russo, M. F., & Beidel, D. C. (1994). Comorbidity of childhood anxiety and externalizing disorders: Prevalence, characteristics, and validation issues. *Clinical Psychology Review, 3,* 199–221.

Ryan, N. D., Puig-Antich, J., Cooper, T. B., Rabinovich, H., Ambrosini, P., Fried, J., Davies, M., Torres, D., & Suckow, R. (1987). Relative safety of single versus divided dose imipramine in adolescent major depression. *Journal of the American Academy of Child and Adolescent Psychiatry, 26,* 400–406.

Sanderson, W. C., Rapee, R. M., & Barlow, D. H. (1987, November). *The DSM-III-R revised anxiety disorder categories: Descriptors and patterns of comorbidity.* Paper presented at the annual meeting of the Association for Advancement of Behavior Therapy, Boston, MA.

Scarr, S. (1969). Social introversion as a heritable response. *Child Development, 40,* 813–822.

Schneider, B. H., & Byrne, B. M. (1987). Individualizing social skills training for behavior-disordered children. *Journal of Consulting and Clinical Psychology, 55,* 444–445.

Schneier, F. R. (1992). *Boundary between social phobia and avoidant personality disorder*. Prepared for the *DSM-IV* subworkgroup on social phobia. Unpublished manuscript, Columbia University.

Schneier, F. R. (1995). Monoamine oxidase inhibitors, selective serotonin reuptake inhibitors, and other antidepressants in pharmacotherapy. In M. B. Stein (Ed.), *Social phobia: Clinical and research perspectives* (pp. 347–374). Washington, DC: American Psychiatric Press.

Schneier, F. R., Chin, S. J., Hollander, E., & Liebowitz, M. R. (1992). Fluoxetine in social phobia. *Journal of Clinical Psychopharmacology, 12,* 62–63.

Schneier, F. R., Johnson, J., Hornig, C. D., Liebowitz, M. R., & Weissman, M. M. (1992). Social phobia: Comorbidity and morbidity in an epidemiologic sample. *Archives of General Psychiatry, 49,* 282–288.

Schneier, F. R., Martin, L. Y., Liebowitz, M. R., Gorman, J. M., & Fyer, A. J. (1989). Alcohol abuse in social phobia. *Journal of Anxiety Disorders, 3,* 15–23.

Schneier, F. R., Saoud, J. B., Fallon, B. A., Hollander, E., Coplan, J., & Liebowitz, M. R. (1993). Buspirone in social phobia. *Journal of Clinical Psychopharmacology, 13,* 251–256.

Schneier, F. R., Spitzer, R. L., Gibbon, M., Fyer, A. J., & Liebowitz, M. R. (1991). The relationship of social phobia subtypes and avoidant personality disorder. *Comprehensive Psychiatry, 32,* 496–502.

Scholing, A., & Emmelkamp, P. M. G. (1993a). Cognitive and behavioural treatments for fear of blushing, sweating or trembling. *Behaviour Research and Therapy, 31,* 155–170.

Scholing, A., & Emmelkamp, P. M. G. (1993b). Exposure with and without cognitive therapy for generalized social phobia: Effects of individual and group treatment. *Behaviour Research and Therapy, 31,* 155–170.

Scholing, A., & Emmelkamp, P. M. G. (1996). Treatment of generalized social phobia: Results at long-term follow-up. *Behaviour Research and Therapy, 34,* 447–452.

Shaffer, D., Fisher, P., Dulcan, M. K., Davies, M., Piacentini, J., Schwab-Stone, M. E., Lahye, B. B., Bourdon, K., Jensen, P. S., Bird, H. R., Canino, G., & Regier, D. A. (1996). The NIMH Diagnostic Interview Schedule for Children Version 2.3 (DISC-2.3): Description, acceptability, prevalence rates, and performance in the MECA study. *Journal of the American Academy of Child and Adolescent Psychiatry, 35,* 865–872.

Sheridan, S. M., Kratochwill, T. R., & Elliott, S. N. (1990). Behavioral consultation with parents and teachers: Delivering treatment for socially withdrawn children at home and school. *School Psychology Review, 19,* 33–52.

Silverman, W. K., & Albano, A. M. (1995). *Anxiety Disorders Interview Schedule for Children.* San Antonio, TX: Psychological Corporation.

Silverman, W. K., & Kurtines, W. M. (1996). *Anxiety and phobic disorders: A pragmatic approach.* New York: Plenum Press.

Simeon, J. G., & Ferguson, H. B. (1987). Alprazolam effects in children with anxiety disorders. *Canadian Journal of Psychiatry, 32,* 570–574.

Simeon, J. G., Ferguson, H. B., Knott, V., Roberts, N., Gautheir, B., Dubois, C., & Wiggins, D. (1992). Clinical, cognitive, and neuropsychological effects of alprazolam in children and adolescents with overanxious disorder and avoidant disorders. *Journal of the American Academy of Child and Adolescent Psychiatry, 31,* 29–33.

Smail, P., Stockwell, T., Canter, S., & Hodgson, R. (1984). Alcohol dependence and phobic anxiety states. I. A prevalence study. *British Journal of Psychiatry, 144,* 53–57.

Spitzer, R. L., Endicott, J., & Robins, E. (1978). Research Diagnostic Criteria: Rationale and reliability. *Archives of General Psychiatry, 35,* 773–782.

Spitzer, R. L., & Williams, J. B. (1986). *Structured Clinical Interview for DSM-III-R axis II.* Unpublished manuscript, Columbia University.

Spitzer, R. L., Williams, J. B., Gibbon, M., & First, M. B. (1992). The Structured Clinical Interview for *DSM-III-R* (SCID) I: History, rationale and description. *Archives of General Psychiatry, 49,* 624–629.

Stein, M. B., Walker, J. R., & Forde, D. R. (1994). Setting diagnostic thresholds for social phobia: Considerations from a community survey of social anxiety. *American Journal of Psychiatry, 151,* 408–412.

Stemberger, R. T., Turner, S. M., Beidel, D. C., & Calhoun, K. S. (1995). Social phobia: An analysis of possible developmental factors. *Journal of Abnormal Psychology, 104,* 526–531.

Strauss, C. C., Lahey, B. B., Frick, P., Frame, C. L., & Hynd, G. W. (1988). Peer social status of children with anxiety disorders. *Journal of Consulting and Clinical Psychology, 56,* 137–141.

Strauss, C. C., & Last, C. G. (1993). Social and simple phobias in children. *Journal of Anxiety Disorders, 1,* 141–152.

Stravynski, A., Lamontagne, Y., & Lavallee, Y. J. (1986). Clinical phobias and avoidant personality disorder among alcoholics admitted to an alcoholism rehabilitation setting. *Canadian Journal of Psychiatry, 31,* 714–719.

Stravynski, A., Marks, I., & Yule, W. (1982). Social skills problems in neurotic outpatients: Social skills training with and without cognitive modification. *Archives of General Psychiatry, 39,* 1378–1385.

Sutherland, S. M., & Davidson, J. R. T. (1995). β-blockers and benzodiazepines in pharmacotherapy. In M. B. Stein (Ed.), *Social phobia: Clinical and research perspectives* (pp. 323–346). Washington, DC: American Psychiatric Press.

Taylor, S. (1996). Meta-analysis of cognitive-behavioral treatments for social phobia. *Behavior Therapy and Experimental Psychiatry, 27,* 1–9.

Thomas, A., & Chess, S. (1977). *Temperament and development.* New York: Brunner/Mazel.

Torgersen, S. (1983). Genetic factors in the anxiety disorders. *Archives of General Psychiatry, 40,* 1085–1089.

Turner, B. G., Beidel, D. C., Hughes, S., & Turner, M. W. (1991). Test anxiety in African American school children. *School Psychology Quarterly, 8,* 140–152.

Turner, S. M., & Beidel, D. C. (1989). Social phobia: Clinical syndrome, diagnosis and comorbidity. *Clinical Psychology Review, 9,* 3–18.

Turner, S. M., & Beidel, D. C. (1996). *Family interactions patterns of anxious parents and their children.* Manuscript in preparation.

Turner, S. M., Beidel, D. C., Borden, J. W., Stanley, M. R., & Jacob, R. G. (1991). Social phobia: Axis I and Axis II correlates. *Journal of Abnormal Psychology, 100,* 102–106.

Turner, S. M., Beidel, D. C., & Cooley, M. R. (1994). *Social Effectiveness Therapy: A program for overcoming social anxiety and social phobia.* Mt. Pleasant, SC: Turndel.

Turner, S. M., Beidel, D. C., & Cooley-Quille, M. R. (1995). Two year follow-up of social phobics treated with Social Effectiveness Therapy. *Behaviour Research and Therapy, 33,* 553–556.

Turner, S. M., Beidel, D. C., Cooley, M. R., Woody, S. R., & Messer, S. C. (1994). A multicomponent behavioral treatment for social phobia: Social Effectiveness Therapy. *Behaviour Research and Therapy, 32,* 381–390.

Turner, S. M., Beidel, D. C., & Costello, A. (1987). Psychopathology in the offspring of anxiety disorders patients. *Journal of Consulting and Clinical Psychology, 55,* 229–235.

Turner, S. M., Beidel, D. C., Dancu, C. V., & Keys, D. J. (1986). Psychopathology of social phobia and comparison to avoidant personality disorder. *Journal of Abnormal Psychology, 95,* 389–394.

Turner, S. M., Beidel, D. C., Dancu, C. V., & Stanley, M. A. (1989). An empirically derived inventory to measure social fears and anxiety: The Social Phobia and Anxiety Inventory. *Psychological Assessment: A Journal of Consulting and Clinical Psychology, 1,* 35–40.

Turner, S. M., Beidel, D. C., & Epstein, L. H. (1991). Vulnerability and risk for anxiety disorders. *Journal of Anxiety Disorders, 5,* 151–166.

Turner, S. M., Beidel, D. C., & Jacob, R. G. (1994). Social phobia: A comparison of behavior therapy and atenolol. *Journal of Consulting and Clinical Psychology, 62,* 350–358.

Turner, S. M., Beidel, D. C., & Larkin, K. T. (1986). Situational determinants of social anxiety in clinic and non-clinic samples: Physiological and cognitive correlates. *Journal of Consulting and Clinical Psychology, 54,* 523–527.

Turner, S. M., Beidel, D. C., Long, P. J., & Greenhouse, J. (1992). Reduction of fear in social phobics: An examination of extinction patterns. *Behavior Therapy, 23,* 389–403.

Turner, S. M., Beidel, D. C., & Townsley, R. M. (1990). Social phobia: Relationship to shyness. *Behaviour Research and Therapy, 28,* 497–505.

Turner, S. M., Beidel, D. C., & Townsley, R. M. (1992a). Social phobia: A comparison of specific and generalized subtypes and avoidant personality disorder. *Journal of Abnormal Psychology, 101,* 326–331.

Turner, S. M., Beidel, D. C., & Townsley, R. M. (1992b). In S. M. Turner, K. S. Calhoun, & H. E. Adams (Eds.), *Handbook of clinical behavior therapy* (pp. 13–37). New York: Wiley.

Turner, S. M., Beidel, D. C., & Wolff, P. L. (1996). Is behavioral inhibition related to the anxiety disorders? *Clincial Psychology Review, 16,* 157–172.

Turner, S. M., Beidel, D. C., Wolff, P. L., Spaulding, S., & Jacob, R. G. (1996). Clinical features affecting treatment outcome in social phobia. *Behaviour Research and Therapy, 34,* 795–804.

Turner, S. M., Cooley-Quille, M. R., & Beidel, D. C. (1995). Behavioral and pharmacological treatment of social phobia: Long-term outcome. In M. Mavissakalian & R. Prien (Eds.), *Anxiety disorders: Psychological and pharmacological treatment* (pp. 343–371). Washington, DC: American Psychiatric Press.

Turner, S. M., McCanna, M., & Beidel, D. C. (1987). Validity of the Social Avoidance and Distress and Fear of Negative Evaluation scales. *Behaviour Research and Therapy, 25,* 113–115.

Turner, S. M., Stanley, M. A., Beidel, D. C., & Bond, L. (1989). The Social Phobia and Anxiety Inventory: Construct validity. *Journal of Psychopathology and Behavioral Assessment, 11,* 221–234.

Van Amerigen, M. V., Mancini, C., & Streiner, D. L. (1993). Fluoxetine efficacy in social phobia. *Journal of Clinical Psychiatry, 54,* 27–32.

Van Amerigen, M., Mancini, C., & Streiner, D. (1994). Social disability in anxiety disorders. *Neuropsychopharmacology, 10*(3S), 615S.

van Vliet, I. M., den Boer, J. A., & Westenberg, H. G. M. (1992). Psychopharmacological treatment of social phobia: Clinical and biochemical effects of brofaromine, a selective MAO-A inhibitor. *European Neuropsychopharmacology, 2,* 21–29.

Vernberg, E. M., Abwender, D. A., Ewell, K. K., & Beery, S. H. (1992). Social anxiety and peer relationships in early adolescence: A prospective analysis. *Journal of Clinical Child Psychology, 21,* 189–196.

Versiani, M., Nardi, A. E., Mundim, F. D., Alves, A. B., Liebowitz, M. R., & Amrein, R. (1992). Pharmacotherapy of social phobia: A controlled study with moclobemide and phenelzine. *British Journal of Psychiatry, 161,* 353–360.

Viesselman, J. O., Yaylayan, S., Weller, E. B., & Weller, R. A. (1993). Antidysthymic drugs (antidepressants and antimanics). In J. S. Werry & M. G. Aman (Eds.), *Practitioner's guide to psychoactive drugs for children and adolescents* (pp. 239–268). New York: Plenum Press.

Wacker, H. R., Mullejans, R., Klein, K. H., & Battegay, R. (1992). Identification of cases of anxiety disorders and affective disorders in the community according to *ICD-10* and *DSM-III-R* using the Composite International Diagnostic Interview (CIDI). *International Journal of Methods in Psychiatric Research, 2,* 91–100.

Warren, S. L., Huston, L., Egeland, B., & Sroufe, L. A. (1997). Child and adolescent anxiety disorders and early attachment. *Journal of the American Academy of Child and Adolescent Psychiatry, 36*, 637–644.

Watson, D., & Friend, R. (1969). Measurement of social-evaluative anxiety. *Journal of Consulting and Clinical Psychology, 33*, 448–457.

Watson, J. B., & Rayner, R. (1920). Conditioned emotional reactions. *Journal of Experimental Psychology, 3*, 1–14.

Weissman, M. M., Leckman, J. F., Merikangas, K. R., Gammon, G. D., & Prusoff, B. A. (1984). Depression and anxiety disorders in parents and children. *Archives of General Psychiatry, 41*, 845–852.

Wergeland, H. (1979). Elective mutism. *Acta Psychiatrica Scandinavica, 59*, 218–228.

Whitehill, M. B., Hersen, M., & Bellack, A. S. (1980). Conversation skills training for socially isolated children. *Behaviour Research and Therapy, 18*, 217–225.

Williams, J. B., Gibbon, M., First, M. B., Spitzer, R. L., Davies, M., Borus, J., Howes, M. J., Krane, J., Pope, Jr., Rounsaville, B., & Wittchen, H. U. (1992). The structured interview for *DSM-III-R* (SCID) II: Multisite test-retest reliability. *Archives of General Psychiatry, 49*, 630–636.

Wlazlo, Z., Schroeder-Hartwig, K., Hand, I., Kaiser, G., & Munchau, N. (1990). Exposure in vivo vs. social skills training for social phobia: Long-term outcome and differential effects. *Behaviour Research and Therapy, 28*, 181–193.

Zitrin, C. M., Klein, D. F., Woerner, M. G., & Ross, D. (1983). Treatment of phobias: A comparison of imipramine and placebo. *Archives of General Psychiatry, 40*, 125–138.

Author Index

Subject Index

About the Authors

Deborah C. Beidel, PhD, is Associate Professor of Psychiatry and Behavioral Sciences and Co-Director of the Anxiety Prevention and Treatment Research Center at the Medical University of South Carolina. She has authored or co-authored over 90 articles, book chapters, and books. In addition, she has served on the editorial boards of numerous psychological journals including *Journal of Consulting and Clinical Psychology, Professional Psychology: Research and Practice,* and *Journal of Anxiety Disorders.* She currently serves as Chair of the Anxiety Disorders Association of America's Children's Task Force and as Chair of the National Institute of Mental Health's Child and Adolescent Psychosocial Interventions Research Consortium. Dr. Beidel was the recipient of the 1990 New Researcher Award from the Association for Advancement of Behavior Therapy. She is a Diplomate of the American Board of Professional Psychology in both clinical and behavioral psychology.

Samuel M. Turner, PhD, is Professor of Psychiatry and Behavioral Sciences and Director of the Anxiety Prevention and Treatment Research Center at the Medical University of South Carolina. Dr. Turner has authored or co-authored over 150 journal articles, book chapters, and books, mostly on the anxiety disorders. He is Associate Editor of *American Psychologist* and has served on the editorial boards of numerous psychological journals including *Journal of Consulting and Clinical Psychology, Behavior Therapy,* and *Behaviour Research and Therapy.* In addition, he has served on numerous national committees and panels including the Extramural Scientific Advisory Board of the National Institute of Mental Health. Dr. Turner was the 1997 recipient of the American Psychological Association's award for Distinguished Contribution

to Professional Knowledge and the award for Distinguished Contribution to Medical Research from the Association of Medical School Psychologists. He is a Diplomate of the American Board of Professional
Psychology in clinical as well as behavioral psychology.